FEDERAL INCOME TAXATION OF ESTATES, TRUSTS, AND BENEFICIARIES

IN A NUTSHELL®

SECOND EDITION

GRAYSON M.P. McCOUCH
Gerald Sohn Professor of Law
University of Florida

WEST
ACADEMIC
PUBLISHING

Nutshell Series, In a Nutshell and the Nutshell Logo are trademarks registered in the U.S. Patent and Trademark Office.

© 2017 LEG, Inc. d/b/a West Academic
© 2020 LEG, Inc. d/b/a West Academic
      444 Cedar Street, Suite 700
      St. Paul, MN 55101
      1-877-888-1330

West, West Academic Publishing, and West Academic are trademarks of West Publishing Corporation, used under license.

Printed in the United States of America

ISBN: 978-1-68467-453-4

PREFACE

Fiduciary income taxation is a dynamic and rewarding field of study. The basic statutory framework, set forth in Subchapter J of the Internal Revenue Code, has remained remarkably stable since its enactment in 1954, although the detailed provisions of the statute and regulations have become increasingly complex. Much of the complexity in Subchapter J flows inexorably from the interplay of federal income tax principles with rules of local law concerning fiduciary accounting and administration and with the separate system of federal estate and gift taxes. In addition, the statute and regulations are replete with technical requirements and restrictions designed to limit opportunities for tax avoidance. Nevertheless, the surface complexity of Subchapter J cannot completely obscure the logical coherence of its underlying structure.

This book, now in its second edition, provides a concise introduction to the federal income taxation of decedents, estates, trusts, and beneficiaries. It is intended to be read by students and by lawyers and other professionals involved in estate planning and administration. Its goal is to provide sufficient background and explanatory discussion to allow the reader to grasp the basic principles of fiduciary income taxation. To that end, the text includes numerous examples illustrating the operation of specific rules as well as occasional discussion of relevant case law and administrative rulings.

Reference is frequently made to provisions of the Internal Revenue Code and the accompanying Treasury regulations, underscoring the importance of having those sources accessible and reading them together with this book. Readers who wish to pursue matters in greater depth can find comprehensive discussions in the leading treatises on fiduciary income taxation.

The topical coverage of this book follows the sequence and organization found in many courses and teaching materials. Chapter 1 provides a general overview of the federal tax treatment of gifts and bequests and introduces some basic principles of fiduciary income taxation. The next two chapters focus on a decedent's income tax liability for the taxable year ending at death (Chapter 2) and the treatment of "income in respect of a decedent" in the hands of an estate or other successor (Chapter 3). Chapter 4 discusses the classification and duration of an estate or a trust as a separate taxable entity, and the following three chapters examine the conduit rules which constitute the heart of Subchapter J. Under those rules, an estate or trust is taxed on income that is accumulated for future distribution (Chapter 5), but income that is distributed during the taxable year is taxed to the beneficiaries who receive it (Chapter 7). The concept of "distributable net income" serves as a measuring rod to determine the amount and character of the distributions received by the beneficiaries (Chapter 6). Chapter 8 deals with "grantor trusts" and explains the circumstances in which a grantor who retains beneficial enjoyment or control of an inter vivos trust may be treated as the trust's owner for income tax purposes. The remaining chapters discuss several types of trusts that qualify for special income tax treatment, including trusts for charitable purposes (Chapter 9), foreign trusts (Chapter 10), accumulation trusts (Chapter 11), and a few other trusts governed by specific statutory provisions (Chapter 12).

In preparing this book I have benefited greatly from the helpful advice and suggestions of current and former colleagues. I am especially grateful to Dennis Calfee and Lawrence Lokken for their friendship, encouragement, and guidance. Finally, I would like to thank Louis Higgins and the West Academic production staff for their invaluable assistance in bringing this book to publication.

GRAYSON M.P. McCOUCH

December, 2019
Gainesville, FL

OUTLINE

TABLE OF CASES

References are to Pages

TABLE OF INTERNAL REVENUE CODE SECTIONS

References are to Pages

TABLE OF TREASURY REGULATIONS

References are to Pages

TABLE OF REVENUE RULINGS

References are to Pages

FEDERAL INCOME TAXATION OF ESTATES, TRUSTS, AND BENEFICIARIES

IN A NUTSHELL®

SECOND EDITION

CHAPTER 1
OVERVIEW

§ 1.1 INTRODUCTION

Citizens and residents of the United States are subject to federal income taxation on income derived from any source, including compensation for personal services, business and investment income, gains from property transactions, and "[i]ncome from an interest in an estate or a trust." I.R.C. § 61(a). The expansive reach of this provision is not unlimited, however. From its earliest days, the income tax has provided an express exclusion from gross income for "the value of property acquired by gift, bequest, devise, or inheritance," subject to the proviso that the exclusion does not extend to "the income from" such property. I.R.C. § 102(a) and (b)(1). Thus, the beneficiary of a gift or bequest is not subject to income tax on the value of the property received, but the beneficiary will be taxed on any income subsequently realized from the property.

The basic statutory scheme seems clear enough, at least in broad outline, as it applies to gifts and bequests made directly to an individual beneficiary. Inevitably, though, details concerning the timing, amount, and character of income realized by the transferor and the beneficiary, respectively, require further elaboration. Moreover, the tax treatment of gifts and bequests is significantly complicated by two additional factors which must be taken into account.

First, gifts and bequests may be subject to gift tax (in the case of a lifetime transfer) or estate tax (in the case of a transfer occurring at death). These taxes on gratuitous transfers of wealth, along with a supplementary tax on generation-skipping transfers, operate largely independently of the income tax. Although the transfer taxes interact with the income tax in important ways, the taxes remain poorly coordinated with each other. At a fairly abstract level (and putting aside significant differences in bases, rates, and exemptions), one might view the wealth transfer taxes as filling a gap created by the income tax's failure to reach gifts and bequests. At a more practical level, however, rising transfer tax exemptions and falling rates have severely curtailed the impact of the transfer taxes in recent years. As a result, taxpayers and their advisers have begun to reevaluate many traditional planning techniques with renewed attention to income tax consequences.

The second complicating factor arises from the interposition of a fiduciary—the trustee of property held in trust, or the executor of a decedent's estate—between the transferor and his or her beneficiaries. By transferring property in trust instead of making a gift directly to a particular beneficiary, a transferor can provide for a highly flexible scheme of beneficial interests extending far into the future. In addition to extensive fiduciary powers and duties relating to management and investment of the trust property, the trustee may be given broad discretion to determine the timing and amount of income and corpus distributions to the beneficiaries, many of whom may be unborn or unascertained when the trust is first created. In administering a decedent's estate (i.e., in collecting property owned at death, paying debts, administration expenses and taxes, and distributing the remaining property to the decedent's testate or intestate successors), the executor performs a role functionally similar to that of a trustee. For income tax purposes, even in the simple case of a trust or estate that has only one beneficiary or a few ascertained beneficiaries with clearly defined interests, it may be awkward to hold each beneficiary directly accountable for his or her share of undistributed income. The problem is far more severe when, as frequently occurs, the trust or estate accumulates income for future distribution to unborn or unascertained beneficiaries whose shares cannot immediately be determined.

For income tax purposes, trusts and estates are generally recognized as taxable entities distinct from the grantor and the beneficiaries. The statutory scheme of fiduciary income taxation is set forth in Subchapter J of the Internal Revenue Code (I.R.C. §§ 641–692) and elaborated in the accompanying Treasury regulations. A fundamental issue under Subchapter J involves the determination of who is responsible for reporting items of income earned by a trust or estate; subsidiary issues involve the timing and character of the amounts to be reported by a particular taxpayer.

In the case of an inter vivos trust, a preliminary question arises concerning the trust's status as a taxable entity. If the grantor retains any of the powers or interests specified in the grantor trust

rules (I.R.C. §§ 671–679), a corresponding portion of
the trust's income may be attributed to the grantor.
In effect, the grantor trust rules determine the extent
to which the grantor's transfer of property in trust is
deemed "incomplete" for income tax purposes. For
example, a grantor who creates an inter vivos trust,
retaining an unrestricted power to revoke or amend
the trust, will continue to be treated as the trust's
owner and will be taxed on the trust's income. Upon
the grantor's death (or earlier termination of all
retained powers and interests), however, the grantor
trust rules will cease to apply and the trust will be
recognized as a taxable entity. Since a decedent's
estate comes into existence only at the time of death,
it is immediately recognized as a taxable entity; the
estate can never be treated as a grantor trust.

A nongrantor trust, like an estate, is recognized as
a taxable entity, and the central mission of
Subchapter J is to allocate the income of the trust or
estate between the entity and the beneficiaries,
ensuring that the income is taxed either to the entity
or to the beneficiaries (but not both). This is
accomplished by allowing the entity a deduction for
amounts distributed to the beneficiaries and
requiring the beneficiaries to include their respective
distributions in gross income. The amounts
distributed retain their income tax characteristics in
the hands of the beneficiaries. In effect, the trust or
estate serves as a "conduit" to the extent that it pays
out its "distributable net income" to the beneficiaries;
the entity itself is subject to tax only on any income
that is accumulated rather than distributed. The

conduit rules governing distributions are set forth in
I.R.C. §§ 651–663.

The basic framework of Subchapter J, including
the grantor trust rules and the conduit rules, has
remained largely unchanged since its enactment in
1954. To be sure, specific statutory provisions have
been added or amended (or repealed, in some cases),
and the Treasury has promulgated a steady stream
of regulations in a tireless quest to forestall real or
perceived abuses. Nevertheless, the underlying
structure has proved remarkably durable. Perhaps
the single most far-reaching change occurred when
Congress enacted a drastically compressed income
tax rate schedule for trusts and estates in 1986 as
part of a comprehensive tax reform package. Under
the rate schedule in effect for 2020, trusts and estates
are taxed at the top marginal rate of 37% on every
dollar of taxable income in excess of $12,950,
compared to a threshold of $518,400 for a single
individual or $622,050 for a married couple filing
jointly. I.R.C. § 1(a), (c), (e), (f), and (j). As a result of
the revised rate schedule, planners have largely
abandoned traditional income accumulation trusts
and have turned their attention to new ways of
channeling trust income to lower-bracket grantors or
beneficiaries.

§ 1.2 INCOME TAX TREATMENT
OF GIFTS AND BEQUESTS

All estates and almost all trusts within the ambit
of Subchapter J arise from a gratuitous transfer of
property made by an individual transferor, typically

in the form of a gift made during life or a bequest occurring at death. Accordingly, in laying the foundation for a discussion of the taxation of estates and trusts under Subchapter J, it is important to review the basic income tax treatment of gifts and bequests.

Treatment of donor or decedent. A gift or bequest clearly constitutes a transfer of property, but because the transfer is gratuitous—meaning that the transferor receives no consideration, at least not in any legally recognized form—it is generally not treated as a sale or exchange for income tax purposes. Thus, the donor or decedent generally recognizes no gain or loss on a transfer of property by gift or bequest. This result is not necessarily inherent in the nature of an income tax. In theory, there is no reason why a gift or bequest of property could not (or should not) cause the transferor to realize gain or loss, and such treatment has been proposed from time to time. Nor does any specific statutory provision prevent a gift or bequest from being treated as a taxable event. Nevertheless, the general rule of nontaxation has been an implicit feature of the statutory structure since 1913, and having prevailed for more than a century, the rule has become thoroughly entrenched.

In a few isolated situations, a transfer by gift is treated as a sale or exchange. For example, a gift may cause the donor to realize gain if the transferred property is subject to liabilities in excess of the donor's basis, or if the gift is conditioned on the donee's payment of the donor's gift tax liability (a "net gift"). Reg. § 1.1001–2(a) and (c) (Example 6);

Diedrich v. Commissioner, 457 U.S. 191 (1982). In addition, a lifetime gift of an installment obligation is treated as a taxable disposition that accelerates built-in gain in the donor's hands. I.R.C. § 453B(a). Rarely if ever does a decedent realize built-in gain or loss in property owned at death. For example, a bequest of an installment obligation generally does not trigger immediate gain realization. Even if gain is accelerated at death, as in the case of a "self-canceling" obligation, the built-in gain will probably be taxed to the decedent's estate (rather than to the decedent on his or her final income tax return). I.R.C. § 453B(c) and (f).

Exclusion of property received as gift or bequest. As previously noted, the value of property received by gift or bequest is excluded from the recipient's gross income, but income generated by the property after the date of the transfer will be taxed to the recipient. I.R.C. § 102(a) and (b)(1); Reg. § 1.102–1(a) and (b). In the simple case of property transferred directly to a donee by gift, the basic distinction between excludable property and post-transfer income is relatively straightforward. For example, if Diane gives a $10,000 bond to her son Eric, Eric receives the bond itself tax-free, and as the new owner of the bond he will be taxed on the subsequent interest payments. Even this simple example, however, raises a potential question concerning interest accrued but not yet realized at the time of the gift. Assume that Diane and Eric are both cash-method, calendar-year taxpayers and that the bond pays interest semi-annually on March 15 and September 15. If the gift occurs on May 15, the first interest payment received by Eric will include two months of interest accrued while Diane owned the bond and four months of post-gift interest. Eric will be taxed only on the interest accruing after the date of the gift; the portion already accrued while Diane owned the bond will be taxed to her as if she had received it and immediately made a gift of the same amount to Eric. Rev. Rul. 72–312, 1972–1 C.B. 22. Diane can make a gift to Eric of the bond, including the right to collect all future interest payments, but she cannot avoid being taxed on interest already accrued at the date of the gift.

The § 102 exclusion also applies to a gift in trust, but the analysis is slightly more complicated. In the previous example, suppose that instead of giving the bond directly to Eric, Diane transfers the bond to an irrevocable inter vivos trust, with income payable to Eric for life and remainder at his death to his surviving issue. The trust, which is recognized as a taxable entity, receives the gift of the bond tax-free under § 102, and the trust must include the subsequent interest payments in gross income (except for any interest accrued at the date of the gift, which will be taxed to Diane). Recall, however, that the trust distributes all of its net income currently to Eric. Under the conduit rules of Subchapter J, the trust is allowed a deduction for the required income distributions, and Eric must include the same amount in gross income. In an early case, the Supreme Court held that amounts of income distributed by a trust to a beneficiary were taxable in the beneficiary's hands and were not excludable from gross income under the predecessor of § 102. The court saw no material difference between "a gift of

the fund for life and a gift of the income from it."
Irwin v. Gavit, 268 U.S. 161 (1925). The Court's
holding, equating a gift of property for a limited
period of time with a gift of the income from the
property, was eventually codified in § 102(b)(2). In its
present form, the statute makes the exclusion of gifts
and bequests expressly subordinate to the conduit
rules of Subchapter J, by providing that any amount
taxable to a beneficiary under the conduit rules shall
be treated as a nonexcludable gift or bequest of
income. I.R.C. § 102(b); Reg. § 1.102–1(c) and (d). In
effect, the § 102 exclusion is reserved for the trust
corpus which is ultimately payable to the remainder
beneficiaries. Thus, when Eric dies and the trust
corpus is distributed to his surviving issue, they will
be taxed on any amounts of income distributed to
them, but they will receive the trust corpus tax-free.
For income tax purposes, they are treated as
receiving a gift of trust corpus which is covered by the
§ 102 exclusion.

The exclusion applies to bequests in much the
same way as to gifts, with two qualifications. First,
the decedent's estate may be interposed as an
intermediate entity between the deceased transferor
and the beneficiaries, as normally occurs when
property is subject to probate administration.
Continuing with the previous example, suppose that
Diane dies and leaves the bond to Eric in her will.
The immediate recipient of the bond is Diane's estate,
which is entitled to exclude the value of the bond (but
not post-death interest payments) from gross income
under § 102. If a decedent's estate distributes its
income currently to a beneficiary, the distributions

are deductible by the estate and includible by the beneficiary under the conduit rules. Typically, however, an estate retains most or all of its net income during the period of administration and is therefore taxable on the accumulated income. Accordingly, to the extent that the post-death interest payments on the bond are accumulated and not distributed currently, they will be taxed to Diane's estate. When the executor eventually winds up the estate administration and distributes the bond (along with accumulated interest), Eric will receive the bond tax-free as an excludable bequest; moreover, he will not be taxed on the interest accumulated in prior years, which has already been taxed to the estate. The income tax consequences would be similar if Diane bequeathed the bond in trust to pay income to Eric for life with remainder at his death to his surviving issue. In that case, the testamentary trust (which constitutes an entity separate from the estate for income tax purposes) would be treated as the distributee. Income distributed to Eric during his life would be taxed to him under the conduit rules, and the remainder beneficiaries would receive the bond tax-free at his death.

The second qualification involves the treatment of income accrued but not yet realized at the time of the transfer. Because a decedent's final taxable year ends at death, the decedent's final return includes only income realized during life; income realized after death must be reported by the person who receives it. Accordingly, in the previous example, any bond interest that was accrued but unpaid at Diane's death would be taxed to the recipient (i.e., Diane's estate or Eric) as "income in respect of a decedent," as discussed in Chapter 3, *infra*.

Recipient's basis in property received by gift or bequest. We have already seen that the value of property received by gift or bequest is excluded from gross income, but the recipient is taxable on income subsequently generated by the property. An important question, not addressed by § 102, involves the recipient's basis in property received by gift or bequest. The basis of the property in the recipient's hands will play a crucial role in computing gain or loss on a subsequent sale or exchange of the property.

In theory, one might expect that the recipient's basis would be the same as the transferor's basis immediately before the transfer. Such a "carryover" basis would be a logical corollary of the general rule treating gifts and bequests as nontaxable both to the transferor and to the transferee. In fact, however, the situation is somewhat more complicated. In the earliest years of the income tax, as a matter of administrative practice, the Treasury allowed the recipient of a gift or bequest to claim a "fresh start" basis equal to the value of the property at the date of acquisition, thereby ensuring that neither the transferor nor the recipient would ever be taxed on pre-transfer gain. In 1921, the statute was amended to provide a bifurcated basis rule: in the case of property "acquired by gift," the donee took a carryover basis, but in the case of property "acquired by bequest, devise, or inheritance," the basis of the inherited property was stepped up (or down) to fair market value at the date of acquisition. Although the rationale for differential treatment of gifts and bequests has always been obscure, the bifurcated approach enacted in 1921 has become firmly entrenched and remains in force, with a few refinements, under current law.

Property acquired by gift. In the case of property "acquired by gift," the donee generally steps into the donor's shoes and takes the property with the same basis it had in the hands of the donor (or the most recent owner who did not acquire the property by gift). I.R.C. § 1015(a). Thus, any built-in gain at the time of the gift is preserved in the hands of the donee and may be recognized on a subsequent sale of the property. For example, suppose that Frieda makes a gift to Gerald of stock that has a basis of $50,000 and a value of $100,000. If Gerald subsequently sells the stock for $120,000, he will be taxed on $70,000 of gain. However, if the donor's basis is greater than the value of the property at the time of the gift, the built-in loss is not recognized. For purposes of computing loss on a subsequent sale, the donee's basis is limited to the property's value at the time of the gift. This limitation was added in 1934 to prevent low-bracket donors from shifting built-in losses to high-bracket donees. Thus, in the previous example, suppose that the stock has a basis of $120,000 in Frieda's hands and a value of $100,000 at the time of the gift. If Gerald subsequently sells the stock for $90,000, he will report a loss of only $10,000; the $20,000 built-in loss is never recognized. What if Gerald sells the stock for $110,000? For purposes of computing gain, Gerald's basis in the stock is $120,000, which is greater than the amount realized ($110,000); for purposes of computing loss, however, his basis is limited to $100,000, the value of the stock at the time of the gift, which is less than the amount realized. Thus, Gerald will recognize neither gain nor loss. Reg. § 1.1015–1(a)(2). In effect, the basis rules of § 1015(a) for property acquired by gift impose a ceiling on the exclusion under § 102, leaving the donee accountable for gain accrued in the hands of the donor as well as the donee while denying the donee the benefit of any built-in loss at the time of the gift.

The donee's basis in property acquired by gift may be increased to reflect the donor's gift tax liability with respect to the transfer. I.R.C. § 1015(d). For gifts made after 1976, the basis increase is limited to the amount of gift tax attributable to the property's "net appreciation" (i.e., the excess, if any, of fair market value over basis) at the time of the gift. I.R.C. § 1015(d)(6); Reg. § 1.1015–5(c). The purpose of this adjustment is to mitigate the burden of taxing the donee on built-in gain that previously gave rise to gift tax liability (imposed on the donor at the time of the gift). Ideally, the amount of the donor's taxable gift would be reduced by the donee's income tax liability on the built-in gain, but since the timing and amount of the donee's future income tax liability is unknown at the time of the gift, the second-best solution allows the donee to increase the basis in the property (but not above fair market value) by the amount of gift tax paid by the donor and attributable to the built-in gain at the time of the gift. (For an analogous allowance in the context of "income in respect of a decedent," see § 691(c), discussed in § 3.5, *infra*.)

In theory, the basis adjustment produces roughly the same total income and gift tax burden (ignoring differences of timing and tax rates), regardless of whether (a) the donee sells appreciated property that was previously subject to gift tax or (b) the donor sells the property and gives the net proceeds to the donee. To illustrate, suppose that Howard owns land worth $100 with a basis of $60 which he plans to give to Irene. Assume a 20% income tax rate on capital gains and a 40% gift tax rate. If Howard sells the property for $100, he will recognize a gain of $40 and pay $8 of tax ($40 × 20%); if he then gives the $92 net proceeds ($100 − $8) to Irene, he will incur a gift tax of $36.80 ($92 × 40%). The total income and gift tax cost is $44.80. Alternatively, if Howard makes a gift of the appreciated property to Irene, he will incur a gift tax of $40 ($100 × 40%), and Irene will take the property with a basis of $76, reflecting a carryover basis of $60 and a $16 adjustment for the gift tax attributable to the built-in gain ($40 gift tax × 40/100 net appreciation); if Irene then sells the property for $100, she will recognize a gain of $24 ($100 − $76 basis) and pay $4.80 of tax ($24 × 20%). Again, the total income and gift tax cost is $44.80. The tax consequences are not exactly equivalent, of course, because in the first case Howard bears the entire tax burden and Irene ends up with $92 after tax, while in the second case Howard pays a larger gift tax and Irene pays a smaller income tax, leaving Irene with $95.20 after tax. (In the second case, the incremental

$3.20 benefit to Irene is matched by an equal increase in the amount of gift tax paid by Howard.)

Some transactions combine elements of a gift and a sale. In a "bargain sale," for example, the transferor may sell property to a family member for a price substantially below fair market value, with the intent of conferring a gratuitous benefit on the purchaser. For income tax purposes, such a transaction is generally treated as part-gift, part-sale. The transferor is treated as selling a portion of the property equal in value to the consideration received, and is allowed to offset all of his or her basis against the amount realized, thereby minimizing the amount of taxable gain. The rest of the property is treated as a gift. Accordingly, the transferor recognizes gain equal to the excess, if any, of the amount realized over the basis of the property, and the transferee takes the property with a basis equal to the greater of the transferor's basis or the amount of consideration paid by the transferee (increased in either case by any gift tax adjustment under § 1015(d)). The transferee's basis is limited to the property's value at the time of the transfer, for purposes of computing any loss on a subsequent sale. Reg. §§ 1.1011–1(e) and 1.1015–4. For example, suppose that Oliver sells land worth $90 to Phoebe for a purchase price of $30; Oliver's basis in the land is $60. Oliver will be treated as selling one-third of the land for $30 and making a gift of the remaining two-thirds to Phoebe. Oliver will recognize no gain, since the amount realized does not exceed his basis in the property, and Phoebe will take the property with a carryover basis of $60 (increased by any gift tax paid by Oliver and attributable to the $30 built-in gain). Alternatively, if Phoebe pays $75 for the property, Oliver will recognize a gain of $15 ($75 amount realized less $60 basis), and Phoebe will take the property with a basis of $75 (increased by any gift tax paid by Oliver and attributable to the $15 built-in gain). A transferor of appreciated property who wishes to shift all of the built-in gain to the transferee while reducing the amount of any taxable gift can do so by selling the property for a price equal to the transferor's basis.

A special rule applies to a bargain sale if the transferee is a charity. To prevent the transferor from offsetting his or her entire basis against the amount realized while deducting the built-in gain as a charitable contribution, the statute requires that basis be allocated proportionately between the sale and gift portions of the transaction. I.R.C. § 1011(b); Reg. § 1.1011–2. In the previous example, suppose that Oliver sells land worth $90, with a basis of $60, to charity for a purchase price of $30. Oliver will be treated as selling one-third of the land for $30 and making a charitable contribution of the remaining two-thirds. Under § 1011(b), he must allocate one-third of his basis to the sale portion and two-thirds to the gift portion; he is not allowed to offset his entire basis against the purchase price. Accordingly, he must recognize a gain of $10 ($30 amount realized less $20 allocable portion of basis), and he may deduct a $60 charitable contribution (subject to the percentage limitations of § 170).

Property acquired from a decedent. Inherited property, unlike property acquired by gift, generally takes a "fresh start" basis in the hands of the recipient. This rule, originally enacted in 1921, now appears in § 1014, which provides that "the basis of property in the hands of a person acquiring the property from a decedent or to whom the property passed from a decedent shall [be] the fair market value of the property at the date of the decedent's death." I.R.C. § 1014(a)(1). The direct consequence of this provision, in conjunction with the failure to treat the transfer of property at death as a taxable event, is that the unrealized appreciation in property owned at death will never be subject to income tax in the hands of the decedent, the recipient, or any other person. Similarly, any built-in losses will never be recognized. Thus, the prospect of obtaining a fresh-start basis offers taxpayers a powerful incentive to retain appreciated assets until death (and to sell or dispose of assets that have declined in value during life). As a matter of tax policy, the tax-free basis step-up for appreciated property is clearly anomalous, but Congress has shown little interest in replacing it with a deathtime tax on unrealized gains or a carryover basis for inherited property. Moreover, while it is sometimes suggested that the estate tax compensates for the nontaxation of unrealized appreciation, the vast majority of estates are completely sheltered from estate tax liability by the ever-expanding unified credit.

Property is eligible for a fresh-start basis only if it was "acquired from" a decedent. For this purpose, property is treated as acquired from a decedent if it falls into one or more enumerated categories, including property passing by bequest, devise, or inheritance (i.e., as part of the probate estate); property transferred by the decedent during life subject to a retained power to revoke or amend; and property otherwise includible in the decedent's gross estate for estate tax purposes. I.R.C. § 1014(b). Furthermore, under a special provision, a surviving spouse's one-half interest in community property is eligible for a fresh-start basis even though only the decedent's half of the property is included in the gross estate. I.R.C. § 1014(b)(6). The statutory definition of property acquired from a decedent provides an express linkage between the income and estate tax treatment of property transferred at death.

In determining the recipient's basis in property acquired from a decedent, the fair market value of the property at the date of death is deemed to be the same as the value determined for estate tax purposes. Reg. § 1.1014–3(a). Thus, if the executor makes an election to use the alternate valuation date, to report farm or business real property based on its special use value, or to exclude land subject to a conservation easement on the estate tax return, the recipient's basis is determined by reference to the estate tax value. I.R.C. § 1014(a)(2)–(a)(4). In some cases, a taxpayer who inherited property from a decedent may seek to establish that the deathtime value of the property (and hence the taxpayer's basis) is higher than the value reported by the executor on the estate tax return. In this situation, the Service has traditionally treated the estate tax valuation as presumptively (but not conclusively) correct, and has allowed the taxpayer (subject to equitable estoppel principles) to rebut the presumption by clear and convincing evidence. Rev. Rul. 54–97, 1954–1 C.B. 113. In 2015, Congress amended § 1014 to limit the basis of property acquired from a decedent to the value finally determined for estate tax purposes (or, if no estate tax return is filed, the value reported by the executor on a separate information statement). I.R.C. § 1014(f). This limitation applies to an item of property only if its inclusion in the decedent's gross estate resulted in an increased estate tax liability (after credits), and thus has no effect on small and moderate estates which incur no estate tax liability because they fall below the threshold for filing a return.

There are two important exceptions to the fresh-start basis provision of § 1014(a). The first exception involves items of "income in respect of a decedent" (IRD). IRD generally refers to amounts that were accrued or substantially earned by the decedent during life, but not realized for income tax purposes before death and therefore not properly includible in the decedent's gross income. Common examples of IRD include accrued but unpaid salary, interest or dividends for the period ending at death, as well as untaxed retirement benefits. Since these amounts were not taxed to the decedent during life, they must be included in gross income by the decedent's estate (or other recipient) when they are actually received. I.R.C. § 691(a). Furthermore, to the extent that an item of IRD was subject to estate tax at the decedent's death and is subsequently included in the recipient's gross income, the combined burden of the estate and income taxes is mitigated by allowing an income tax deduction for an allocable portion of the estate tax. I.R.C. § 691(c). As a corollary of this statutory scheme, § 1014(c) denies a fresh-start basis to IRD items, in order to ensure that they do not escape tax in the hands of the recipient. In effect, the recipient takes IRD items with a carryover basis. To illustrate, suppose that on October 1 Zipco declares a dividend of $1 per share, payable on December 15 to shareholders of record as of November 1. Cindy, who owned 10 shares of Zipco stock, dies on November 5, and her estate receives a $10 dividend on December 15. Because Cindy died after the record date and before the payment date, the dividend constitutes an item of IRD which must be included in gross income by her estate. The estate does not take the dividend with a stepped-up basis, but it is entitled to an income tax deduction for any estate tax attributable to the dividend. (For a more detailed discussion of IRD, see Chapter 3, *infra.*)

The second exception to fresh-start basis consists of an anti-abuse rule aimed at "basis-laundering" transactions. Under the anti-abuse rule, property passing from a decedent takes a carryover basis in the recipient's hands if the recipient (or the recipient's spouse) transferred the property by gift to the decedent during the one-year period ending on the date of death at a time when the value of the property exceeded its basis. I.R.C. § 1014(e). To illustrate the abuse at which this provision is aimed, suppose that Martha makes a gift of stock to Norman when the stock has a value of $100 and a basis of $20, and Norman dies six months later leaving the stock (still worth $100) to Martha by will. Instead of allowing Martha to inherit the stock with a stepped-up basis, § 1014(e) prescribes a carryover basis. As a result, the basis of the stock in Martha's hands is the same as Norman's basis, which of course was the same as Martha's basis when she gave the stock to Norman. Thus, by denying a fresh-start basis, § 1014(e) eliminates the tax advantage of this sort of transaction. The result would be the same if Norman left the stock to Martha's spouse, or if Norman's executor sold the stock and Martha (or her spouse) was entitled to the sale proceeds.

Uniform basis. The rules governing the basis of property acquired by gift or bequest apply not only to property in the hands of an estate or a trust but also to the interests of the entity's beneficiaries. The regulations explain that, under the principle of "uniform basis," the basis of property "will be the same, or uniform, whether the property is possessed or enjoyed by the executor or administrator, the heir, the legatee or devisee, or the trustee or beneficiary of a trust created by a will or an inter vivos trust." Reg. § 1.1014–4(a); see also Reg. § 1.1015–1(b). In most cases, the basis of property held by an estate or a trust is of little concern to the beneficiaries until the entity distributes the property to a particular beneficiary, whereupon the distributee receives the property with the same basis it had in the entity's hands, adjusted for any gain or loss recognized by the entity on the distribution. I.R.C. § 643(e)(1). If an executor or a trustee sells property and reinvests the proceeds, the entity will have a cost basis in the newly acquired assets, and upon distribution those assets will have the same basis (adjusted for any gain or loss recognized by the entity on the distribution) in the beneficiary's hands.

To illustrate, suppose that Claudia dies leaving her entire estate to Duncan by will. Claudia's property, including Blackacre (worth $200) and Whiteacre (worth $100), has a basis equal to its value at the date of her death. In the course of administering her estate, the executor sells Whiteacre, purchases Greenacre for $150, and eventually distributes Blackacre and Greenacre (along with the other property remaining after paying debts, taxes and administration expenses) tax-free to Duncan as sole beneficiary under the will. The basis of the distributed property in Duncan's hands is the same as in the estate's hands, $200 for Blackacre (the value at Claudia's death) and $150 for Greenacre (the purchase price paid by the estate).

In the previous example, suppose that instead of devising her estate to Duncan, Claudia creates a testamentary trust to pay income to Duncan for life with remainder at his death to Elmo. As in the previous example, Claudia's property has a basis in the estate's hands equal to its date-of-death value, and when the executor distributes property to the testamentary trust (a taxable entity separate from the estate), the trust will receive the property with the same basis it had in the estate's hands. Duncan will be taxed on the net trust income distributed to him during his lifetime under the conduit rules of Subchapter J, but unless he receives distributions of trust corpus he will not be directly affected by the trust's basis in its assets. At Duncan's death, the trust will terminate and distribute its property tax-free to Elmo as remainder beneficiary. The basis of the distributed property in Elmo's hands will be the same as in the trust's hands. Thus, property that was owned by Claudia and passed through her estate and testamentary trust will have a basis in Elmo's hands equal to its date-of-death value, while property purchased by the estate or the trust will have a basis equal to its acquisition cost, adjusted in either case for depreciation, capital improvements, and the like. Note that Duncan is not entitled to amortize his life income interest, and Elmo recognizes no gain or loss when his remainder interest becomes possessory. The basis of property distributed by an estate or a trust is the same in the hands of the distributee as it was in the entity's hands immediately before the distribution. The analysis would be the same in the case of an irrevocable inter vivos trust, except that the trust would receive its initial property by gift directly from the grantor with a carryover basis under § 1015. (Any property added to the trust at death would receive a fresh-start basis if it was included in the grantor's gross estate and was therefore acquired from a decedent under § 1014.)

If a beneficiary sells his or her interest in an estate or a trust, it may be necessary to apportion the uniform basis in the trust property to determine the shares of the respective beneficiaries. In the previous example, suppose that Claudia's testamentary trust holds only two assets: Blackacre, worth $600, with a basis of $200 (the value at Claudia's death), and Greenacre, worth $300, with a cost basis of $150.

While Duncan is still alive, Elmo sells his remainder interest in the trust to a third party for its actuarial value of $360 (determined under the Treasury tables). In computing his gain from the sale of his remainder, Elmo is entitled to recover his basis, which consists of a share of the uniform basis in the trust property proportionate to the actuarial value of Elmo's remainder. Since his remainder is assumed to be worth 40% of the trust property ($360 ÷ $900), his share of the uniform basis is $140 (40% × $350), and he is taxed on a capital gain of $220 ($360 amount realized less $140 basis). Reg. § 1.1014–5(c). Note that Elmo's share of the uniform basis consists of a ratable share of the trust's basis in the property, reflecting a carryover basis in property acquired by gift, a fresh-start basis in property acquired from a decedent, and a cost basis in property purchased by the trustee, adjusted for depreciation, capital improvements, and the like. Reg. §§ 1.1014–4, 1.1014–5, and 1.1015–1(b). Note also that while Duncan is alive he too has a share of the uniform basis proportionate to the actuarial value of his income interest, but if he sells his income interest to a third party (not in conjunction with a sale of Elmo's remainder) his basis will be disregarded and he will therefore be taxed on the full amount realized. I.R.C. § 1001(e); Reg. § 1.1001–1(f).

Finally, note that while the amount of uniform basis (as adjusted) of property in the hands of an estate or a trust is always the same as the beneficiaries' aggregate bases in their interests, the beneficiaries' respective shares of uniform basis (reflecting the actuarial values of their interests) vary according to the passage of time and changes in interest rates. According to the regulations, the purpose of the uniform basis rule, as applied to property acquired from a decedent, is "on the one hand, to tax the gain, in respect of such property, to [the person] who realizes it (without regard to the circumstance that at the death of the decedent it may have been quite uncertain whether the taxpayer would take or gain anything); and, on the other hand, not to recognize as gain any element of value resulting solely from the circumstance that the possession or enjoyment of the taxpayer was postponed." Reg. § 1.1014–4(a)(2).

§ 1.3 DISTRIBUTIONS FROM ESTATE OR TRUST TO BENEFICIARIES

For income tax purposes, an estate or a trust is recognized as a taxable entity separate from its beneficiaries, and all of the entity's income is taxable in much the same way as that of an individual taxpayer. A primary function of Subchapter J is to allocate the income of an estate or a trust between the entity and its beneficiaries, so that the income will be taxed either to the entity or to the beneficiaries but not to both. The statutory scheme allocates income to the beneficiaries to the extent of the amounts currently distributable to them, and allocates any remaining income to the entity. To accomplish this result, the entity is allowed a deduction for amounts distributed to the beneficiaries, and the beneficiaries are required to include the same aggregate amount in gross income, apportioned in proportion to their respective distributions. In effect, an estate or a trust functions as a conduit to the extent that it distributes its income currently to the beneficiaries, leaving the entity to report any residual amounts held or accumulated for distribution in future years. If the estate or the trust makes no current distributions and accumulates all of its income, all of the income will be taxed to the entity. Under the compressed rate schedule applicable to estates and trusts, the potential tax savings from accumulating taxable income in a single entity (or even in multiple trusts) are severely limited. Accordingly, the beneficiaries will generally not be subject to a second level of tax when the accumulated amounts are distributed to them in a subsequent year.

Amounts distributed by an estate or a trust may be viewed as "carrying out" taxable income to the beneficiaries to the extent that those amounts are deductible by the entity and includible by the beneficiaries under the conduit rules. Conversely, to the extent that a distribution does not give rise to a deduction and matching inclusion, it may be viewed as a tax-free distribution of corpus. Under pre-1954 law, the income tax treatment of distributions often varied depending on whether the amounts in question were treated as coming from income or principal for fiduciary accounting purposes. In 1954, Congress adopted "distributable net income" (DNI) as a statutory mechanism to measure the extent to which distributions are deductible by an estate or a trust and includible by its beneficiaries under the conduit rules. The concept of DNI minimizes the need to trace the source of distributions to fiduciary accounting income or principal under local law, and instead provides a more uniform federal standard for determining the amount and character of an entity's tentative taxable income that is available for distribution to the beneficiaries during the taxable year. Technically, DNI of an estate or a trust is defined in the same manner as taxable income but without regard to any distribution deduction or personal exemption and subject to additional modifications. For example, DNI takes account of tax-exempt interest (an item of fiduciary accounting income that is excluded from gross income), and excludes undistributed capital gains (which are generally allocated to corpus but are included in gross income). These adjustments represent an attempt to refine DNI as a measure of amounts that, if distributed, are properly reportable by the beneficiaries, while excluding items that are properly reportable by the entity for income tax purposes. In sum, DNI serves two important functions: it places a ceiling on the amount of distributions that an estate or a trust may deduct and that the beneficiaries must include in gross income; and it establishes the character of distributions in the hands of the beneficiaries. (For a more detailed discussion of DNI, see Chapter 6, *infra.*)

Under the conduit rules, amounts distributed by an estate or a trust to its beneficiaries are generally deductible by the entity and includible by the beneficiaries up to the DNI ceiling. DNI is allocated first to mandatory distributions of current income, and then to any other amounts properly paid, credited, or required to be distributed, whether from income or corpus, and the items entering into DNI are allocated among the beneficiaries in each category in proportion to their respective shares. Any amounts in excess of DNI are deemed to be tax-free distributions of corpus. For example, suppose that a trust is required to pay its net income to Sandra for life, with remainder at her death to her surviving issue. The trust's net income consists of $200 interest and $200 qualified dividends; it also has a $100 capital gain (allocated to corpus) and a deductible trustee fee of $100 (also charged to corpus). The trust has $400 of fiduciary accounting income and $300 of DNI (reflecting the $100 deduction for the trustee fee). Thus, although the trust distributes $400 of fiduciary accounting income to Sandra, the amount deductible by the trust and includible by Sandra is limited to $300; for tax purposes, the remaining $100 is treated as a tax-free distribution of corpus. The $100 capital gain, which is excluded from DNI, is taxable to the trust itself (though it may be offset by a personal exemption). Although it may seem unfair that the $100 trustee fee produces a tax benefit for Sandra even though it is actually paid from corpus, the deduction might otherwise be wasted if it could not be used to offset other taxable income in the trust's hands. More generally, by allowing most deductions to reduce DNI regardless of whether the corresponding items are charged to income or corpus for fiduciary accounting purposes, the conduit rules tend to avoid wasting deductions while minimizing the need for tracing.

In the previous example, suppose that the trustee is not required to distribute any income currently but has discretion to pay income or corpus to Sandra or Tyler. The trustee exercises its discretion by paying $100 of fiduciary accounting income to Sandra and $500 of corpus to Tyler; the remaining $300 of fiduciary accounting income is accumulated in the trust. Under the conduit rules, it generally does not matter whether discretionary distributions are traceable to fiduciary accounting income or corpus; in the absence of required current income distributions, all distributions carry out a ratable share of DNI. Here, the trust's DNI of $300 establishes a ceiling on the amount of distributions deductible by the trust and includible by the beneficiaries. Thus, the trust is allowed a distribution deduction of $300, and Sandra and Tyler must include their respective shares of DNI in gross income. Sandra will be taxed on $50 ($300 × 100/600) and Tyler will be taxed on $250 ($300 × 500/600); for tax purposes, the remaining amounts paid to them are treated as tax-free distributions of corpus.

Not all distributions carry out DNI from an estate or a trust to its beneficiaries. If the governing instrument provides for a gift or bequest of a specific sum of cash or of specific property, payment of the cash or property may be excluded from the conduit rules and treated as a tax-free distribution of corpus. (For a more detailed discussion of taxable and tax-free distributions under the conduit rules, see Chapter 7, *infra*.)

For many years, if a trust did not distribute all of its income currently, the accumulated amounts were subject to a second level of tax when distributed to the beneficiaries in a subsequent taxable year. Under current law, however, the compressed rate schedule neutralizes most of the tax advantage of accumulating income in trust, and the additional tax was repealed in 1997 for most domestic trusts. (For a discussion of the "throwback" rules, see Chapter 11, *infra*.)

§ 1.4   TRUST INCOME ATTRIBUTED TO GRANTOR

Subchapter J generally recognizes a trust as a taxable entity separate from its grantor. However, an inter vivos trust may be disregarded for tax purposes, even though it is validly created and enforceable under local law, if the grantor retains substantially unfettered beneficial enjoyment or control of the trust. For example, under a pair of "grantor trust" provisions originally enacted in 1924, a trust's income will be taxed directly to the grantor if the grantor retains either a power to revoke the trust or a right to receive trust income. (The modern versions of those provisions appear in §§ 676 and 677.) Prior to 1954, these were the only statutory provisions that dealt specifically with the use of trusts as devices for shifting taxable income from a grantor to family members. Confronted with a wide range of trusts, gifts, and other income-shifting arrangements that were not specifically covered by the grantor trust provisions, the courts developed an expansive assignment-of-income doctrine to identify the appropriate taxpayer under the predecessor of § 61. The doctrine remains important under current law, although its field of application has been narrowed by statutory developments including the enactment of expanded grantor trust provisions, joint returns for married couples, and the "kiddie tax" on unearned income of minor children.

In the landmark case of Lucas v. Earl, 281 U.S. 111 (1930), the Supreme Court held that an agreement between a husband and wife to share all of their respective earnings equally during marriage was ineffective for tax purposes, even if the agreement was enforceable under local law. Consequently, each spouse was taxable on his or her own earnings under the predecessor of § 61; the tax could not be avoided by an "anticipatory" assignment of income. The doctrine announced in *Lucas v. Earl* makes it virtually impossible for an individual taxpayer to avoid tax on personal service income by directing that the income be paid to a family member or a trust. For an unsuccessful attempt to deflect a grantor's future earnings to a "family trust," see Schulz v. Commissioner, 686 F.2d 490 (7th Cir. 1982).

Courts have applied the assignment-of-income doctrine somewhat less rigorously to transfers of income-producing property. As previously noted, property transferred by gift generally takes a carryover basis in the donee's hands, with the result that any unrealized appreciation at the time of the gift is preserved and taxed to the donee upon a subsequent sale of the property. In this sense, a lifetime gift of the donor's entire interest in property, with no retained interests or powers, is an effective technique for shifting future income (including unrealized appreciation) from the donor to the donee.

(In the case of a bequest, appreciation not realized before death may escape tax altogether.) However, the assignment-of-income doctrine does constrain the donor's ability to assign a time-limited income interest while retaining ownership of the underlying property.

In the leading case of Helvering v. Horst, 311 U.S. 112 (1940), a father who owned interest-bearing bonds made a gift to his son of coupons representing the right to collect the current year's interest, while retaining ownership of the bonds. The Supreme Court saw no reason to treat the gift of interest coupons differently from the income-splitting agreement in *Lucas v. Earl*, and held that the father was taxable on the interest payments that were actually made (at his direction) to the son. The doctrine applies with equal force to a trust beneficiary's assignment of his or her beneficial interest. For example, one year after its decision in *Horst*, the Court held that an income beneficiary remained taxable on the income of a trust despite her assignment to her children of specified dollar amounts of the following year's income. Harrison v. Schaffner, 312 U.S. 579 (1941). In contrast, a life income beneficiary who irrevocably assigned specified dollar amounts of annual income to his children succeeded in shifting a corresponding portion of the corresponding income tax liability to the children, apparently because the transfer was complete, without reservation, and the transferred payments were coterminous with the assignor's outstanding life income interest. Blair v. Commissioner, 300 U.S. 5 (1937).

The Supreme Court's willingness to attribute the income of an inter vivos trust to its grantor reached its high-water mark in Helvering v. Clifford, 309 U.S. 331 (1940). In *Clifford*, the grantor created an irrevocable short-term trust to pay income to his wife and then to return the underlying property to himself; as sole trustee, the grantor retained control over the trust administration, including the timing of income distributions. Although the trust escaped the reach of the rudimentary grantor trust provisions under pre-1954 law, the Court held that the trust's income was taxable to the grantor under the predecessor of § 61, based on the grantor's continuing "dominion and control." The scope and reasoning of the *Clifford* decision generated considerable confusion and uncertainty which persisted until 1954 when Congress enacted a comprehensive new set of statutory grantor trust provisions.

The grantor trust provisions, which now appear in §§ 671–679, enumerate the circumstances in which a grantor will be treated as the deemed owner of an inter vivos trust for income tax purposes by reason of specified powers or interests. In addition to the obvious examples of a retained power of revocation and a retained interest in present or future income, the statute provides that grantor trust status may be triggered by specified powers of disposition or administration as well as by a retained reversionary interest. In some cases, a power of withdrawal held by a person other than the grantor may cause the power holder to be treated as the deemed owner of a corresponding portion of the trust. The grantor trust provisions supersede the open-ended *Clifford* doctrine, replacing "dominion and control" with a detailed list of specific powers and interests that will trigger grantor trust status. Conversely, a trust that scrupulously avoids all of the statutory triggers will not be treated as a grantor trust by reason of the grantor's retained dominion and control.

To the extent that a trust is treated as a grantor trust, its income is taxable directly to the grantor (or other deemed owner) and in effect the trust itself is disregarded for substantive income tax purposes. Consequently, the normal conduit rules of Subchapter J do not apply to a wholly-owned grantor trust. As a practical matter, the impact of grantor trust status is likely to be greatest where the grantor is taxed on trust income that is actually paid to other beneficiaries; if the income is payable to the grantor, the difference between grantor and nongrantor status may be less important. Traditionally, tax planners generally sought to avoid grantor trust status, and nongrantor trusts were widely used to shift income to lower-bracket beneficiaries or to accumulate income at relatively low tax rates. Ironically, however, the compressed rate schedule applicable to trusts under current law has made grantor trust status increasingly attractive because trust income is often taxed at a lower marginal rate in the grantor's hands than it would be if it were taxed to the trust as a separate taxable entity. The grantor trust provisions are discussed in more detail in Chapter 8, *infra*.

§ 1.5 GIFT AND ESTATE TAXES

The transfer of property by gift or bequest is not treated as a taxable event for income tax purposes. The transferor generally recognizes no gain or loss, and the recipient does not include the transferred property in gross income. Instead, gratuitous transfers of property are subject to a separate scheme of gift and estate taxation (supplemented in some cases by a tax on generation-skipping transfers). As a policy matter, the income tax and the wealth transfer taxes may be viewed as complementary components of a larger federal tax system in evaluating the revenue and distributional effects of current law or proposed reforms. Moreover, as a practical matter, in planning and implementing a particular transaction, taxpayers should consider the transaction's gift and estate tax treatment as well as its income tax consequences (and nontax implications). Nevertheless, for the most part—aside from a few specific points of intersection, such as the fresh-start basis rule of § 1014(a) for property acquired from a decedent, and the adjustments for gift and estate taxes under §§ 1015(d) and 691(c)— the gift and estate taxes are conceptually and operationally separate and distinct from the income tax, and accordingly they are touched on here only in passing.*

The gift and estate taxes are imposed on gratuitous transfers of property made by individual taxpayers

---

* For a more detailed discussion of wealth transfer taxation, see McNulty & McCouch, Federal Estate and Gift Taxation (9th ed. 2020).

during life or at death. The two taxes have been
closely but imperfectly coordinated with each other
from their inception, and since 1976 they have been
"unified" in the sense that they share a common rate
schedule and exemption amount. The tax base
consists of cumulative taxable transfers made during
life or at death; as implied by their respective names,
the gift tax applies to lifetime transfers and the
estate tax applies to transfers occurring at death.
Very generally, the taxes are imposed at a flat 40%
rate on cumulative taxable transfers in excess of a
$10 million exemption (indexed for inflation).
Because the gift and estate taxes are imposed on the
transfer (not on the receipt) of property, the
responsibility for reporting a taxable transfer and
paying any resulting tax falls primarily on the donor
or the decedent's executor (not on the recipient).

Although the gift and estate taxes nominally apply
to all taxable transfers made during life or at death,
very few taxpayers actually incur any gift or estate
tax liability. There are several reasons for the limited
reach of the gift and estate taxes. Most obviously, the
$10 million exemption (indexed for inflation) far
exceeds the net worth of all but the wealthiest
taxpayers. Consequently, in the vast majority of
cases, any property owned at death passes to the
decedent's beneficiaries completely free of estate and
income taxes, with a fresh-start basis equal to its
date-of-death value. Moreover, the $10,000 (indexed
for inflation) per-donee annual gift tax exclusion
allows most routine lifetime gifts to escape gift tax
entirely; because such gifts are excluded from taxable
gifts, they do not count against the donor's lifetime

exemption and in most cases need not even be reported. Finally, both the gift tax and the estate tax allow unlimited deductions for transfers made (in qualifying form) to a spouse or to charity, with the result that even very large fortunes often escape gift and estate taxes either temporarily (in the case of a bequest to a surviving spouse) or permanently (in the case of a charitable bequest).

To avoid potential confusion, it should be emphasized that certain terms and concepts may have subtly different meanings depending on the context in which they appear. In the gift tax context, for example, a "transfer by gift" generally refers to a transaction in which a donor gratuitously confers a beneficial interest in property on another person, receiving less than full money's-worth consideration in return. The test is essentially objective, focusing on the lack of full consideration, and the donor's donative intent (or lack thereof) is only tangentially relevant. Commissioner v. Wemyss, 324 U.S. 303 (1945). By contrast, in the income tax context, a transfer of property may qualify as an excludable gift in the recipient's hands if the transfer was motivated by "detached and disinterested generosity" or by considerations of "affection, respect, admiration, charity or like impulses." Commissioner v. Duberstein, 363 U.S. 278 (1960).

A more significant difference arises in determining whether a transfer is deemed wholly or partially "complete" for gift, estate, and income tax purposes. For gift tax purposes, a gift of property is generally complete (and therefore subject to gift tax) when the donor relinquishes dominion and control and retains no power to change the beneficial enjoyment of the property. Reg. § 25.2511–2. Thus, for example, a grantor who transfers property in trust subject to a retained power of revocation initially makes no completed gift; a completed gift will occur only to the extent that the trust property passes beyond the grantor's control (e.g., upon distribution to another beneficiary or upon termination of the retained power during the grantor's lifetime). Moreover, a gift may be partially complete and partially incomplete. For example, a grantor who transfers property in trust subject to a retained life income interest makes a completed gift of the remainder interest but not the retained income interest. To the extent that a retained interest or power prevents a gift from becoming complete during the donor's lifetime, the transfer will almost always be includible in the gross estate at death. In other words, a transfer that is treated as incomplete during life (and therefore not subject to gift tax) by reason of a retained interest or power is treated as being completed at death (and therefore subject to estate tax). Thus, in the two examples just given, the donor's retained power of revocation or retained life income interest would cause the underlying trust property to be included in the gross estate. I.R.C. §§ 2036 and 2038. Indeed, in a few cases a single transfer may be subject to overlapping gift and estate taxes, giving rise to an automatic adjustment in the estate tax computation to mitigate the risk of double taxation.

A grantor's retained interest in or power over a trust may cause the grantor to be treated as the deemed owner of the trust (or a portion thereof) under the grantor trust provisions. I.R.C. §§ 671–679. In effect, those provisions define the extent to which a transfer in trust remains incomplete for income tax purposes. If the grantor retains a proscribed interest or power, the trust income (or a portion thereof) will be attributed to the grantor; the normal conduit rules of Subchapter J apply to the trust (or a portion thereof) only if the grantor retains none of the enumerated taxable strings. The specific definition of an incomplete transfer set forth in the grantor trust provisions diverges in material respects from its counterparts in the gift and estate taxes. For example, various powers of administration or disposition held by the grantor's spouse or by a nonadverse third party may trigger grantor trust status without preventing a completed gift for gift tax purposes. This disparity between the income and transfer taxes has prompted widespread interest in a form of "intentionally defective" grantor trust which gives rise to a taxable gift on creation but escapes inclusion in the grantor's gross estate at death, while leaving the grantor personally liable for the income tax on income generated by the trust during the grantor's lifetime. As a result, the trust and the beneficiaries are relieved of the burden of paying income tax on the trust income, which falls instead on the grantor, who makes the annual tax payments with no additional gift tax liability. Rev. Rul. 2004–64, 2004–2 C.B. 7.

§ 1.6 STATE FIDUCIARY INCOME TAXES

Although the present discussion focuses primarily on the federal income taxation of estates, trusts, and beneficiaries, the income tax consequences under state law also deserve at least a brief mention. States that impose a fiduciary income tax typically follow the federal model, treating an estate or a trust as a conduit with respect to amounts of income currently distributed to beneficiaries and taxing the entity itself only on its accumulated income. Income of a grantor trust is taxed to the grantor (or other deemed owner) under principles similar to those of federal law. Importantly, estates, trusts, and beneficiaries are generally taxable on income from all sources if they are residents of the taxing state, while nonresident taxpayers are taxable only on income derived from sources within the taxing state. To mitigate the risk of double taxation, a resident taxpayer is typically allowed a credit for income tax paid to another state on income derived from sources in the other taxing state. Nevertheless, in selecting trustees and designating the place of administration, taxpayers should give careful consideration to state income tax consequences.

A state's taxing jurisdiction is limited by the statutory definition of a "resident" for income tax purposes. An individual taxpayer (including a grantor or beneficiary) is generally treated as a resident of a state based on domicile or physical presence during the taxable year. The residence of a decedent's estate is generally aligned with the place of primary probate administration, which is normally in the state of the decedent's domicile; if ancillary jurisdiction in another state is necessary, the other state's taxing jurisdiction extends only to income derived from sources within its borders. In the case of a trust, the concept of residence is far from uniform. Several states treat a trust as a resident only if the trust is administered within the state or has at least one resident trustee. Some states impose an additional or alternative requirement that the trust have at least one resident beneficiary. And some other states treat a trust as a resident if the grantor (or the testator, in the case of a testamentary trust) is a resident at the time the trust is created or becomes irrevocable. Given the number and variety of relevant factors, it is often uncertain whether a trust qualifies as a resident of one or more states during a particular taxable year. In theory, several states may simultaneously claim the same trust as a resident, and assert taxing jurisdiction over its income from all sources, based on different local definitions of residence. Moreover, a state which claims the trust as a resident may deny any credit for income taxes imposed by other states on the trust's investment income, on the ground that income from intangible property is not deemed to be derived from any source outside the state of the trust's residence. Consequently, trusts face a heightened risk of multiple taxation by two or more states.

Nevertheless, the taxing jurisdiction of the states is subject to two significant limitations under the federal constitution. The first constraint arises from the Due Process Clause, which has been interpreted to require a "minimum connection" between a state and the person, property or transaction being taxed, as well as a rational relationship between the income attributed to the state and values connected with the state. North Carolina Department of Revenue v. Kaestner Family Trust, 139 S.Ct. 2213 (2019). These requirements are easily satisfied when a state taxes the income of a trust that is administered within the state or has one or more resident trustees. The situation is less clear when a state asserts its taxing jurisdiction over a trust based on the residence of the grantor or the beneficiaries. In *Kaestner*, for example, North Carolina sought to tax all of the income accumulated by an out-of-state trust for beneficiaries who lived in North Carolina. During the relevant years, the beneficiaries did not receive any income from the trust and had no right to demand any distributions or to control, possess, or enjoy the trust property; indeed, because of the discretionary nature of the trust, none of the beneficiaries could count on receiving any specific amount of future distributions. Given the attenuated relationship between the resident beneficiaries and the trust property, the Supreme Court held that "the presence of in-state beneficiaries alone does not empower a State to tax trust income that has not been distributed to the beneficiaries where the beneficiaries have no right to demand that income and are uncertain ever to receive it." Similar considerations have led other courts to hold on due process grounds that a state lacks jurisdiction to tax the income of an out-of-state trust based solely on the grantor's status as a resident when the trust was created and when it became irrevocable. Fielding v. Commissioner, 916

N.W.2d 323 (Minn. 2018), cert. denied, 139 S.Ct. 2773 (2019) (inter vivos trust); see also Swift v. Director of Revenue, 727 S.W.2d 880 (Mo. 1987) (testamentary trust); but cf. Chase Manhattan Bank v. Gavin, 733 A.2d 782 (Conn.), cert. denied, 528 U.S. 965 (1999) (contra, testamentary trust).

Even if a state's fiduciary income tax survives scrutiny under the Due Process Clause, it may nevertheless be struck down under the Commerce Clause if it creates an impermissible burden on interstate commerce. As previously noted, any state that taxes its own residents on income from all sources and also taxes nonresidents on income derived from sources within the taxing state creates a risk of double taxation, but the possibility of double taxation alone is not fatal. Under prevailing doctrine, the tax will satisfy the "dormant" Commerce Clause if it (1) applies to an activity that has a substantial nexus with the taxing state, (2) is fairly apportioned, (3) does not discriminate against interstate commerce, and (4) is fairly related to services provided by the taxing state. South Dakota v. Wayfair, Inc., 138 S.Ct. 2080 (2018). Thus, even if a state clearly has jurisdiction to tax the income of resident trusts, a taxing statute that fails to provide some mechanism of apportionment or credit to mitigate the burden of double taxation may be vulnerable to a constitutional challenge on the ground that it imposes excessive burdens or discriminates against interstate commerce.

The patchwork of disparate state fiduciary income tax systems can also give rise to tax planning opportunities. One notable example is the "incomplete nongrantor trust," which is created and administered entirely in a state that has no fiduciary income tax. The trust is an irrevocable, inter vivos trust that has no contacts with (and is therefore not subject to tax by) the state where the grantor resides. To ensure that the trust is treated as a nongrantor trust, the grantor must avoid retaining any interests or powers that might trigger grantor trust status. However, the grantor does retain powers sufficient to prevent the funding of the trust from giving rise to a completed gift for gift tax purposes. These powers may include (1) a power to consent to discretionary distributions directed by a "distribution committee," (2) a nonfiduciary power to distribute corpus to family members subject to an ascertainable standard, and (3) a nongeneral testamentary power of appointment. Moreover, if properly structured, the trust may provide protection from the grantor's creditors while allowing the grantor to receive discretionary distributions directed by the distribution committee. The main purpose of this elaborate arrangement is to remove the trust's income from the taxing jurisdiction of any state that imposes a fiduciary income tax. The trust produces no federal income or transfer tax saving. Indeed, income accumulated in the trust will likely be subject to federal income tax at the top marginal rate, and the trust property will be includible in the grantor's gross estate for federal estate tax purposes. Nevertheless, any incremental federal tax burden may be more than offset by the complete avoidance of state income taxes.

§ 1.7 SUPPLEMENTARY READING

The primary sources of federal income tax law include the Internal Revenue Code, Treasury regulations, and reports of cases decided by the Tax Court, the federal appellate courts and other federal courts. In addition, the Internal Revenue Service provides guidance in the form of published revenue rulings. These authorities are of paramount importance in researching questions of federal tax law and reaching informed and reliable conclusions. There is no substitute for a careful reading of the applicable provisions of the statute, regulations, and case law.

It would hardly be realistic, however, to expect the primary sources to provide a definitive answer for every inquiry. Fortunately, there is a rich body of secondary sources that offer broader and often more nuanced perspectives on issues arising in the income taxation of estates, trusts, and beneficiaries. Helpful explanations of statutory enactments can be found in the relevant legislative committee reports as well as in "general explanations" compiled by the staff of the Joint Committee on Taxation. Numerous published articles in law reviews and professional journals provide detailed and often insightful commentary on a range of theoretical and practical issues.

Finally, several excellent books and treatises provide comprehensive coverage of federal fiduciary income taxation. Among the leading treatises in the area are Bittker & Lokken, Federal Taxation of Income, Estates and Gifts (3d ed. 2003 & Supp.); and Ferguson & Ascher, Federal Income Taxation of

Estates, Trusts, and Beneficiaries (4th ed. updated 2019). Valuable practical discussions can also be found in Abbin & Schafer, Income Taxation of Fiduciaries and Beneficiaries (2019); Berek, Federal Income Taxation of Decedents, Estates and Trusts (2019); Boyle & Blattmachr, Blattmachr on Income Taxation of Estates and Trusts (17th ed. 2018); Peschel & Spurgeon, Federal Taxation of Trusts, Grantors and Beneficiaries (3d ed. 1997 & Supp.); and Zaritsky, Lane & Danforth, Federal Income Taxation of Estates and Trusts (3d ed. 2001 & Supp.). Helpful explanations of state fiduciary income taxation appear in Hellerstein, Hellerstein & Swain, State Taxation (3d ed. 1998 & Supp.) (ch. 20); and Schoenblum, Multistate and Multinational Estate Planning (2009) (ch. 22).

CHAPTER 2

DECEDENT'S FINAL
INCOME TAX RETURN

§ 2.1   FILING AND PAYMENT

A deceased individual's final taxable year ends on the date of death. If the decedent reported income on a calendar-year basis (as nearly all individuals do), the due date for filing the final income tax return and paying the tax is April 15 of the year following the year of death. I.R.C. § 6072; Reg. § 1.6072–1(b). The decedent's executor is responsible for filing the decedent's tax returns, including not only the final income tax return but also any other required income or gift tax returns that the decedent may have failed to file during life. I.R.C. § 6012(b)(1). Of course, the executor will also be responsible for filing an estate tax return and income tax returns for the estate, if required. Thus, for example, if the decedent died on March 1, 2020, the executor has until April 15, 2021 to file the decedent's income tax return for the short taxable year ending on the date of death and to pay the resulting tax; however, the 2019 return, if not filed before death, is still due, with payment of the tax, by April 15, 2020.

§ 2.2   ITEMS REPORTED ON
THE FINAL RETURN

Because the decedent's final taxable year ends on the date of death, that year will normally be a short one (unless the decedent happens to die on December

31). The taxpayer's "deceased" status, along with the date of death, should be noted on the final income tax return. The fact of death has relatively little direct impact on the items of income, deduction or credit to be reported on the final return, or on the method of accounting. If the decedent reported income using the cash method (as nearly all individuals do), the same method must be used on the final return. Consequently, only items of gross income that the taxpayer actually or constructively received before death are included on the final return. By the same token, if the taxpayer used the accrual method (e.g., as sole proprietor of a business), items of gross income accrued during life (and not solely by reason of death) are included. I.R.C. § 451(b); Reg. § 1.451–1(b). Items of "income in respect of a decedent," to which the decedent was entitled but which were not yet realized before death, are not included on the decedent's final return; instead, such items are taxed to the estate (or other successor) upon receipt after death, as discussed in Chapter 3, *infra*. The decedent is allowed a full personal exemption under § 151 and, in the case of a nonitemizer, a standard deduction under § 63, without proration, on the final return.

U.S. savings bonds. The decedent may have owned U.S. savings bonds (Series EE or Series I) on which interest accrues currently but is not payable until redemption or maturity. If the decedent reported income using the cash method, the interest need not be included in gross income until the bond matures or is redeemed or disposed of (unless the decedent elected to report the accrued interest on a current basis). I.R.C. § 454(a); Reg. § 1.454–1(a). In such a case, the executor should consider making an election to report the accrued interest on the final return. Rev. Rul. 68–145, 1968–1 C.B. 203. The amount to be included will be the full amount of interest accrued on the bond in the decedent's hands (but not previously reported) to the date of death. The election may be advantageous if the decedent's marginal tax rate is relatively low (e.g., because of the short taxable year ending at death), or if the incremental income can be offset on the final return by deductions (e.g., large charitable contributions or loss carryovers) that might otherwise be wasted. Furthermore, the executor's election will not constrain the estate or any other successor holder in deciding how to report interest accruing after the date of death. The successor holder can choose freely whether to defer reporting post-death interest or to include it currently in gross income. Rev. Rul. 58–435, 1958–2 C.B. 370. If the executor does not elect to include any pre-death interest on the final return, such interest will constitute income in respect of a decedent and will eventually be taxed to the successor holder. See § 3.2, *infra*.

Interests in partnerships, S corporations, estates and trusts. Upon the death of a member of a general or limited partnership, the partnership's taxable year closes with respect to the decedent but remains open with respect to the remaining partners. I.R.C. § 706(c)(2). Accordingly, the decedent's distributive share of items of partnership income, loss, deduction and credit for the period ending on the date of death passes through and is reported on the decedent's final return; the distributive share for the balance of the

partnership's taxable year is taxed directly to the
decedent's estate (or other successor). If the
partnership uses a fiscal year rather than a calendar
year, the result of this bifurcated computation may
be a "bunching" on the final return of the decedent's
distributive share both for the short taxable year
ending at death and for the entire preceding taxable
year. For example, suppose that the partnership's
taxable year ends on June 30 and the decedent dies
on September 30 of the same calendar year. The
decedent's distributive share for the partnership's
taxable year ending June 30 as well as for the three-
month period ending at death will be reported on the
decedent's final return.

Similar rules apply to a decedent's share of pass-
through items with respect to S corporation stock.
I.R.C. §§ 1366(a)(1) (proration of S corporation's year-
end items) and 1377(a) (elective bifurcation of S
corporation's taxable year). The death of an S
corporation shareholder may cause the corporation to
lose its S status if the decedent's stock passes directly
from the decedent to a successor who is not a
permitted shareholder (e.g., a nonresident alien, or a
trust not enumerated in the statute). The
corporation's S status will not be jeopardized while
the executor has possession of the decedent's stock for
purposes of administration, since the estate is a
permissible shareholder. I.R.C. § 1361(b)(1); Rev.
Rul. 62–116, 1962–2 C.B. 207. However, the
corporation will cease to be an S corporation if the
decedent's stock is actually or constructively
distributed to an impermissible shareholder. The
statute allows a two-year grace period for stock

already held in a grantor trust at the decedent's death or subsequently transferred to a trust under the decedent's will, but the corporation may lose its S status at the end of the grace period if the trust continues to hold the decedent's stock. I.R.C. § 1361(c)(2).

If the decedent was a cash-method beneficiary of an estate or trust, only distributions actually made before death will be reported on the decedent's final return, although the amount and character of taxable items will be determined based on distributable net income of the estate or trust for its full taxable year. See § 7.8, *infra*. Income that accrued before death and was required to be distributed currently, but is actually distributed after death, will be taxed to the decedent's estate (or other successor) as income in respect of a decedent. Reg. §§ 1.652(c)–2 and 1.662(c)–2. See § 3.2, *infra*.

Medical expenses. The Code allows a deduction for unreimbursed medical expenses to the extent they exceed 10% of the taxpayer's adjusted gross income. I.R.C. § 213(a). Because the deduction is allowed only for expenses paid during the taxable year, and a decedent's final taxable year ends on the date of death, medical expenses incurred before death but paid afterward generally would not be deductible on the decedent's final return. Moreover, if paid by the estate, such expenses would not be deductible by the estate because they were not incurred for medical care of the taxpayer or a spouse or dependent. Fortunately, a special rule allows a deduction on the decedent's final return for medical expenses of the decedent that are paid by the estate within one year after death. I.R.C. § 213(c)(1); Reg. § 1.213–1(d)(1). Although the deduction is allowed "below the line" as an itemized deduction, it is expressly excluded from the category of "miscellaneous itemized deductions" and accordingly is not subject to the 2% floor. I.R.C. § 67(b)(5). Consistent with the prohibition of § 642(g) on double deductions, the statute requires a waiver of the estate tax deduction otherwise allowable under § 2053 as a condition for claiming the income tax deduction for medical expenses. I.R.C. § 213(c)(2); Reg. § 1.213–1(d)(2). Although qualifying expenses may be deducted, in whole or in part, either on the estate tax return or on the decedent's final income tax return, any amount claimed as an income tax deduction will be subject to the 10% floor. For example, suppose that Abigail's adjusted gross income for the year of her death was $50,000 and that she incurred $20,000 of medical expenses which were paid by her estate within one year after her death. Abigail's executor can elect to deduct $15,000 on the final income tax return, or $20,000 on the estate tax return. However, the executor cannot circumvent the 10% floor by claiming $15,000 as an income tax deduction and the remaining $5,000 as an estate tax deduction. Rev. Rul. 77–357, 1977–2 C.B. 328.

If the decedent was the beneficiary of a tax-advantaged "health savings account" that passes to the decedent's estate (rather than to a surviving spouse or another designated beneficiary), the value of the account at death must be included in the decedent's gross income on the final return. I.R.C. § 223(f)(8)(B). A deathtime tax can be avoided if the account passes directly to the surviving spouse, who is allowed to step tax-free into the decedent's shoes as the new beneficiary. I.R.C. § 223(f)(8)(A). However, if the account passes directly to a designated beneficiary other than the spouse, the new beneficiary will be taxed on the value of the account at death, reduced by any qualified medical expenses incurred by the decedent and paid within one year after death. I.R.C. § 223(f)(8)(B).

Charitable contributions, losses and carryovers. An individual taxpayer generally can deduct qualifying charitable contributions made during the taxable year, subject to percentage limitations based on the taxpayer's "contribution base" (i.e., adjusted gross income) as well as the nature of the contribution and the charitable organization. I.R.C. § 170(a) and (b)(1). Contributions in excess of the percentage limitations may be carried forward, generally for up to five years. When the taxpayer dies, the decedent's charitable contributions for the year of death, as well as any amounts carried forward from previous years, are deductible on the final return up to the applicable percentage limitations. No deduction will be allowed to the estate (or any other successor) for any excess amounts; the carryover expires with the decedent. Even if the decedent left a surviving spouse and filed a joint income tax return, the spouse can carry over only the portion of any excess contributions attributable to the spouse's own contributions (based on hypothetical separate returns). Reg. § 1.170A–10(d)(4). To the extent that additional income can properly be reported on the decedent's final return, the decedent's contribution base, and hence the amount allowable as a charitable deduction, may be increased.

Similar considerations apply to capital losses and net operating losses, whether realized in the year of the decedent's death or carried forward from previous years. Such losses are deductible, if at all, only on the decedent's final income tax return, and are not deductible by the estate (or any other successor) after death. Reg. §§ 1.1212–1 and 1.172–7; Rev. Rul. 74–175, 1974–1 C.B. 52.

The decedent may have engaged in a "passive activity" (i.e., a trade or business in which the decedent did not materially participate, or a rental activity), and may have incurred net losses which were not currently deductible but were carried forward to subsequent years. I.R.C. § 469. In general, suspended passive activity losses carried forward from previous years can be deducted when the taxpayer disposes of his or her entire interest in the passive activity in a taxable transaction. I.R.C. § 469(g)(1). For this purpose, death is treated as a taxable disposition; as a result, the excess passive activity losses can be deducted on the decedent's final return. However, the deductible amount of the excess losses must be reduced to the extent that the transferee's basis in the interest acquired from the decedent exceeds the decedent's adjusted basis immediately before death. I.R.C. § 469(g)(2). This adjustment prevents the deathtime transfer from generating a double income tax benefit: the amount of unrealized gain that escapes tax in the transferee's hands by reason of a tax-free basis step-up should not also be allowed as a deductible loss on the decedent's final return. To illustrate, suppose that Amy dies owning rental property with a fair market value of $100 and an adjusted basis (immediately before death) of $90; she also has $30 of suspended passive activity losses from prior years. Amy can use the suspended losses to offset non-passive income on her final return, but the deductible amount is limited to $20; the $10 loss disallowed on Amy's final return is preserved by stepping up the property's basis from $90 to $100 in the hands of her successor.

Annuities. One final item with special relevance for the decedent's final return arises in the context of an annuity. In its simplest form, an annuity is a contract that provides for regular, periodic payments beginning on a specified date and lasting for the annuitant's lifetime (or, in the case of a survivor annuity, for the lifetimes of the annuitant and another specified individual). For income tax purposes, the owner's basis (i.e., the amount invested in the contract) is generally recovered ratably over the expected duration of the measuring life, and annuity payments in excess of basis are taxable to the annuitant upon receipt. The excludable portion of each annuity payment is computed by applying a fixed "exclusion ratio" (i.e., the investment in the contract divided by the expected return) to the amount of the payment; the balance of the payment is included in the annuitant's gross income. I.R.C. § 72(a) and (b).

Until 1986, the exclusion ratio applied uniformly to all annuity payments throughout the term of the annuity, regardless of whether the annuitant died prematurely or outlived his or her life expectancy. To measure mortality gains and losses more accurately, Congress amended the statute in 1986 to limit the total amount excluded from gross income to the owner's actual investment in the contract. As a result, once the owner's basis is fully recovered (i.e., at the end of the annuitant's life expectancy), all subsequent annuity payments must be included in gross income. I.R.C. § 72(b)(2). This ensures that when the annuitant outlives his or her life expectancy, the resulting "mortality gain" is fully taxable. Conversely, if the annuity payments cease by reason of the annuitant's premature death before the owner's basis is fully recovered, the resulting "mortality loss" (i.e., the unrecovered investment in the contract) is deductible on the deceased annuitant's final income tax return. I.R.C. § 72(b)(3). Although this deduction is technically allowed "below the line" as an itemized deduction, it is expressly excluded from the category of "miscellaneous itemized deductions" and accordingly is not subject to the 2% floor. I.R.C. § 67(b)(10).

Special relief may be available if the decedent was killed while in active military service in a combat zone. I.R.C. § 692.

§ 2.3 JOINT RETURN

If the decedent was married and left a surviving spouse, the executor may join with the surviving spouse in filing a joint return which covers the decedent's short taxable year ending at death and the spouse's full taxable year. I.R.C. § 6013(a). Of course, the usual requirements for filing a joint return must also be met: the spouses must have been married to each other and not divorced or separated pursuant to a court decree at the date of death. I.R.C. § 6013(d)(1) and (d)(2). If the surviving spouse remarries before the end of her taxable year, the spouse may file a joint return with her new spouse but not with the decedent. I.R.C. § 6013(a)(2); Reg. § 1.6013–1(d)(2).

The executor is normally the only person authorized to consent to filing a joint return on behalf of the decedent, either for the decedent's final taxable year or for previous taxable years. The surviving spouse can act unilaterally in filing a joint return only if the decedent has not already filed a return for the taxable year in question and no executor has been appointed before the filing of the joint return or before the due date (including any extension) for filing the spouse's return. Even then, the spouse's election to file jointly can be disaffirmed by a subsequently appointed executor for a period of up to one year. I.R.C. § 6013(a)(3); Reg. § 1.6013–1(d)(3)–(d)(5).

Filing a joint return may be advantageous for both spouses from a tax perspective. For example, a joint return may allow use of the decedent's excess deductions (e.g., for charitable contributions, capital losses, or operating losses) or unused loss carryovers that otherwise would expire at death by offsetting them against the surviving spouse's income for the full taxable year. At the same time, a joint return subjects the estate and the surviving spouse to joint and several liability for their combined tax obligations. I.R.C. § 6013(d)(3). The portion of the couple's combined tax liability allocable to the decedent is deductible for estate tax purposes as a claim against the estate. For this purpose, the amount of the joint liability is presumed to be allocated between the spouses in proportion to their respective liabilities based on hypothetical separate returns, unless the executor and the spouse agree on a different allocation. I.R.C. § 2053(a)(3); Reg. § 20.2053–6. By the same token, if the couple is entitled to a refund, the decedent's allocable portion of the refund is includible as an asset of the gross estate for estate tax purposes.

§ 2.4 FIDUCIARY LIABILITY

The executor has a duty to notify the Service of the decedent's death and the executor's identity by filing a Notice Concerning Fiduciary Relationship (Form 56). Upon giving notice, the executor assumes the powers, rights and duties of the decedent with respect to federal taxes. I.R.C. § 6903. According to the regulations, the executor "shall" give notice of the fiduciary relationship and "must" thereupon assume the powers, rights and duties provided in the statute. Reg. § 301.6903–1(a). Thus, giving notice appears to be mandatory rather than optional, and the executor cannot avoid the potentially burdensome consequences of the statute by simply failing to give the required notice. The purpose of giving notice is essentially procedural, to inform the Service of the executor's identity, authority and standing as a fiduciary to deal with the Service in matters concerning the decedent's taxes. In fact, the executor has a strong incentive to give the required notice, because failure to do so may result in a valid deficiency notice being mailed to the decedent's last known address (rather than to the executor), causing the executor to miss the deadline for seeking review in the Tax Court and ultimately triggering fiduciary liability under local law. I.R.C. § 6901(g); Reg. § 301.6903–1(c). In any event, the executor is generally liable only in a representative capacity; in other words, the decedent's tax liability will normally be asserted only against the estate, not against the executor personally. I.R.C. § 6903; Reg. § 301.6903–1(a).

In some circumstances, however, the executor may become liable personally and not merely as a representative of the estate. The decedent's federal tax liability represents a claim of the federal government which takes priority over other general creditors, and an executor who violates that priority by paying other debts from an insolvent estate is personally liable, to the extent of the improper payment, for the unpaid federal claim. 31 U.S.C. § 3713. The threat of personal liability, however, is subject to three material limitations. First, the estate must be insolvent, i.e., claims against the estate must exceed the assets available to pay creditors. As long as there are sufficient assets in the estate to pay all outstanding claims, the federal government can collect its claims without proceeding against the executor personally. Second, the priority for federal claims is not absolute, but is subject to an implied exception for prior secured debts and certain other items, including administration expenses, funeral expenses, and family allowances (e.g., homestead and family support) which are afforded priority under applicable local law. Rev. Rul. 80–112, 1980–1 C.B. 306. These items can be paid with impunity, even if the remaining assets are insufficient to pay federal claims. Third, although the executor's personal liability is not conditioned on intentional misconduct, the statute is interpreted to apply only if the executor had personal knowledge of the federal claim, or at least knowledge of facts that would put a reasonably prudent person on inquiry notice. Rev. Rul. 66–43, 1966–1 C.B. 291. Thus, as long as the executor exercises due diligence in investigating potential claims against the estate, the executor should be immune from personal liability for failure to give priority to an unknown federal tax claim.

An executor who has satisfied all known claims against the estate may wish to wind up administration before the end of the limitation period for assessment of income (or gift) tax. As a practical matter, the executor can file a Request for Prompt Assessment (Form 4810), which will shorten the normal limitation period from three years to 18 months. I.R.C. § 6501(d). A request for prompt assessment generally ensures that any adjustments to the returns as filed will be resolved expeditiously, although the shorter deadline may result in heightened scrutiny of the returns. Also, the request has no effect on the six-year limitation period for substantial omissions or the open-ended limitation period for failure to file. I.R.C. § 6501(c), (d), and (e). To be released from personal liability for the decedent's income (and gift) tax obligations, the executor can file a Request for Discharge From Personal Liability (Form 5495). The Service has nine months from the date of the request to notify the executor of the amount of any such taxes, and upon payment of any amount due (or in the absence of notification, upon expiration of the nine-month period), the executor is discharged from personal liability for such taxes. I.R.C. § 6905. At the end of the estate administration, the executor should also file a Notice Concerning Fiduciary Relationship (Form 56), to inform the Service of the termination of fiduciary status. I.R.C. § 6903.

If no executor is appointed (e.g., in the absence of a proceeding for estate administration), the heir or other person in charge of the decedent's property is responsible for filing the decedent's final income tax return. I.R.C. § 6012(b)(1). Furthermore, if the decedent's tax liabilities remain unpaid, the Service may collect the unpaid tax from the successors, to the extent of the property they received from the decedent, pursuant to the transferee liability provisions of § 6901.

CHAPTER 3
INCOME IN RESPECT
OF A DECEDENT

§ 3.1 OVERVIEW

Most income earned by an individual taxpayer, whether arising from personal services, property, or other sources, is properly reportable by the taxpayer on his or her final income tax return or in some earlier taxable year. Some items of income, however, may not be fully realized before death or may not have been taken into account under the taxpayer's accounting method during the taxpayer's lifetime. For example, wages earned but not yet paid at the time of death, interest or dividends accrued but not yet paid, and gain reported on the installment method for payments to be made after death, would all escape inclusion on the final return of a cash-method taxpayer. All of these items would eventually have been includible in the taxpayer's gross income if he or she had lived long enough to collect them; but death intervened before the items were taken into account and prevented them from showing up on the taxpayer's final return. Moreover, although these items will eventually be collected by the deceased taxpayer's estate (or other successor), they might escape income tax permanently if they qualified for a fresh-start basis as property acquired from a decedent under § 1014(a).

One possible response to the problem of disappearing income would be to require all individuals to adopt an accrual method of accounting for the year of death. In fact, Congress adopted this approach in 1934, but the resulting "bunching" of income on the decedent's final return, combined with lingering uncertainty concerning the criteria for accrual, prompted a change of course after only eight years. In 1942, Congress enacted the predecessor of § 691(a), which provides generally that items of "income in respect of a decedent" (IRD), if not properly includible in the year of death (or any previous taxable year), must be included in gross income by the deceased taxpayer's estate (or other successor) when the items are eventually collected. Upon collection, items of IRD give rise to gross income of the same amount and character in the recipient's hands as they would have had in the hands of the decedent had he or she lived to collect them. In effect, the successor who collects items of IRD steps into the decedent's shoes. To ensure that items of IRD retain their built-in tax liability in the successor's hands, § 1014(c) specifically denies them the fresh-start basis that applies to other property acquired from a decedent. A parallel provision allows the estate (or other successor) to claim a deduction (or credit) for certain expenses that were incurred by the decedent during life but not paid until after death. The provision for "deductions in respect of a decedent," contained in § 691(b), is discussed in § 3.4, *infra*.

Items of IRD will eventually be subject to income tax in the hands of the decedent's successors, and they may also be subject to estate tax at the decedent's death. To the extent that items of IRD give rise to estate tax liability with no offsetting reduction to reflect the built-in income tax liability in the hands of the successors, there is a potential problem of double taxation. In contrast, the income tax liability incurred by the decedent on amounts included in his or her final return reduces the size of the decedent's taxable estate, either directly (if paid before death) or indirectly (if deductible as a claim against the estate under § 2053(a)(3)). In the case of items of IRD, however, it is practically impossible to provide a comparable *estate tax* deduction because the successor's income tax liability may not yet be ascertainable when the estate tax return is filed. To mitigate the problem of double taxation, § 691(c) allows the successor who reports an item of IRD to claim an *income tax* deduction for a ratable portion of the estate tax, if any, that was imposed on the item at the decedent's death. The § 691(c) deduction produces a combined estate and income tax burden that is roughly equivalent to the result where the income tax was incurred before death, although the successor who benefits from the income tax deduction may be someone other than the person who bears the burden of the estate tax. The § 691(c) deduction is discussed in § 3.5, *infra*.

As a practical matter, when an estate (or other successor) receives a right to income that is classified as IRD, the two most important consequences, discussed below, are the inclusion of the item in the recipient's gross income (with no fresh-start basis) and the availability of an income tax deduction for any estate tax attributable to the item.

§ 3.2 INCOME IN RESPECT OF A DECEDENT

The Code and the regulations repeatedly refer to "income in respect of a decedent" but provide no precise definition of the term. The regulations suggest that it includes "amounts to which a decedent was entitled as gross income but which were not properly includible" on the final return or for any previous taxable year under the decedent's method of accounting. Reg. § 1.691(a)–1(b). This is a good starting point, but the courts have given the term a somewhat more flexible and occasionally expansive interpretation. Courts and commentators have emphasized several factors, including the origin of IRD in the decedent's efforts or property ownership during life, the impending or nearly complete realization at the time of death, and the transfer of a passive right to collect income after death. Perhaps the best approach is to examine some commonly encountered examples of income rights that have been held to constitute IRD, while keeping in mind that the general rule allowing a fresh-start basis remains undisturbed for property (other than IRD) acquired from a decedent.

Personal service income. For a decedent who reported income using the cash method (as nearly all individuals do), IRD clearly covers items that were accrued but not yet received before death. An obvious example is salary or wages earned during life but paid after death, including amounts accrued during the decedent's final pay period as well as any arrearages from previous pay periods. Reg.

§ 1.691(a)–2(b) (Example 1). Similarly, fees and commissions billed but not collected before death easily qualify as IRD. The concept of IRD, however, is not limited to amounts technically accrued at death. Indeed, post-death payments derived from the decedent's lifetime services may qualify as IRD even if they remained contingent at death and had not yet ripened into a legally enforceable right in the decedent's hands. For example, the regulations recognize that a widow's right to receive renewal commissions on life insurance sold by the decedent during his lifetime constitutes an item of IRD. Reg. § 1.691(a)–2(b) (Example 2). The same is true of contingent fees attributable to a lawyer's work in progress at the time of death, as well as a discretionary bonus declared and paid by an employer after death to a deceased employee's estate or other successor. Rev. Rul. 65–217, 1965–2 C.B. 214; O'Daniel's Estate v. Commissioner, 173 F.2d 966 (2d Cir. 1949); Rollert Residuary Trust v. Commissioner, 752 F.2d 1128 (6th Cir. 1985). Note that a purely discretionary death benefit may be an item of IRD even though it is not includible in the decedent's gross estate.

Investment income. If a decedent owned bonds or real property that generated regular current income in the form of interest or rent, payments received after death may be apportioned on a daily basis between the period ending on the date of death and the period after death. In the case of a cash-method taxpayer, amounts accrued but unpaid at death are not properly reportable on the final return and therefore constitute an item of IRD, whereas amounts accruing after death are taxed directly to the estate (or other successor). A similar result holds for the amount of interest accrued but unpaid at death on unmatured U.S. savings bonds. In some cases the accrued interest on a U.S. savings bond is reportable only when the bond matures or upon its earlier redemption or disposition (unless the holder elects to include the interest in gross income on a current basis). The interest accrued on such a bond to the date of death constitutes an item of IRD in the successor's hands (unless the decedent's executor elected to include the accrued interest on the final return). Rev. Rul. 64–104, 1964–1 C.B. 223. To the extent that interest on state or local bonds is excluded from gross income (see I.R.C. § 103), it arguably falls outside the scope of § 691, though the same result could be reached by treating the interest as an item of IRD that retains its tax-exempt character in the hands of the recipient. See Reg. § 1.691(a)–1(d).

Dividend income, unlike interest and rent, is not apportioned on a daily basis but accrues on the "record date" on which shareholders of record become entitled to a dividend to be paid on a specified future date. Accordingly, if a shareholder dies after a dividend is declared but before the record date, the dividend is taxable directly to the estate (or other successor); if death occurs on or after the record date and before the date of payment, the successor will report the dividend as an item of IRD; and if death occurs after the date of payment, the dividend is includible on the deceased shareholder's final return.

Sale proceeds. A taxable sale or exchange of property that occurred before death may give rise to IRD, to the extent that proceeds are received after death and the resulting gain is not properly includible on the decedent's final return. For example, if the decedent sold property in the year of death and received payment in the form of an installment note, the excess of the face amount of the note over the decedent's basis (immediately before death) is an item of IRD. I.R.C. § 691(a)(4). The decedent's basis in the note carries over in the hands of the estate (or other successor), who will report the same amount and character of taxable gain upon receipt of post-death installment payments as the decedent would have done if those payments had been received before death. Reg. § 1.691(a)–5(a).

Even if the sale or exchange is not actually consummated until after death, the resulting gain may constitute IRD if the decedent had substantially completed the necessary arrangements during life, leaving only formal or ministerial steps to be taken after death. For example, suppose that a cash-method decedent entered into a binding agreement for the sale of real property and substantially fulfilled the prerequisites for completing the transaction but died before the closing date; after death, the decedent's executor completes the sale and delivers the deed pursuant to the agreement. The estate will take a carryover basis in the property and report any gain on the sale as IRD, of the same character and in the same amount that the decedent would have done had the decedent survived the closing date. Rev. Rul. 78–32, 1978–1 C.B. 198.

Nevertheless, when a decedent dies owning appreciated property and has taken no steps to dispose of it during life, the estate (or other successor) generally takes a fresh-start basis under § 1014(a), thereby eliminating any tax on unrealized appreciation accrued to the date of death. To determine whether preparations for a sale or other disposition were merely preliminary at the time of death, or had reached a sufficiently advanced stage to give rise to IRD, may require close attention to the facts and circumstances of the particular case. The regulations offer an illustrative example involving a farmer who owned and operated an apple orchard. Before his death, he entered into negotiations to sell a specified quantity of apples to a canning factory, and after his death his executor completed the sale and delivered the apples. On these facts, the sale completed by the executor does not give rise to IRD. However, if the decedent disposed of the apples before death by delivering them to a cooperative association for processing and sale, and the association eventually distributed the decedent's share of the proceeds to his estate, the post-death proceeds would constitute IRD. Reg. § 1.691(a)–2(b) (Example 5); cf. Commissioner v. Linde, 213 F.2d 1 (9th Cir.), cert. denied, 348 U.S. 871 (1954).

Courts have drawn similar distinctions in cases involving the post-death redemption of a decedent's stock in a closely held corporation, focusing on the question of how far the transaction had progressed toward completion at the time of death and what acts remained to be performed. Compare Estate of Sidles v. Commissioner, 65 T.C. 873 (1976), aff'd mem., 553

F.2d 102 (8th Cir. 1977) (liquidating distribution to estate of sole shareholder, pursuant to plan adopted before death, constituted IRD; post-death actions of corporate board were "mere formalities" and "ministerial acts") with Keck v. Commissioner, 415 F.2d 531 (6th Cir. 1969) (no IRD where planned liquidation was contingent on regulatory approval and shareholder agreement which occurred only after death; decedent had no "right" at death to compel liquidation or receive proceeds).

In a case involving an executory contract for the sale of livestock, the Tax Court inquired whether the decedent's estate acquired "a right to receive proceeds from an asset's disposition" or instead acquired "the asset itself," noting that IRD would arise in the former case but not the latter. The court distilled the basic elements of IRD in a four-part test: (1) the decedent entered into a "legally significant arrangement" concerning the sale, giving rise to a right "beyond the level of a mere expectancy"; (2) the decedent performed the "substantive (nonministerial) acts" required as preconditions to the sale; (3) at the time of death there were no "economically material contingencies" that might have disrupted the sale; and (4) the decedent would have received the sale proceeds, actually or constructively, if death had not intervened. Estate of Peterson v. Commissioner, 74 T.C. 630 (1980), aff'd, 667 F.2d 675 (8th Cir. 1981).

The regulations confirm that a disposition which by its terms will occur only at or after death does not give rise to IRD. For example, if a deceased shareholder entered into an enforceable buy-sell agreement providing for sale or redemption of the decedent's stock at death, the transaction does not give rise to IRD. Reg. § 1.691(a)–2(b) (Example 4). Because the sale or redemption would take place only at death, the shareholder could never have received the proceeds during his or her lifetime. Accordingly, the decedent's stock is eligible for a fresh-start basis in the hands of the estate (or other successor), and the resulting gain, if any, will be limited to the excess of the sale proceeds over the value of the stock at death.

Survivor annuities. In the case of a single-life annuity, the annuity payments cease at the annuitant's death; in the absence of a refund feature, no further amounts are payable to the decedent's estate or other beneficiary. Moreover, if the annuitant dies before recovering the investment in the contract, the unrecovered amount is allowed as a deduction on the decedent's final return under § 72(b)(3) (see § 2.2, *supra*). By contrast, in the case of a survivor annuity, the amounts payable to the surviving beneficiary after the decedent's death are treated as IRD. The beneficiary steps into the decedent's shoes and takes over the decedent's basis and exclusion ratio. The annuity payments do not take a fresh-start basis in the recipient's hands, even though the value of those payments is included in the decedent's gross estate for estate tax purposes. I.R.C. § 1014(b)(9)(A). Thus, once the investment in the contract has been recovered, the beneficiary is fully taxable on the remaining annuity payments.

Retirement benefits. A decedent may have accumulated substantial retirement benefits in a qualified plan or a traditional individual retirement account. To the extent not taxed to the decedent during life, those benefits will be taxed to the estate or other successor as IRD upon distribution after death. The retirement account receives no fresh-start basis at the decedent's death. Often the retirement account will have been funded entirely with tax-deductible contributions and will have a zero basis, but to the extent it was funded with after-tax contributions the account may have a positive basis. In any event, the decedent's basis in the retirement account carries over in the successor's hands. Amounts distributed from the account after death will be taxable to the recipient as IRD under the rules of § 72 relating to annuities, subject to an exclusion ratio reflecting the decedent's basis, if any. If the retirement account was funded entirely with tax-deductible contributions, post-death distributions will be fully taxable as ordinary income to the recipient, just as they would have been to the decedent if made before death.

Interests in partnerships, S corporations, estates and trusts. The death of a partner causes the partnership's taxable year to close with respect to the deceased partner but not with respect to the remaining partners. As a result, the decedent's distributive share of items of partnership income for the short taxable year ending at death passes through and is reported on the decedent's final return, while the distributive share for the period after death is taxed directly to the decedent's estate (or other successor). This bifurcated computation generally ensures that the decedent's entire distributive share is properly included on his or her final return, and avoids generating IRD in the successor's hands. The same holds true for a decedent's share of pass-through items with respect to S corporation stock. See § 2.2, *supra*.

In the case of a deceased partner, the estate (or other successor) generally takes the partnership interest with a fresh-start basis equal to its value at death, including the partner's share of partnership liabilities. (For estate tax purposes, the value of the decedent's partnership interest is determined net of partnership liabilities, which must be added back in computing the successor partner's income tax basis under § 1014.) The successor partner's basis must be reduced, however, to the extent the partnership interest consists of IRD. This can happen, for example, when payments made in liquidation of a deceased partner's interest exceed the value of the decedent's share of partnership property, or to the extent that liquidating payments are attributable to a deceased general partner's share of unrealized receivables or unstated goodwill in a service partnership. I.R.C. §§ 736(a) and 753. In addition, the courts have held that a partnership interest consists of IRD to the extent that the partnership holds income rights (e.g., zero-basis accounts receivable) that would constitute items of IRD if held directly by a deceased partner. Quick Trust v. Commissioner, 444 F.2d 90 (8th Cir. 1971); Woodhall v. Commissioner, 454 F.2d 226 (9th Cir. 1972). The successor partner's basis in the partnership interest must be reduced by his or her share of such items, in order to prevent the successor partner from escaping tax on the items when they are eventually collected. A similar statutory "look-through" rule expressly applies to S corporation stock. I.R.C. § 1367(b)(4).

If the decedent was a cash-method beneficiary of an estate or trust, income that accrued before death and was required to be distributed currently, but is actually distributed after death to the decedent's estate (or other successor), is taxed to the recipient as IRD. Reg. §§ 1.652(c)–2 and 1.662(c)–2.

§ 3.3 AMOUNT, CHARACTER, AND TIMING OF INCLUDIBLE ITEMS

Items of IRD are generally includible in the gross income of the estate (or other successor) "when received." I.R.C. § 691(a)(1). For this purpose, items of IRD are received only when they are actually collected. In effect, the successor must report items of IRD on the cash method, even if it normally uses a different accounting method. Reg. § 1.691(a)–2(a). The inclusion in gross income is buttressed by § 1014(c), which denies a fresh-start basis to items of IRD and hence leaves the successor with a carryover basis in those items. The portion, if any, of the amount received that would have been a tax-free recovery of basis in the decedent's hands is not included in gross income by the successor as IRD.

Moreover, the Code preserves the character of the amount includible in gross income in the hands of the successor, who is treated as stepping into the decedent's shoes with respect to the IRD item. I.R.C.

§ 691(a)(3). In some cases, the tax consequences may be quite favorable. For example, if a lifetime sale would have generated a long-term capital gain for the decedent, proceeds received after death as IRD will have the same character in the successor's hands. Reg. § 1.691(a)–3(b). Similarly, if a portion of the gain on a lifetime sale of the decedent's principal residence would have been excludable under § 121, the exclusion applies equally to proceeds received after death as IRD. Rev. Rul. 82–1, 1982–1 C.B. 26. By the same token, however, the tax consequences may be distinctly unfavorable, as in the case of gain on the sale of inventory or other property that carries an ordinary income taint.

Section 691(a)(1) identifies three categories of the decedent's successors who may become taxable on items of IRD: (1) the decedent's estate, with respect to items subject to probate administration; (2) a successor who acquires an item outside of probate by reason of the decedent's death (e.g., a surviving joint tenant, annuitant, or pay-on-death beneficiary); and (3) a successor who acquires an item by "bequest, devise, or inheritance" upon "distribution by the decedent's estate." These categories are comprehensive and mutually exclusive; they cover all possible successors who may be required to include IRD items in gross income under § 691.

Items of IRD which are subject to probate administration are taxed to the estate if they are collected directly by the executor (first category). Items which pass outside of probate to a surviving joint tenant or a designated beneficiary are taxed to the successor when they are collected (second category). Alternatively, if the estate distributes an item of IRD to a testate or intestate beneficiary in satisfaction of a specific gift of the distributed item, or in satisfaction of a residuary or intestate share, the distributee (and not the estate) is treated as the recipient of the distributed item and becomes taxable when the item is eventually collected (third category). In this case, the distribution by the estate is not treated as a taxable transfer. Reg. § 1.691(a)–4(b). In a case involving an IRD item that was distributed by the decedent's estate to a residuary beneficiary and subsequently collected by the beneficiary, the court held that the taxation of the item was governed exclusively by § 691 and was not subject to the normal conduit rules. Accordingly, the beneficiary was taxed on the entire amount collected in the year of receipt. Rollert Residuary Trust v. Commissioner, 752 F.2d 1128 (6th Cir. 1985).

Ordinarily, items of IRD are collected by the estate (or other successor) who became entitled to them at the decedent's death. However, if the estate or other successor makes a "transfer" of an item of IRD before collecting it, the transferor must include in gross income the value of the IRD item at the time of the transfer (or the amount of consideration received, if greater). For this purpose, a transfer is broadly defined as a "sale, exchange, or other disposition," including a transfer by gift. I.R.C. § 691(a)(2). The effect of this provision is merely to accelerate the timing of inclusion, without changing the character of the amount reported by the transferor. As a corollary, the transferee takes the item of IRD with a basis equal to its value at the time of the transfer (or the consideration paid, if greater). Thus, for example, if the decedent's executor distributes a $100 claim for unpaid wages (an IRD item) to a general legatee in satisfaction of a $100 bequest, the estate must report $100 of compensation income, and the legatee takes the claim with a basis of $100. A similar result occurs whenever an estate distributes an item of IRD in satisfaction of a pecuniary legacy or a beneficiary's claim to another specific asset. This result is to be distinguished from a nontaxable distribution to a beneficiary in the third category described above.

If a successor described in § 691(a)(1) becomes entitled to receive an item of IRD but dies before collecting it, the item will retain its character as IRD as it passes to a new successor, who will include the item in gross income when it is eventually collected. The deathtime transfer to a new successor described in § 691(a)(1) is not treated as a taxable transfer under § 691(a)(2). Reg. § 1.691(a)–4(b). To illustrate the serial application of § 691, suppose that Alice dies and leaves her individual retirement account (an IRD item), funded entirely with tax-deductible contributions, to her son Bart, who dies before receiving any distributions from the account and leaves the account to his sister Chloe. Neither Alice's death nor Bart's death is treated as a taxable transfer. Instead, Chloe takes the account with a carryover basis of zero and must report all distributions from the account as ordinary income. If Chloe transfers the account to another person during her lifetime, the remaining account balance will be taxable to her under § 691(a)(2). (She will also be allowed to deduct a portion of the estate taxes, if any, imposed on the account in Alice's and Bart's estates under § 691(c).)

Section 691 makes special provision for transfers of installment obligations, mirroring the rules set out in I.R.C. § 453B. As a general matter, the transfer of an installment obligation at the original holder's death does not constitute a taxable disposition under § 453B(c), but the excess of the obligation's face amount over the decedent's basis constitutes an item of IRD. I.R.C. § 691(a)(4). The obligation takes a carryover basis in the hands of the estate (or other successor), who includes the same portion of each post-death payment in gross income that the decedent would have done if living. Reg. § 1.691(a)–5(a). A cancelation of the obligation is treated as a taxable transfer; if cancelation occurs at the holder's death, the value of the obligation (or the amount of consideration received, if greater), reduced by the decedent's basis, is includible in gross income of the estate (or other successor). For this purpose, if the decedent and the obligor were related persons (as defined in § 453(f)(1)), the value of the obligation is deemed to be not less than its face amount. I.R.C. § 691(a)(2) and (a)(5); Reg. § 1.691(a)–5(b). To illustrate, suppose that Archie dies intestate, survived by his only child Belle, owning an installment note with a face amount of $100, a value of $80, and a basis of $60. If Belle collects the full face amount of $100, she will report taxable gain of $40 ($100 amount realized less $60 basis); if she collects only $90, her taxable gain is $30; if she gives the note to her own child, her taxable gain is only $20 ($80 value less $60 basis). Reg. § 1.691(a)–5(c). Alternatively, if Belle is the obligor and the note is automatically canceled at Archie's death, Archie's estate must report taxable gain of $40 ($100 face amount less $60 basis). See Rev. Rul. 86–72, 1986–1 C.B. 253 (self-canceling installment note); Frane v. Commissioner, 998 F.2d 567 (8th Cir. 1993) (same).

As a matter of planning, a charitably inclined testator may find it advantageous to satisfy a charitable bequest with items of IRD, thereby relieving other beneficiaries of the built-in income tax liability. A charitable gift of IRD can be accomplished either by a nonprobate transfer or by a bequest under the testator's will. For example, suppose that Gisela has a $100 individual retirement account which constitutes an item of IRD. If she designates a tax-exempt charity as the successor beneficiary, the account will pass directly to the charity at Gisela's death, completely bypassing her estate, and post-mortem distributions from the account will be tax-free by virtue of the charity's tax-exempt status. Alternatively, in the absence of a nonprobate beneficiary designation, Gisela might bequeath the retirement account to charity in her will. In that case, the account must pass through the hands of her executor on its way to the charity. If the estate distributes the account to the charity pursuant to a specific bequest or as part of the residuary estate, the distribution will generally be tax-free and the charity will receive subsequent distributions from the account free of tax. However, if the estate liquidates the account and then distributes the proceeds to the charity, the estate must include the amount received in gross income. Similarly, if the estate distributes the account in satisfaction of a pecuniary bequest, the estate will be taxed on a deemed transfer of the account. If the estate includes either the proceeds of the account or the value of the account itself in gross income, it may still be entitled to an offsetting charitable deduction under § 642(c). The charitable deduction, though, is available only if the will authorizes or directs the payment of amounts of gross income to charity; in the absence of an express testamentary provision, the deduction may be lost (see § 5.8, *infra*). To protect the estate from potential income tax exposure, the testator should include a provision in the will authorizing the executor to satisfy charitable bequests with items of IRD.

§ 3.4 DEDUCTIONS IN RESPECT OF A DECEDENT

Conceptually, a "deduction in respect of a decedent" (DRD) is the mirror image of income in respect of a decedent. Just as a decedent may have earned income that is not received until after death, the decedent may also have incurred expenses that are not paid until after death and are therefore not properly deductible on the decedent's final return. Unless the estate (or other successor) is allowed to step into the decedent's shoes and deduct these items when paid after death, the deduction might be lost altogether, resulting in overstatement of taxable income. To mitigate this problem, § 691(b) allows a deduction (or credit) for some of these items. Unlike the open-ended inclusion of IRD items, however, the statutory definition of DRD items is limited to six enumerated categories. Specifically, DRD items consist of the deductions allowable under §§ 162 (business expenses), 163 (interest), 164 (taxes), 212 (expenses of producing nonbusiness income), and 611 (depletion), as well as the foreign tax credit allowable under § 27. Conspicuously absent from the enumerated categories are several commonly encountered items, including alimony payments (under a pre-2019 divorce or separation instrument), charitable contributions, and business or investment losses. Thus, for example, if the decedent made charitable contributions or incurred capital losses or net operating losses in excess of the limited deductions allowable on the final return, the excess amounts will not carry over and will not be deductible by the estate (or any other successor).

An item of DRD that falls within any of the enumerated categories is allowable, when paid, as a deduction (or credit) to the estate or, if the estate is not liable for the obligation, to the successor who received property from the decedent subject to the obligation. I.R.C. § 691(b). For example, suppose that Mary, a cash-method taxpayer, dies owning real property that is subject to liens for mortgage interest and real property taxes that are accrued but unpaid at her death. If Mary's estate is liable for the interest and taxes under local law, the estate can deduct those amounts when paid. Rev. Rul. 58–69, 1958–1 C.B. 254. However, if the property was not subject to probate administration but passed directly to an heir who pays the interest and taxes, the heir is entitled to the deduction. Similarly, a successor who receives an item of IRD subject to foreign income tax can elect to claim a credit under § 27 (in lieu of a deduction under § 164) upon payment of the tax. Reg. § 1.691(b)–1(a). Percentage depletion does not involve a cash outlay and is deductible only by the successor who receives the related item of IRD (e.g., rent or royalty income from mineral property). Reg. § 1.691(b)–1(b).

Items of DRD are expressly exempt from the prohibition on "double deductions" in § 642(g). Accordingly, some items of DRD may be deductible both on the estate tax return as a claim against the estate (see I.R.C. § 2053(a)(3)) and also on the income tax return of the estate (or other successor).

§ 3.5 DEDUCTION FOR ESTATE TAX

To alleviate the burden of overlapping income and estate taxes imposed on items of IRD, § 691(c) allows a deduction to each successor who includes an item of IRD in gross income. In general, the statutory formula calls for a computation of the federal estate tax attributable to the net value of all IRD items included in the decedent's gross estate (reduced by estate tax deductions constituting DRD items), coupled with an apportionment of the estate tax among the various recipients of IRD items. Each recipient who includes items of IRD in gross income is entitled to deduct the amount of estate tax, if any, attributable to those items.

More specifically, the statute prescribes a three-step formula for computing the § 691(c) deduction. The first step involves a computation of the "net value" of IRD items that were subject to estate tax in the decedent's estate. This amount is equal to the value (as determined for estate tax purposes) of all items of IRD included in the gross estate, reduced by the amount of all items of DRD allowed as estate tax deductions. (Note that this computation does not necessarily take account of all items of IRD and DRD, but only those that are includible in the gross estate or deductible in arriving at the taxable estate. Special rules for survivor annuities and statutory stock options appear in §§ 691(d) and 421(c)(2), respectively.) The second step requires a computation of the estate tax attributable to inclusion of the net value of IRD items in the estate. This amount is equal to the excess of the actual estate tax over a hypothetical estate tax calculated as if no items of IRD or DRD were included in the estate. Finally, the third step involves a computation of the deduction available to a successor who includes a particular item of IRD in gross income. The deductible amount is equal to (a) the estate tax attributable to the net value of IRD items in the estate (i.e., the amount determined in step two), multiplied by (b) the estate tax value of the particular IRD item (or the amount included in gross income, if less), divided by (c) the estate tax value of all items of IRD included in the gross estate. I.R.C. § 691(c)(1) and (c)(2); Reg. § 1.691(c)–1(a).

For example, suppose that Alice collects a $10 item of IRD that was previously included at the same amount in her brother Bart's gross estate. For estate tax purposes, the estate included IRD items with a total value of $100 and deducted DRD items of $20.

The estate incurred an estate tax of $50, but if the IRD and DRD items had been excluded from the estate, the estate tax would have been only $30. If Alice includes $10 in gross income on account of the IRD item, she is entitled to a § 691(c) deduction of $2, computed as follows: (a) $20 estate tax attributable to net IRD items ($50 actual tax less $30 hypothetical tax), multiplied by (b) $10 estate tax value of the IRD item collected by Alice, divided by (c) $100 estate tax value of all IRD items. If Alice collected only $5, her § 691(c) deduction would be limited to $1. Even if she collects $15, her § 691(c) deduction cannot exceed the $2 of estate tax attributable to the IRD item. Reg. § 1.691(c)–1(d) (Example 1).

It is possible that an item of IRD may have passed through the hands of two (or more) decedents before it is finally collected by the ultimate recipient and included in gross income. If this happens, the item retains its character as IRD in the hands of the ultimate recipient, who is entitled to a § 691(c) deduction for the estate tax attributable to the item in each decedent's estate. Reg. § 1.691(c)–1(b) and (d) (Example 2).

The § 691(c) deduction is allowed to the same person who includes the corresponding item of IRD in gross income. If an estate or a trust collects an item of IRD and distributes the proceeds to a beneficiary within the same taxable year, the proceeds retain their character as IRD in the beneficiary's hands, and the beneficiary (rather than the estate) is entitled to the corresponding § 691(c) deduction. However, if the proceeds are not distributed within the same taxable year, the § 691(c) deduction remains with the entity. Reg. § 1.691(c)–2(a).

The § 691(c) deduction is intended to mitigate the cumulative burden of estate and income taxes on items of IRD. Although the deduction is allowed "below the line" as an itemized deduction, it is expressly excluded from the category of "miscellaneous itemized deductions" and accordingly is not subject to the 2% floor. I.R.C. § 67(b)(7). Moreover, the practical advantages of the § 691(c) deduction are limited in two important respects. First, the deduction provides a tax benefit only to the extent that an item of IRD generated an estate tax in the decedent's estate. The unlimited marital deduction, coupled with an ever-expanding estate tax exemption, ensure that only a very small number of very large estates will incur any estate tax liability. In the vast majority of cases, items of IRD attract no estate tax liability even if they are included in a decedent's gross estate. Consequently, these items take a carryover basis in the hands of the decedent's successors and must be included in gross income with no offsetting § 691(c) deduction. The second limitation arises from a potential mismatch between the benefit of the § 691(c) deduction and the burden of the underlying estate tax liability. Even when an item of IRD generates an estate tax liability, there is no assurance that a successor who bears the burden of that liability will also reap the benefit of the corresponding § 691(c) deduction. Indeed, if a decedent leaves a specific bequest of IRD items to one beneficiary and directs that the estate tax be paid from the residuary share left to another beneficiary, the former receives the IRD item free of estate tax but nevertheless enjoys the benefit of a § 691(c) deduction for the estate tax actually paid from the latter's share.

CHAPTER 4

INCOME TAX CLASSIFICATION OF ESTATES AND TRUSTS

§ 4.1 OVERVIEW

For federal income tax purposes, an estate or a trust is generally treated as a taxable entity separate and distinct from its beneficiaries, and Subchapter J provides detailed rules for determining whether and how the income of an estate or a trust will be taxed— to the entity itself or to the beneficiaries (or to the deemed owner of a "grantor trust," see Chapter 8, *infra*). The statute contains no specific definition of an "estate" or a "trust," although it does offer some fragmentary clues to the meaning of those terms, and the regulations provide further guidance.

It is important to remember that the meaning of terms like "estate" or "trust" depends on the context in which they are used. Under the local law governing administration of a decedent's estate, for example, the "probate estate" generally consists of property owned at death which passes by will or intestacy subject to administration by a court-appointed executor or administrator. Essentially the same assets are treated as part of the estate for federal income tax purposes, as discussed in § 4.2, *infra*. In contrast, the "gross estate" for federal estate tax purposes is not limited to property passing by will or intestacy, but may also include joint tenancy property, survivor annuities, life insurance proceeds, and lifetime transfers subject to retained enjoyment or control.

At common law, a trust is generally defined as a fiduciary relationship in which a trustee holds title to property for the benefit of beneficiaries (or for charitable purposes) in accordance with the grantor's manifested intent. This rather open-ended definition provides a useful starting point for understanding the federal tax concept of a trust, but the creation of a valid trust under local law does not necessarily lead to the conclusion that the arrangement will be treated as a trust within the meaning of Subchapter J. Indeed, in some cases a revocable trust may be treated as part of the deceased grantor's estate for federal income tax purposes, if the executor so elects (see § 4.4, *infra*). The classification of a particular arrangement for income tax purposes is obviously a matter of federal tax law, but the nature and extent of the rights and obligations of fiduciaries and beneficiaries with respect to the underlying property are determined under applicable local law. In borderline situations, a question may arise whether a particular arrangement is properly classified for federal income tax purposes as a trust, as a business entity, or in some other way, as discussed in § 4.3, *infra*.

Once it is determined that a fiduciary arrangement is properly classified as an estate or a trust under Subchapter J, additional questions may arise concerning the duration of the taxable entity. The question of duration, like the issue of classification, involves an interplay of federal tax law and local law.

If the administration of an estate or a trust in the hands of a fiduciary is unreasonably prolonged, the entity may be considered to have terminated and distributed property to the beneficiaries, with potentially serious tax consequences, as discussed in § 4.5, *infra*.

The executor of an estate or the trustee of a trust is responsible for filing income tax returns on behalf of the taxable entity. In general, the executor or trustee is liable only in a fiduciary capacity, meaning that the entity's tax liabilities will be asserted against the entity's assets rather than against the fiduciary personally. However, a fiduciary who violates the federal statute governing the priority of federal claims (including tax liabilities) by paying other debts from an insolvent estate or trust may incur personal liability, as discussed in § 2.4, *supra*.

§ 4.2 ESTATES

A decedent's estate comes into existence as a taxable entity immediately upon the decedent's death, even though the formal opening of the estate administration and the appointment of the executor may be delayed for several weeks, months, or even longer. (For tax purposes, the fiduciary of an estate is generally referred to as the executor. Thus, the term also includes the administrator of an intestate estate.) Ordinarily there is little room for doubt concerning the existence or classification of an estate for federal income tax purposes. (But note the election under § 645, discussed in § 4.4, *infra*.) Instead, the primary question is whether particular

items of income, deduction or credit are reportable by
the estate and its beneficiaries under the provisions
of Subchapter J or instead by another person or
entity under a different part of the Code.

For federal income tax purposes, a decedent's
estate generally comprises property included in the
probate estate, i.e., property passing by will or
intestacy and subject to custody or management by
the executor for purposes of administration. The
income produced by such property during the period
of administration or settlement must be reported by
the estate on its income tax return. I.R.C. § 641(a)(3).
In contrast, property that passes directly to a
successor outside the probate system is not part of
the estate for purposes of Subchapter J, and income
from nonprobate assets is reported directly by the
successor. For example, suppose that Austin died
leaving his sister Bertha as sole legatee. At the time
of his death, Austin owned a mutual fund account in
his own name, as well as an insurance policy on his
life with Bertha as the designated beneficiary; Austin
and Bertha also owned a lake cabin as joint tenants
with right of survivorship. The mutual funds, which
pass through the hands of Austin's executor as part
of his probate estate, are also part of the estate under
Subchapter J. Accordingly, the executor will report
all items of income, deduction and credit attributable
to the mutual funds, from Austin's death until the
funds are distributed to Bertha, on the estate's
income tax return. The life insurance proceeds and
the joint tenancy property are not subject to probate
administration; they pass directly to Bertha outside
Austin's will and are not available to pay creditors'

claims or administration expenses. Therefore Bertha is treated as the owner of those assets for tax purposes from the date of Austin's death, and she will account for all post-death income and expenses attributable to them on her own individual income tax return. (The life insurance proceeds are excludable from her gross income under § 101, and the joint property is excludable under § 102.)

If, under applicable local law, real property is subject to administration, i.e., the executor is entitled to possess and control the property and to collect the rents and profits therefrom, the income from the property received by the executor during the period of administration is taxable to the estate. This is so even if the property itself is not treated as an asset of the estate because legal title passes directly to the decedent's heirs or devisees. Rev. Rul. 57–133, 1957–1 C.B. 200; Reg. § 1.661(a)–2(e). In contrast, if the executor is not entitled to possession or control of the real property, the income from the property is taxable directly to the heir or devisee and not to the estate. Even in this latter situation, the executor may be authorized to sell the real property to pay debts or administration expenses if other assets of the estate are insufficient. If the executor actually exercises such a power, the portion of the property needed to pay debts and administration expenses is treated as part of the estate for income tax purposes and a ratable portion of any gain from the sale is taxable to the estate. Rev. Rul. 59–375, 1959–2 C.B. 161.

In some states, real property which qualifies as homestead is exempt from claims of creditors and is not subject to administration as part of the probate estate. Such property should not be treated as part of the estate for income tax purposes.

When a married decedent dies owning community property, the community terminates and the community property is owned by the decedent's estate and the surviving spouse in equal shares as tenants in common. Only the one-half undivided interest over which the decedent had a testamentary power of disposition becomes part of the decedent's estate for income tax purposes; the other half of the community property passes to the surviving spouse by operation of law. The income from the surviving spouse's share of community property is taxed directly to the spouse and not to the decedent's estate, even if both halves of the community property are technically subject to administration and available to pay community debts and administration expenses. Rev. Rul. 55–726, 1955–2 C.B. 24.

§ 4.3 TRUSTS

For federal tax purposes, a trust is generally defined as "an arrangement created either by a will or by an inter vivos declaration whereby trustees take title to property for the purpose of protecting or conserving it for the beneficiaries under the ordinary rules applied in chancery or probate courts." Reg. § 301.7701–4(a). Although this definition largely coincides with the common law elements of an express private trust, it implicitly excludes business entities that are validly formed and recognized as trusts under applicable local law, and at the same time fails to account for some fiduciary arrangements that are treated as trusts under Subchapter J because of their functional resemblance to trusts, even though they are not recognized as such under local law. In short, in asking whether a particular arrangement will be taxed as a trust under Subchapter J, it is neither necessary nor sufficient to determine that the arrangement constitutes a trust under local law or that it is labeled as a "trust." Apart from the core case of a family trust created by will or by inter vivos gift to manage and invest property for the benefit of ascertainable beneficiaries, the income tax treatment of borderline cases depends on whether the income from the underlying property is appropriately taxed under Subchapter J or under some other provision of the Code.

A trust should be contrasted with a debtor-creditor relationship. A debt usually consists of an obligation to pay a fixed principal amount on a specified date, with interest, from the borrower's general assets or from property pledged as security; no fiduciary obligation arises with respect to any specific property. An obligation that has the substantive characteristics of a debt will be treated as a debt for federal tax purposes, even if it is labeled as a trust. For example, if a life insurance company agrees to hold the proceeds of a matured policy "as trustee" and to pay interest to the designated beneficiary from the company's general funds, pursuant to a settlement option under the terms of the policy, no trust is created and the interest payments are taxable directly to the beneficiary. Rev. Rul. 68–47, 1968–1 C.B. 300.

A trust must also be distinguished from an agency. An agent acts only on behalf of the principal and subject to direction by the principal; although the relationship is a fiduciary one, the agent's fiduciary duties are owed only to the principal and not to any other beneficiary. Therefore, an agent who acts merely as nominee for the principal will not be treated as a trustee for federal tax purposes, even if the agent holds title to the principal's property. Reg. § 301.7701–6(b)(2). In some states a grantor can create a passive trust under which the nominal trustee holds bare legal title to the grantor's real property but the grantor retains the entire beneficial interest in the property as well as exclusive control over the management of the property and power to direct the conveyance of legal title. Such an arrangement may be effective to transmute the grantor's ownership of real property into intangible personalty under local property law, but it is functionally indistinguishable from an agency and may be treated as such for federal tax purposes. Rev. Rul. 92–105, 1992–2 C.B. 204 (Illinois land trust).

Whether a guardianship or a custodianship for a minor child should be classified as a trust for tax purposes presents a closer question. Both a guardian and a custodian (under the Uniform Transfers to Minors Act or its predecessor, the Uniform Gifts to Minors Act) have similar broad powers to manage and dispose of a minor child's property; both owe fiduciary duties to the minor child, much like those of a trustee, but neither a guardian nor a custodian holds legal title to the property under their control. The main difference between a guardian and a custodian is that the former is appointed by court order and subject to continuing court supervision, while the latter is not. Although both a guardianship and a custodianship bear a functional resemblance to a trust for the minor child, there is no reason to recognize either one of these nontrust arrangements as a separate taxable entity. In the case of a guardianship or a custodianship, the underlying property is already owned by the minor child; there are no other present or future beneficiaries who might become entitled to distributions of income or corpus. Accordingly, for federal income tax purposes, the minor child is treated as the owner of the property and is directly taxable on the income therefrom. Reg. § 1.641(b)–2(b) (guardianship); Anastasio v. Commissioner, 67 T.C. 814, aff'd mem., 573 F.2d 1287 (2d Cir. 1977) (custodianship). Note, however, that the minor child's net unearned income may be taxable at the parent's marginal rate under the "kiddie tax" provisions of § 1(g). Also, the child's parent may be taxable on custodianship income to the extent it is used to discharge the parent's support obligation. Rev. Rul. 59–357, 1959–2 C.B. 212.

Another arrangement that bears a close functional resemblance to a trust is a legal life estate coupled with a power to consume or sell the underlying property. In one often-cited case, a testator left property (not in trust) to his daughter for life with remainder at her death to her surviving issue; the daughter was also given a broad power to consume the property for her needs, maintenance and comfort. The court found that, "notwithstanding her extensive powers of beneficial use," the life tenant "occupie[d] a fiduciary relationship with the remaindermen" which was "clothed with the characteristics of a trust," and held that the capital gain from a sale of the property was taxable to the trust as a separate taxable entity (rather than directly to the daughter). United States v. DeBonchamps, 278 F.2d 127 (9th Cir. 1960); see also Rev. Rul. 61–102, 1961–1 C.B. 245 (power of sale); Rev. Rul. 75–61, 1975–1 C.B. 180 (power in trust). This result may be viewed as a pragmatic solution to the problem of identifying a taxpayer who could plausibly be taxed on the gain from the sale of the property. The daughter herself held only a life estate coupled with a power to consume the property for her own needs; her power was not unlimited, and presumably the remainder takers could have blocked any excessive or arbitrary exercise of the power. Since the daughter did not have an unlimited power to make the property her own, she could not be taxed directly on the gain from the sale. Nor could the gain be taxed to the remainder takers because their identities and the extent of their interests would not be ascertainable until the daughter's death. Therefore, the only plausible taxpayer who could be summoned into existence and taxed on the gain was a notional trust with the daughter as trustee. The outcome might well have been different if the daughter had held an unrestricted power of invasion, since then she could have been treated for tax purposes as the owner of the underlying property. See Hirschmann v. United States, 309 F.2d 104 (2d Cir. 1962).

A similar problem arises in connection with an "honorary trust" created for a noncharitable purpose such as the care of an animal or the maintenance of a cemetery lot. Assuming that the arrangement is enforceable under local law, at least if the named caretaker is willing to act, the difficulty for tax purposes is that there is no human beneficiary who can be taxed directly on the income from the underlying property. Accordingly, the Service has ruled that such an arrangement will be classified as a trust and treated as a taxable entity, even though the payments for noncharitable purposes will not be deductible as distributions because they are not made to a human beneficiary. Rev. Rul. 76–486, 1976–2 C.B. 192 (care of animal); Rev. Rul. 58–190, 1958–1 C.B. 15 (cemetery lot).

In an influential early decision, the Supreme Court held that a business trust, which had been validly created under local law to develop and sell residential real estate lots adjoining a golf course, was properly classified as an association (taxable as a corporation) rather than as a trust for federal income tax purposes. The Court found that the arrangement more closely resembled a business association than a traditional trust: it was formed with the objective of carrying on a business; the beneficiaries purchased their interests in the trust, joining together in a common enterprise for profit in much the same way as shareholders of a corporation; and, by further analogy to a corporation, the business trust provided for centralized management, continuity of life, limited liability, and freely transferable interests. Morrissey v. Commissioner, 296 U.S. 344 (1935).

The "resemblance" test announced in *Morrissey* is echoed in the regulations, which warn that merely casting an organization in the form of a trust will not prevent the trust from being classified in accordance with its "real character." Thus, a business trust may be taxed as a corporation or a partnership if it is "created by the beneficiaries simply as a device to carry on a profit-making business which normally would have been carried on through business organizations that are classified as corporations or partnerships." Reg. § 301.7701–4(b). In contrast, an arrangement will generally be taxed as a trust if "the purpose of the arrangement is to vest in trustees responsibility for the protection and conservation of property for beneficiaries who cannot share in the discharge of this responsibility and, therefore, are not associates in a joint enterprise for the conduct of business for profit." Reg. § 301.7701–4(a).

A trust is unlikely to be classified as a business entity for tax purposes if it was created by gift or by will for beneficiaries other than the grantor. Even if the trust was formed with the objective of carrying on a business for profit, the Tax Court has rejected the Service's attempts to tax the trust as a corporation, in the absence of evidence that the beneficiaries purchased their interests or voluntarily joined together in a common enterprise. Bedell Trust v. Commissioner, 86 T.C. 1207 (1986) (acq.); Elm Street Realty Trust v. Commissioner, 76 T.C. 803 (1981) (acq.). As a practical matter, the tax advantages of creating trusts to accumulate income largely disappeared in 1986 with the enactment of severely compressed tax rates for trusts. Consequently, both the risk of misclassification and the need to rectify it have receded in recent years. Furthermore, under the "check the box" regulations promulgated in 1996, an unincorporated business is classified as a partnership for tax purposes unless the owners elect to have the entity treated as a corporation. Reg. § 301.7701–3.

The regulations provide that an "investment trust" generally will be classified as a trust for tax purposes if (1) the trust has only one class of ownership interests representing undivided beneficial interests in the trust assets, and (2) the trustee has no power under the trust agreement to vary the investment of the trust assets. Reg. § 301.7701–4(c); Rev. Rul. 2004–86, 2004–2 C.B. 191 (Delaware statutory trust). For example, suppose that a grantor purchases a portfolio of residential mortgage loans and transfers them to a bank as trustee, in exchange for certificates of beneficial interest representing undivided fractional interests in the pooled loans and their proceeds. The grantor then offers the certificates for sale to the public. If the trustee merely collects the payments of principal and interest on the loans and distributes them to the certificate holders, and has no power to vary the trust investments or reinvest the loan proceeds, the trust is properly classified as a trust for tax purposes. Furthermore, the certificate holders are generally treated as grantors and deemed owners of the trust assets under the grantor trust rules. Rev. Rul. 84–10, 1984–1 C.B. 155. An investment trust with multiple classes of beneficial interests may still be classified as a trust for tax purposes if the multiple-class structure is merely incidental to the primary purpose of facilitating direct investment in the trust assets. However, if the trustee has the power to vary the trust investments, the trust will be classified as a business entity for tax purposes.

A "liquidating trust" that receives assets in connection with the winding up of a business organization is classified as a trust for tax purposes if it is formed for the primary purpose of liquidating and distributing the assets transferred to it, and not to carry on a profit-making business that would normally be conducted by a business entity. Reg. § 301.7701–4(d).

An "environmental remediation trust" that constitutes a valid trust under local law is also treated as a trust for tax purposes if is created for the primary purpose of collecting and disbursing amounts for environmental remediation of an existing waste site, and not to carry on a profit-making business that would normally be conducted by a business entity. Reg. § 301.7701–4(e).

Even if an entity is properly classified as a trust, its income is not necessarily governed by Subchapter J. Various types of trusts are subject to special rules, some of which are discussed in Chapter 12, *infra*. Furthermore, Subchapter J has no application to employee trusts or other tax-exempt trusts (see I.R.C. §§ 401 et seq. and 501 et seq.), or to bankruptcy estates (see I.R.C. § 1398). For special treatment of other types of trusts, see I.R.C. §§ 468B (qualified settlement funds), 646 (Alaska native claims settlement trusts), 584 (common trust funds), and 856–859 (real estate investment trusts).

§ 4.4 QUALIFIED REVOCABLE TRUSTS

As long as the grantor of a revocable trust is alive and holds a power of revocation, the grantor is treated as the owner of the trust under the grantor trust rules (see Chapter 8, *infra*). In effect, the trust is disregarded for income (as well as gift and estate) tax purposes. At the grantor's death, however, the grantor's power of revocation expires and the trust becomes irrevocable. From the date of death, the trust is generally treated as a separate taxable entity, distinct from the decedent's estate, with its own exemption and rate brackets. The distinction between the (formerly revocable) trust and the estate creates few serious difficulties, but it ignores the functional equivalence between a will and a revocable trust and may give rise to minor inconveniences of accounting and reporting, especially where assets "pour over" from the estate to the trust under the decedent's will or where the trust assets can be reached to pay claims against the estate. For example, a pourover will typically directs that the residuary estate be added to a separate revocable inter vivos trust. The trust may have been partially funded during the decedent's lifetime, but the decedent's power of revocation causes the trust's income and assets to be attributed to the grantor until the power terminates at death. Therefore, the trust comes into existence as a separate taxable entity only at or after the decedent's death, and distributions of assets from the residuary estate to the trust will be taxed under the conduit rules (see Chapter 7, *infra*). To the extent that a revocable trust is funded during the grantor's lifetime, the trust property may be subject to creditors' claims under local law, even though the property is technically not part of the probate estate and therefore not subject to probate administration. In addition, estates enjoy a few tax advantages that are not generally available for revocable trusts, such as eligibility to elect a fiscal year, to hold stock in an S corporation beyond a two-year grace period after the decedent's death, and to deduct amounts permanently set aside for charitable purposes.

To minimize the tax disadvantages of revocable trusts (compared to estates) while preserving their nontax advantages, Congress amended the Code in 1997 to allow a "qualified revocable trust" (QRT) to be treated as part of the deceased grantor's estate for income tax purposes, if the executor and the trustee so elect. I.R.C. § 645. A QRT is a trust that was treated as owned by the grantor on the date of death under § 676 by reason of a power exercisable by the grantor (alone or with the consent of a spouse or nonadverse party) to regain title to the trust property. The term does not include a trust that was treated as owned by the grantor solely by reason of a power held by the grantor's spouse or by a nonadverse party. I.R.C. § 645(b)(1); Reg. § 1.645–1(b)(1).

The election to treat a QRT as part of the deceased grantor's estate is made jointly by the executor and the trustee on Form 8855, which must be filed by the due date (including any extension) for filing the estate's income tax return for its first taxable year. If no executor has been appointed, the trustee of the QRT may make the election by filing Form 8855 by the due date (including any extension) for the trust's first taxable year. Reg. § 1.645–1(c)(1) and (c)(2). However, if an executor is appointed after the trustee has already made a § 645 election, the election terminates as of the day before the executor's appointment unless the executor agrees to join in making the election and files a revised Form 8855 within 90 days after the appointment. Reg. § 1.645–1(g). If there are two or more QRTs, the election may be made separately by some or all of them, and if no executor has been appointed one trustee must be appointed to file income tax returns on behalf of the combined electing trusts. Reg. § 1.645–1(c)(3). Once made, the election is irrevocable. I.R.C. § 645(c).

The effect of the election is that the electing trust will be treated as part of the deceased grantor's estate for purposes of the substantive income tax provisions of the Code. Thus, the executor will report the combined income of the estate and the electing trust on the estate's income tax return. As long as the estate files a return on behalf of both entities and the election remains in effect, the trust normally need not file a separate return, although it is recognized as a separate entity with its own tax identification number. If no executor is appointed, the electing trust will be treated as an estate and will file an income tax return accordingly. Reg. § 1.645–1(d) and (e).

The election relates back to the date of the grantor's death and remains in effect until the earlier of (1) the date when both the estate and the electing trust have distributed all of their assets, or (2) the day before the "applicable date," which is two years after the date of death if the estate was not required to file an estate tax return, or six months after the date of final determination of the estate tax liability if the estate was required to file an estate tax return. I.R.C. § 645(b)(2); Reg. § 1.645–1(f). For this purpose, the estate tax liability is considered to be finally determined on any of the following, whichever first occurs: six months after the issuance of a closing letter (unless a refund claim is filed within one year); final disposition of a claim for refund (unless a suit is instituted within six months); execution of a settlement agreement; entry of a final court judgment (unless appealed); or expiration of the statute of limitations on assessment of the estate tax. Reg. § 1.645–1(f)(2). At the end of the "election period," the § 645 election terminates automatically and the electing trust ceases to be treated as part of the estate. The assets in the trust are deemed to be distributed on the last day of the election period from the estate to a newly created trust which is treated as a separate taxable entity. From then on, the new trust reports its income in the usual manner. Reg. § 1.645–1(h).

§ 4.5   DURATION OF ESTATE OR TRUST

A decedent's estate is generally recognized as a taxable entity from the date of death, and it reports the income received "during the period of administration or settlement." I.R.C. § 643(a)(3). The regulations define this as "the period actually required by the administrator or executor to perform the ordinary duties of administration, such as the collection of assets and the payment of debts, taxes, legacies, and bequests," which may be longer or shorter than the period specified under applicable local law. Reg. § 1.641(b)–3(a). In the normal course of events, if the executor is diligent in settling the estate, the taxable entity is considered as terminated when all of its assets have been distributed (except for a reasonable reserve for administration expenses and contingent liabilities). To guard against the risk of an "unduly prolonged" administration, however, the regulations provide that the estate may be deemed to have terminated for income tax purposes "after the expiration of a reasonable period for the performance by the executor of all the duties of administration." Reg. § 1.641(b)–3(a).

There may be sound reasons in a particular case for delay in settling an estate. For example, substantial disputes may arise concerning the ownership of estate assets, the validity or construction of the decedent's will, the enforceability of creditors' claims, or the amounts payable on account of administration expenses or estate tax liability. The regulations acknowledge that if a § 645 election has been made with respect to a qualified revocable trust (see § 4.4, *supra*), no deemed termination will occur as long as the election remains in effect. The Service has also ruled that if an estate elects to defer payment of estate taxes under I.R.C. § 6166, administration will not be treated as unreasonably prolonged during the deferral period, which may last up to 14 years after the decedent's death. Rev. Rul. 76–23, 1976–1 C.B. 264 (estate continued as permitted shareholder of S corporation). However, because of the "inherently factual nature" of the question involved, the Service has announced that it will not issue private letter rulings on "[w]hether the period of administration or settlement of an estate or a trust . . . is reasonable or unduly prolonged." Rev. Proc. 2020–3, § 3.01(87), 2020–1 I.R.B. 131. The compressed tax rates applicable to estates and trusts since 1986 have greatly reduced the potential tax advantages of protracted fiduciary administration, leaving taxpayers with little incentive to test the limits of the reasonable period allowed by the regulations.

If the estate is deemed to have terminated, its assets will thereafter be treated as owned by the persons succeeding to the property of the estate, and the income from those assets will be taxed directly to those persons (rather than to the estate). Reg. § 1.641(b)–3(d). The consequences of an inadvertent deemed termination can be quite unpleasant both for the estate and for the deemed owners. In one case, a decedent left stock in a closely held corporation to a testamentary trust for his wife and children. The estate administration was substantially completed within five years after the decedent's death, but the executors retained the stock in the estate and 13 years later consented to the corporation's Subchapter S election. Following the deemed termination of the estate, the constructive owner of the stock for income tax purposes was not the estate (a permissible S shareholder) but rather the testamentary trust (an impermissible S shareholder). The corporation's Subchapter S election was therefore invalid. Old Virginia Brick Co. v. Commissioner, 367 F.2d 276 (4th Cir. 1966).

The duration of trusts for income tax purposes raises issues similar but not identical to those involving decedents' estates. The main difference concerns the time when a trust comes into existence as a taxable entity. A trust created during life normally comes into existence for income tax purposes when it is funded with identifiable property and becomes enforceable under applicable local law. However, if the trust is treated as a grantor trust by reason of powers or interests retained by the grantor (e.g., a power of revocation), it may be disregarded for income tax purposes until the retained powers or interests expire, typically at the grantor's death. A grantor trust that was already funded in whole or in part during the grantor's lifetime will be recognized as a taxable entity from the date of the grantor's death. A testamentary trust normally comes into existence for tax purposes only when it is funded after death. The funding of a testamentary trust may be postponed for a reasonable period during administration of the decedent's estate, even if a beneficiary is entitled to receive income from the date of death, but if the estate administration is unduly prolonged, the trust may be treated as coming into existence for tax purposes before it is actually funded.

Once a trust has come into existence, it generally continues to be recognized as a taxable entity until all of the trust property (except for a reasonable reserve for administration expenses and contingent liabilities) is distributed to the persons who are entitled to succeed to it upon termination of the trust. The trust does not automatically terminate upon the happening of the event by which the duration of the trust is measured. Instead, the trustees have a reasonable time thereafter "to perform the duties necessary to complete the administration of the trust." Reg. § 1.641(b)–3(b). For example, if by its terms the trust is to terminate at the death of a life income beneficiary and the trust property is to be distributed to the remainder beneficiaries, the trust remains in existence as a taxable entity for a reasonable period after the death of the income beneficiary while the trustee winds up the affairs of the trust. The regulations warn, however, that the winding up of the trust cannot be "unduly postponed" and that the trust may be considered terminated for income tax purposes after the expiration of a reasonable period for completing the administration of the trust. After a deemed termination, the persons who succeed to the trust assets will be treated as the owners of the assets, and the income from those assets will be taxed directly to those persons (rather than to the trust). Reg. § 1.641(b)–3(d).

CHAPTER 5

TAXABLE INCOME OF
ESTATES AND TRUSTS

§ 5.1 OVERVIEW

Estates and trusts are taxed in much the same manner as individual taxpayers, with several important differences. The taxable income of an estate or a trust is computed in three basic steps. First, gross income is determined under the provisions of the Code generally applicable to individuals (I.R.C. § 641(b)), and the resulting amount is reduced by deductions, subject to certain modifications set forth in § 642, to arrive at a tentative taxable income. Those modifications are discussed in more detail in this chapter. Second, "distributable net income" (DNI) is computed by taking the tentative taxable income of the estate or trust and making the adjustments required by § 643. DNI functions as a measure of the amount and character of income and deductions that may be passed through to beneficiaries who receive distributions during the taxable year, as discussed in Chapter 6, *infra*. Third, a deduction is allowed for amounts of income required to be distributed currently and other amounts properly paid, credited or distributed to beneficiaries during the taxable year, to the extent such amounts do not exceed DNI (adjusted to exclude net tax-exempt income). I.R.C. §§ 651 and 661. The amount allowed as a deduction to the estate or trust is matched by inclusion of the same amount in gross income by the beneficiaries who received (or were entitled to receive) the distributions. Thus, conduit treatment for the amount passing through to the beneficiaries is limited to DNI, and distributions in excess of DNI are neither deductible to the entity nor taxable to the beneficiaries. The tax treatment of distributions is discussed in Chapter 7, *infra*. The entity is subject to tax on its taxable income (i.e., its tentative taxable income, further reduced by the deductions for distributions and for a personal exemption) at the rates applicable to estates and trusts, subject to any allowable credits against the resulting tax. I.R.C. § 641(a).

Estates and trusts are not subject to the phaseout of itemized deductions for high-income taxpayers. I.R.C. § 68(e).

Estates and trusts may also be subject to the alternative minimum tax. I.R.C. §§ 55–59. The alternative minimum tax is imposed only to the extent that it exceeds the entity's regular income tax liability. As a result of applicable rates and exemptions, the regular income tax imposed on an estate or a trust is often equal to or greater than the alternative minimum tax, and the impact of the alternative minimum tax is correspondingly limited.

§ 5.2 REPORTING

All trusts (other than tax-exempt trusts and charitable trusts) are required to report income on a calendar-year basis. I.R.C. § 644. Estates, however, are permitted to elect a fiscal year (i.e., one that ends on the last day of a month other than December). I.R.C. § 441. (Since distributions are deemed to be made on the last day of the entity's taxable year, a fiscal year election offers a limited opportunity for deferral of income passing through from an estate to its beneficiaries. See § 7.8, *infra*.) The first taxable year of an estate or a trust begins when the entity comes into existence, and the executor or trustee is responsible for filing the fiduciary income tax return and paying any tax owed. I.R.C. § 6012(b)(4). The due date for filing the return and paying the tax is the 15th day of the fourth month following the close of the taxable year (e.g., April 15 for a calendar-year taxpayer). I.R.C. §§ 6072(a) and 6151(a). An estate or a trust is required to file a return if it has $600 or more of gross income for the taxable year or if any beneficiary is a nonresident alien; a trust must also file a return if it has any taxable income, even if its gross income is less than $600. I.R.C. § 6012(a)(3)– (a)(5). For example, suppose that a decedent dies on January 17 and the executor elects a fiscal year ending January 31. If the estate has gross income of less than $600 during its first taxable year (i.e., the period beginning at death and ending two weeks later), the executor need not file a return for that year; the return for the estate's second taxable year will not be due until May 15 of the year following the decedent's death.

In reporting its taxable income, the estate or trust must compute its distributable net income (DNI) for the taxable year (see Chapter 6, *infra*) and determine the amount and character of DNI carried out by distributions to each of the beneficiaries (see Chapter 7, *infra*). The results of these computations appear in information schedules (Schedule K-1) which are attached to the entity's fiduciary income tax return and are also sent to the beneficiaries to use in reporting their own taxable income.

Estates and trusts (other than charitable trusts) are generally required to make quarterly payments of estimated tax. However, this requirement does not apply to an estate, or to a former grantor trust that receives a pourover bequest of the deceased grantor's residuary estate, for taxable years ending less than two years after the date of the decedent's death. I.R.C. § 6654(*l*). Any portion of estimated tax payments made by a trust for a taxable year may be treated as paid by a beneficiary (rather than by the trust), following a constructive distribution to the beneficiary of the amount involved, if the trustee so elects. I.R.C. § 643(g)(1). The same election is available to the executor of an estate for a taxable year that is "reasonably expected" to be the estate's final taxable year. I.R.C. § 643(g)(3).

§ 5.3   EXEMPTION AND TAX RATES

Estates and trusts are allowed a deduction—in effect, an exemption—in lieu of the personal exemption provided for individual taxpayers.* The

---

*   The personal exemption for individual taxpayers is set at zero for taxable years beginning after 2017 and before 2026. I.R.C. § 151(d)(5). The § 642(b) exemption for estates and trusts, however, remains unchanged.

amount of the exemption is $600 for an estate, $300 for a trust that is required to distribute all of its income currently, and $100 for any other trust (except a "qualified disability trust," which is eligible for a larger exemption). I.R.C. § 642(b). The exemption, which is not indexed for inflation, affords a very limited opportunity for an estate or a trust to shelter its gross income from tax at the entity level. Moreover, any temptation to take advantage of multiple exemptions by creating several trusts is likely to run afoul of the rule of § 643(f), discussed in § 5.4, *infra*. The exemption is allowed "above the line" in computing the entity's adjusted gross income. I.R.C. § 67(e)(2). If an estate or a trust has insufficient income, after other deductions, to make full use of the exemption at the entity level, the unused amount is wasted; the exempt amount is not allowed as a deduction in computing DNI and therefore cannot be passed through to the beneficiaries. I.R.C. § 643(a)(2). No standard deduction is allowed to an estate or a trust. I.R.C. § 63(c)(6)(D).

Estates and trusts are subject to tax on their taxable income at the rates set forth in I.R.C. § 1(e), (h), and (j). The statutory rate brackets are severely compressed, and an entity with a relatively modest amount of taxable income will find itself subject to the top marginal rate of 37%. The rate brackets are indexed for inflation. In 2020, an estate or a trust was subject to a tax of $3,129 on its first $12,950 of taxable income and 37% of taxable income in excess of $12,950. Before 1986, the rate brackets for trusts and estates were considerably broader, and the opportunities for using separate taxable entities to report income at relatively low tax rates were correspondingly greater. The compressed rate schedule enacted in 1986, however, has largely eliminated the traditional incentives for shifting income from individual grantors to trusts and for accumulating trust income instead of distributing it to individual beneficiaries. Indeed, the incentives are often reversed, and grantors may find it advantageous to be treated as the owners of their trusts, at least for income tax purposes, under the grantor trust rules. See Chapter 8, *infra*. Similarly, nongrantor trusts may be able to reduce the tax burden on their income by making distributions to beneficiaries in lower tax brackets. See Chapter 7, *infra*. In many cases the compressed tax rates, coupled with the additional costs of administration and fiduciary income tax return preparation, will outweigh the very limited tax savings flowing from the status of an estate or a trust as a separate taxable entity.

An estate or a trust that has adjusted gross income in excess of the threshold for the 37% regular income tax rate is subject to an additional 3.8% tax on its undistributed net investment income. I.R.C. § 1411(a)(2). To the extent that net investment income enters into the computation of DNI, it may be possible to mitigate the burden of this tax by making current distributions of such income to lower-bracket beneficiaries. See § 6.7, *infra*.

§ 5.4 MULTIPLE TRUSTS

A taxpayer may be tempted to create several trusts, each with its own separate exemption and rate brackets, in order to reduce the total tax burden on trust income. The problem of "multiple trusts" was especially acute before the enactment of the compressed rate schedule in 1986. In 1972 the Treasury addressed the problem by issuing an anti-abuse regulation. Although the Tax Court held the regulation invalid in Stephenson Trust v. Commissioner, 81 T.C. 283 (1983), Congress responded in 1984 by codifying the substance of the regulation. The Service now has statutory authority to consolidate two or more trusts and treat them as a single trust, for purposes of Subchapter J, if the trusts have "substantially the same" grantor and "substantially the same" primary beneficiaries as well as a "principal purpose" of avoiding income tax. I.R.C. § 643(f); Reg. § 1.643(f)–1. The consolidation rule applies to trusts created after March 1, 1984 (and to preexisting irrevocable trusts to the extent funded thereafter).

The legislative history illustrates the application of § 643(f) with an example in which a grantor creates four discretionary trusts for the benefit of his four siblings, naming three of them (in various combinations) as the beneficiaries of each separate trust. The statute expressly treats a married couple as a single person for this purpose, and the legislative history indicates that the consolidation rule cannot be avoided merely by using different nominal grantors or by naming different contingent beneficiaries. However, the rule does not apply if the trusts have "substantial independent purposes" which negate the requisite principal purpose of tax avoidance.

§ 5.5   ADMINISTRATION EXPENSES

Section 212 allows a deduction for "ordinary and necessary expenses" paid or incurred during the taxable year (1) for the "production or collection of income," (2) for the "management, conservation, or maintenance of property held for the production of income," or (3) in connection with the "determination, collection, or refund of any tax." Most administration expenses of an estate or a trust fit comfortably within one or more of these categories. Indeed, the regulations confirm that a deduction is generally allowed under § 212 for "[r]easonable amounts paid or incurred by the fiduciary of an estate or trust on account of administration expenses, including fiduciaries' fees and expenses of litigation, which are ordinary and necessary in connection with the performance of the duties of administration." Reg. § 1.212–1(i); see also Bingham's Trust v. Commissioner, 325 U.S. 365 (1945) (allowing deduction for expenses of contesting income tax deficiency and winding up testamentary trust on termination).

Nevertheless, no deduction is allowed for expenditures that are properly classified as "personal, living, or family expenses" of a beneficiary. I.R.C. § 262. A leading example of this sort of nondeductible personal expenditure is DuPont

Testamentary Trust v. Commissioner, 514 F.2d 917 (5th Cir. 1975), in which a testamentary trust sought to obtain a § 212 deduction for the expense of maintaining a mansion for rent-free occupancy by the grantor's widow. Affirming the Tax Court's denial of the deduction, the Fifth Circuit noted that the mansion served as the widow's "private residence" and was "the antithesis of income producing property." See also DuPont Testamentary Trust v. Commissioner, 66 T.C. 761 (1976), aff'd, 574 F.2d 1332 (5th Cir. 1978) (on remand, denying distribution deduction for amounts paid by trust pursuant to contractual obligation).

An expenditure is also nondeductible if it represents a capital outlay for the acquisition or improvement of property. I.R.C. § 263. Such expenditures generally must be treated as part of the cost of the property. When an executor or a trustee participates in a proceeding involving the validity or interpretation of a contested will or trust instrument, there is a risk that the expenses of litigation incurred by the fiduciary may be treated as nondeductible capital expenditures incurred in "defending or perfecting title to property." Reg. § 1.212–1(k). See Manufacturers Hanover Trust Co. v. United States, 312 F.2d 785 (Ct. Cl.), cert. denied, 375 U.S. 880 (1963) (no deduction for amounts paid to settle dispute over continuing validity of trust). Nevertheless, a deduction may be allowed if the litigation expenses were incurred primarily for the purpose of facilitating fiduciary administration rather than defending title to property. See Moore

Trust v. Commissioner, 49 T.C. 430 (1968) (deduction allowed for litigation expenses paid by trust to determine timing of distributions to remainder beneficiaries).

Any deduction otherwise allowable under § 212 for fiduciary administration expenses may be wholly or partially disallowed if the estate or trust holds assets (e.g., state or municipal bonds) that produce tax-exempt interest. In computing its taxable income, the entity must determine the portion of each expense that is properly allocable to the production of tax-exempt interest, and the amount of the deduction must be correspondingly reduced. I.R.C. § 265(a)(1); Reg. §§ 1.212–1(i) and 1.265–1(c). The allocation of expenses to tax-exempt interest is discussed in § 7.3, *infra*.

The deduction for administration expenses under § 212 is generally allowed "below the line" as an itemized deduction in computing the taxable income of an estate or a trust. Moreover, administration expenses are not among the deductible items enumerated in § 67(b) (e.g., interest expense, state and local taxes, and charitable contributions) which are categorically exempt from the 2% floor on "miscellaneous itemized deductions" imposed by § 67(a). Instead, the statute provides a safe harbor for costs of administration which "would not have been incurred if the property were not held in such trust or estate," which are allowed "above the line" in computing the entity's adjusted gross income. I.R.C. § 67(e)(1). Thus, except to the extent that they fall within the safe harbor (or are attributable to property held for the production of rents or royalties, which qualify independently as an "above-the-line" deduction under § 62(a)(4)), administration expenses are treated as "miscellaneous itemized deductions" and are subject to the 2% floor.*

In Knight v. Commissioner, 552 U.S. 181 (2008), the Supreme Court interpreted the statutory safe harbor to allow a full deduction only for costs that "would not 'commonly' or 'customarily' be incurred by individuals," and held that investment advisory fees incurred by a trustee generally fall outside the safe harbor because "[i]t is not uncommon or unusual for individuals to hire an investment adviser." The Court's analysis is echoed in the regulations (promulgated in 2014), which provide that administration expenses are subject to the 2% floor to the extent that they "commonly or customarily" would be incurred by a hypothetical individual holding the same property. Reg. § 1.67–4(a). Examples of such expenses include "ownership costs" incurred simply by virtue of owning property (and not otherwise deductible as a business expense or a state or local tax), tax preparation fees relating to gift tax returns, and investment advisory fees. In unusual circumstances an investment advisory fee might include a "special, additional charge" for fiduciary accounts or an incremental cost attributable to an "unusual investment objective" or the "need for a specialized balancing of the interests of various

---

    * Miscellaneous itemized deductions are not allowed to individual taxpayers (or to estates and trusts) for taxable years beginning after 2017 and before 2026. I.R.C. § 67(g).

parties (beyond the usual balancing of the varying interests of current beneficiaries and remaindermen)," and the regulations acknowledge that in such a case the incremental additional cost might escape the 2% floor. Reg. § 1.67–4(b). Administration expenses customarily incurred by fiduciaries and not by individuals (e.g., probate court fees and costs of fiduciary bonds, published notices, and fiduciary accountings) are not subject to the 2% floor. Similarly, tax preparation fees relating to estate or generation-skipping transfer tax returns, fiduciary income tax returns, or a decedent's final income tax return are not subject to the 2% floor. Reg. § 1.67–4(b). In the case of a "bundled fee" charged by a fiduciary, attorney or accountant, the regulations generally require that the fee be allocated (using any "reasonable method") between the costs that are subject to the 2% floor and those that are not. If a bundled fee is not computed on an hourly basis, however, the 2% floor applies only to the portion of the fee that is attributable to investment advice; the rest of the fee is fully deductible. Reg. § 1.67–4(c).

§ 5.6 EXCESS DEDUCTIONS AND LOSSES

During the course of administration, an estate or trust routinely pays or incurs many deductible expenses which directly reduce the entity's taxable income. The entity may also be able to deduct net capital losses (in excess of capital gains) up to $3,000, as well as losses incurred in a trade or business. I.R.C. §§ 1211(b) and 165. With the exception of capital losses, most deductible items enter into DNI and thereby reduce the potentially taxable amount of distributions made to beneficiaries during the current taxable year. If an estate or trust has expenses or losses in excess of gross income for a taxable year, the excess amount generally produces no current tax benefit to the entity or the beneficiaries. The entity's taxable income cannot be less than zero, and the same is true of DNI. As a general rule, in the absence of a statutory provision to the contrary, excess administration expenses, losses, and other deductible items incurred by an estate or trust during a taxable year do not flow through to the beneficiaries and cannot be carried forward to subsequent years by the entity; such excess expenses and losses are wasted. Nevertheless, the statute expressly provides that net capital losses may be carried forward indefinitely. I.R.C. § 1212(b). Net operating losses arising in taxable years ending after 2017 may also be carried forward indefinitely. I.R.C. §§ 172(b) and 642(d).* For an estate or trust, net operating losses are defined rather narrowly to exclude net capital losses and net nonbusiness losses, as well as the entity's § 642(b) exemption, any § 642(c) charitable deduction, and any distribution deduction. I.R.C. § 172(c), (d)(2), and (d)(4); Reg. § 1.642(d)–1(b). Consequently, the carryforward for

---

* Under prior law, net operating losses could be carried forward up to 20 years, or carried back up to two years. A loss carryback could give rise to a recomputation of DNI and hence a reduction in taxable distributions to beneficiaries for the years in question. Rev. Rul. 61–20, 1961–1 C.B. 248.

net operating losses is basically limited to excess business deductions.

Year of termination. The statute provides a special rule for the final taxable year of the estate or trust, i.e., the year of termination. In that year, any excess deductions (other than the § 642(b) exemption and any § 642(c) charitable deduction), as well as any unused capital losses and net operating losses that would otherwise carry over to a subsequent year, are allowed as deductions to "the beneficiaries succeeding to the property of the estate or trust." I.R.C. § 642(h). Those beneficiaries are generally defined as the residuary beneficiaries of the estate or trust because the burden of the excess deductions and carryover losses falls on their share, rather than on specific gifts or pecuniary legacies. Reg. § 1.642(h)–3. For example, suppose that a decedent's will leaves a $100,000 legacy to Amy and the residuary estate in equal shares to Ben and Casey. If the estate has $50,000 of excess deductions in its final taxable year (e.g., from executor's commissions and attorney's fees paid in that year), the deductions will normally be allocated $25,000 to Ben and $25,000 to Casey, in proportion to their residuary shares. Similarly, if half of the residuary estate is left in trust for Casey (rather than outright), the $25,000 excess deduction will flow through to the testamentary trust. However, if the estate has insufficient assets to pay the full amount of Amy's legacy, she is entitled to a priority allocation of the excess deductions up to the amount of the shortfall. In the preceding example, if the estate had only

$90,000 of assets available (after taxes, debts, and administration expenses) to satisfy Amy's legacy, $10,000 of the excess deductions would be allocated to Amy. The residuary shares of Ben and Casey would be worthless, but they would share the remaining $40,000 of excess deductions equally. Reg. § 1.642(h)–4.

When a beneficiary succeeds to excess deductions upon termination of an estate or trust, the items that gave rise to the deductions in the entity's hands do not retain their character in the beneficiary's hands. The excess amount is treated as a miscellaneous itemized deduction and is subject to the 2% floor. Reg. § 1.642(h)–2(a).* If the successor beneficiary is itself a trust, the excess deduction may reduce the successor trust's DNI and thereby indirectly reduce the amount of taxable distributions made by that trust to its beneficiaries. Rev. Rul. 57–31, 1957–1 C.B. 201 (excess deductions on termination of estate passed to testamentary trust as successor beneficiary).

In contrast, any unused carryovers of capital losses or net operating losses generally do retain their character in the beneficiary's hands and are allowed "above the line" in computing adjusted gross income. (In the case of a corporate beneficiary, however, a capital loss carryover is treated as a short-term

---

* Miscellaneous itemized deductions are not allowed to individual taxpayers (or to estates and trusts) for taxable years beginning after 2017 and before 2026. I.R.C. § 67(g).

capital loss incurred by the estate or trust in its final taxable year.) Reg. § 1.642(h)–1(b).

Passive activity losses. The ability of an estate or a trust to deduct net losses from "passive activities" is limited by § 469. A passive activity is generally defined as a trade or business in which the taxpayer does not materially participate, as well as any rental activity. I.R.C. § 469(a) and (c). The statute provides a safe harbor, however, for certain rental real estate activities of a taxpayer who performs substantial personal services in one or more real estate businesses in which the taxpayer materially participates. I.R.C. § 469(c)(7). To satisfy the material participation requirement, a taxpayer must be involved in the operations of the activity on a regular, continuous and substantial basis. I.R.C. § 469(h). In the absence of regulations specifically addressing the application of the passive activity loss rules to estates and trusts, a question arises as to whether personal services performed by an executor or a trustee, acting on behalf of an estate or a trust, should be attributed to the entity in determining whether the taxpayer (i.e., the entity) satisfies the material participation requirement. In a case involving a trust that owned rental real estate properties and engaged in other real estate activities, the Tax Court held that services performed by three of the trust's six trustees could be attributed to the trust, and concluded that the trust satisfied the material participation requirement. The court did not need to decide whether the activities of the trust's other employees could also be taken into account. Aragona Trust v. Commissioner, 142 T.C. 165 (2014).

§ 5.7 DEPRECIATION

If an estate or a trust holds depreciable property that is used in a trade or business or for the production of income, any available depreciation deduction must be apportioned between the entity and the beneficiaries. The beneficiaries deduct their allocable shares of depreciation directly on their personal income tax returns, and the entity's deduction is limited to any residual amount that is not allocated to the beneficiaries. I.R.C. § 642(e); Reg. § 1.642(e)–1.

In the case of a trust, the depreciation deduction is apportioned between the trust and the "income beneficiaries" in accordance with the terms of the trust or, in the absence of such provisions, based on their shares of the trust's income. I.R.C. § 167(d). The regulations interpret this to mean that if the trustee is required or permitted by the terms of the trust (or under local law) to maintain a depreciation reserve, the depreciation deduction is allocated to the trust to the extent of any amount set aside from income for the reserve, and the balance of the deduction, if any, is apportioned between the trust and the beneficiaries in proportion to their respective shares of the trust's fiduciary accounting income. If no provision is made for a depreciation reserve, or if no income is set aside, the depreciation deduction must be apportioned based on the respective shares of the trust and the beneficiaries in fiduciary accounting income. Reg. § 1.167(h)–1(b). Aside from the reserve rule, the regulations do not allow any departure from the income-based apportionment rule. Any provision in the trust instrument for a different method of apportioning the deduction is ineffective. Dusek v. Commissioner, 376 F.2d 410 (10th Cir. 1967) (disregarding trustee's purported allocation of depreciation deduction by trustee pursuant to discretionary power granted in trust instrument).

To illustrate, suppose that a trust has rental income of $250 and related expenses of $100, and that the trust property is eligible for a depreciation deduction of $100. If there is no depreciation reserve and the trustee distributes the net fiduciary accounting income of $150 to a beneficiary, the entire depreciation deduction must be allocated directly to the beneficiary. If the trustee distributes half the net income to the beneficiary and accumulates the other half, the deduction is split equally between the beneficiary and the trust. Alternatively, suppose that the trustee, exercising discretion granted by the trust instrument, sets aside $80 of income as a depreciation reserve. Of the remaining $70 of net income, the trustee distributes half to the beneficiary and accumulates the other half. The trust is entitled to an $80 priority allocation of the depreciation deduction, and the remaining $20 deduction is allocated $10 to the beneficiary and $10 to the trust in proportion to their respective shares of net income (reduced by the $80 set aside for the reserve). If the amount set aside as a reserve exceeds the amount of the depreciation deduction, the entire deduction is allocated to the trust.

The reserve rule for trusts does not apply to estates, presumably because the limited duration of an estate normally does not warrant the creation of a depreciation reserve. In the case of an estate, the depreciation deduction must be apportioned between the estate and the "heirs, legatees, and devisees" in proportion to their respective shares of the estate's fiduciary accounting income. I.R.C. § 167(d); Reg. § 1.167(h)–1(c). In one case, a testator devised depreciable real property to a testamentary trust. During the course of administration and before the trust was funded, the executor distributed income from the property directly to the trust's income beneficiary. The court held that the estate was required to allocate a portion of the depreciation deduction to the beneficiary based on "her status vis-a-vis the real property under the trust." Lamkin v. United States, 533 F.2d 303 (5th Cir. 1976); but cf. Estate of Nissen, 345 F.2d 230 (4th Cir. 1965) (testamentary trust beneficiaries who received income distributions from estate were not heirs, legatees, or devisees).

In sum, the effect of these rules is to apportion the depreciation deduction between an estate or a trust and its beneficiaries based on their respective shares of fiduciary accounting income (including, in the case of a trust, any amount set aside as a depreciation reserve). Because distributable net income is computed by reference to the entity's tentative taxable income, the depreciation deduction enters into DNI only to the extent that it is allocated to the entity. Any portion of the depreciation deduction allocated directly to a beneficiary is reported on the beneficiary's personal income tax return and is allowed "above the line" in computing adjusted gross income. I.R.C. § 62(a)(5).

At first glance, it may seem unfair, or at least counterintuitive, to require that the depreciation deduction be allocated between an entity and its beneficiaries in proportion to their shares of fiduciary accounting income. Tax depreciation is an accounting mechanism that allows a taxpayer to recover the tax cost (i.e., basis) of depreciable assets over a specified period. It is not a cash outlay, and it does not reduce the carrying cost of the underlying assets on the fiduciary's books. Since depreciable assets have (or are deemed to have) a limited useful life, they may be viewed as wasting assets that skew the entity's investment return in favor of the income beneficiaries at the expense of the remainder beneficiaries. If the income beneficiaries enjoy the tax benefit of a depreciation deduction, in addition to an enhanced stream of fiduciary accounting income, they arguably receive an unwarranted windfall. The problem of unfairness may be mitigated if the fiduciary is directed, or at least authorized, to restore the presumed decline in value of depreciable assets by making periodic transfers from income to corpus. This is the basic function of a depreciation reserve. (Recall that, as a matter of tax accounting, amounts set aside as a depreciation reserve on a trust's books trigger an equivalent allocation of the depreciation deduction to the trust.) In the absence of a depreciation reserve, the potential problem of unfairness must be weighed against the risk of allocating the tax deduction to a taxpayer who cannot make effective use of it. If the depreciation deduction is allocated to an estate or a trust in a taxable year when the entity has little or no taxable income, the deduction may be wasted. In contrast, an allocation based on fiduciary accounting income tends to avoid this sort of wastage. The amount of tax depreciation is not limited by the amount of fiduciary accounting income, and the depreciation deduction allocated to a particular beneficiary may exceed the beneficiary's share of current fiduciary accounting income. Rev. Rul. 74–530, 1974–2 C.B. 188.

The Code and the regulations contain identical provisions for allocating the deduction for depletion relating to natural resources between an estate or trust and its beneficiaries. I.R.C. § 611(b); Reg. § 1.611–1(c)(4) and (c)(5). Similar rules also apply to the deductions for amortization relating to pollution control facilities, goodwill and other intangibles. I.R.C. § 642(f); Reg. § 1.642(f)–1.

§ 5.8 CHARITABLE CONTRIBUTIONS

Estates and trusts are allowed to deduct "any amount of the gross income, without limitation," which is paid during the taxable year for a qualifying charitable purpose "pursuant to the terms of the governing instrument." I.R.C. § 642(c)(1). Although the § 642(c) deduction is allowed "below the line" as an itemized deduction in computing taxable income, it is expressly excluded from the category of "miscellaneous itemized deductions" and is not subject to the 2% floor. I.R.C. § 67(b)(4). The § 642(c) deduction is in lieu of the charitable deduction provided in § 170, and is not subject to the percentage limitations (or the related carryforward rules) of that provision. Thus, an estate or trust may reduce its taxable income to zero by paying its gross income (whether earned in the current year or accumulated in previous years) for qualified charitable purposes. Reg. § 1.642(c)–1(a)(1). The deduction is available not only for qualifying charitable payments made during the current taxable year, but also, at the election of the executor or trustee, for amounts that are actually paid during the following taxable year. Reg. § 1.642(c)–1(b). This election allows the executor or trustee to make supplementary charitable payments based on a review of the financial and tax position of the estate or trust after the end of the taxable year for which the deduction is claimed. Qualified charitable purposes are defined somewhat more broadly under § 642(c) than under § 170, allowing, for example, gifts to foreign charities. Moreover, payments made for charitable purposes may be deducted under § 642(c), even if they are not made to or for the use of a qualifying charitable organization. Nevertheless, § 642(c) contains its own set of requirements and restrictions.

The requirement that a charitable contribution be paid from "gross income" prevents the estate or trust from obtaining an unwarranted deduction for amounts paid to charity from tax-exempt income or corpus that will not be subject to tax in any event. If a deduction were allowed for such payments, it could be used to shelter current or future distributions to private beneficiaries from tax. Accordingly, the allowable deduction for a charitable contribution does not include any amount that is allocable to tax-exempt interest or other items not entering into the gross income of the estate or trust. Reg. § 1.642(c)–3(b)(1). Furthermore, the gross income requirement implies a need to trace charitable payments to a particular source. A charitable gift of specific property (or its proceeds) under the terms of a will or trust instrument presents no difficulty in this regard, since any income generated by the property (or its sale) is clearly part of the gift. The same holds true for income allocable to a charitable residuary gift. Tracing the source of funds paid to satisfy a gift of a specific dollar amount may be more difficult. The regulations acknowledge the controlling effect of a provision in a will or trust instrument that specifically identifies the source of such payments "to the extent such provision has economic effect independent of income tax consequences," but otherwise presume that the payments consist of a ratable share of each class of items of income of the estate or the trust. Reg. § 1.642(c)–3(b)(2). For example, a provision that purports to characterize a pecuniary charitable gift as being paid from various classes of income in a specified order (e.g., ordinary income, then capital gain, then tax-exempt income, then corpus) will not be respected for tax purposes because it has no independent economic effect. In contrast, a provision that defines the charitable gift as consisting of all of the current year's ordinary income will be respected because the size of the gift depends on the amount of ordinary income earned by the estate or trust in the current year.

The requirement that a charitable contribution be made "pursuant to the terms of the governing instrument" is satisfied if the contribution is authorized by terms of the will or trust instrument, even if it is not required. Thus, the Supreme Court has upheld a deduction for charitable contributions made by trustees in the proper exercise of discretion expressly granted under a deed of trust. Old Colony Trust Co. v. Commissioner, 301 U.S. 379 (1937). Nevertheless, the weight of judicial authority suggests that the governing instrument must affirmatively indicate some charitable purpose or intent; it is not enough that the instrument does not prohibit charitable contributions. For example, one court held that a testamentary trust was not entitled to deduct any portion of amounts paid to charity pursuant to a beneficiary's exercise of a general power of appointment. Because the will creating the trust gave the beneficiary an unrestricted power to appoint the trust property as she saw fit, without indicating any preference for private beneficiaries or charitable organizations, the court found that the will did not sufficiently express a charitable intent on the part of the testator. Brownstone v. United States, 465 F.3d 525 (2d Cir. 2006).

The deduction also applies to amounts of gross income, without limitation, which are "permanently set aside" for qualifying charitable purposes by an estate pursuant to the terms of the decedent's will. I.R.C. § 642(c)(2). This provision allows an estate to deduct amounts which are not actually paid but are accumulated to be used for charitable purposes in the future. No deduction is allowed for amounts set aside by an estate for charitable purposes unless, under the terms of the will and the circumstances of the particular case, the risk that those amounts might be diverted or dissipated is "so remote as to be negligible." Reg. § 1.642(c)–2(d). The set-aside deduction is generally available only for estates and not for trusts. Under pre-1969 law, trusts were also allowed to deduct amounts set aside for future charitable payments, but the scope of the set-aside deduction was narrowed in 1969 in order to prevent nonexempt trusts from being used to circumvent newly-enacted restrictions on tax-exempt private foundations. (See § 9.1, *infra*.) Under current law, the § 642(c)(2) set-aside deduction does not apply to any trust other than a "qualified revocable trust" that elects to be treated as part of a decedent's estate (see § 4.4, *supra*) or a trust that is grandfathered under pre-1969 law. A related provision also disallows a charitable deduction for any amount allocable to unrelated business income of a trust. I.R.C. §§ 642(c)(4) and 681(a).

If a charitable payment is deductible under § 642(c), it cannot be deducted a second time as a distribution under § 661. I.R.C. § 663(a)(2). The prohibition of a double tax benefit makes perfectly good sense as far as it goes, but the regulations go further and state categorically that amounts paid by

an estate or trust for charitable purposes are
deductible "only" as provided in § 642(c). Reg.
§ 1.663(a)–2. Relying on the regulations, the
government has taken the position that if a
charitable payment fails for any reason to qualify for
a deduction under § 642(c), it cannot be deducted
instead as a distribution under § 661. Although this
position has been criticized by commentators as
unduly harsh and contrary to the language and
purpose of the statute, the courts have nevertheless
accepted the government's interpretation of the
regulations. In the leading case, an estate made
payments to charity in satisfaction of a pecuniary
bequest. Because the payments were made from
corpus (rather than from gross income), they were
not deductible under § 642(c), and the estate sought
to deduct them instead under § 661 as amounts
"properly paid" to the charity. In response, the
government argued that the deduction under § 661
should be available only for distributions to
noncharitable beneficiaries. The court accepted the
government's view as "consistent with the statutory
scheme and a reasonable interpretation thereof."
Mott v. United States, 462 F.2d 512 (Ct. Cl. 1972),
cert. denied, 409 U.S. 1108 (1973).

§ 5.9 DOUBLE DEDUCTIONS

The prohibition on "double deductions" in § 642(g)
generally prevents estates and trusts (and other
taxpayers) from deducting any item for income tax
purposes to the extent that the same item qualifies
for an estate tax deduction under § 2053 (relating to

claims and administration expenses) or § 2054 (relating to losses). For example, if an executor deducts an administration expense (e.g., an executor's commission or attorney's fee) on the estate tax return, she cannot deduct the same item on the fiduciary income tax return. Similarly, if the executor deducts the cost of selling property on the estate tax return, she cannot offset the same item against the sale price of property in determining gain or loss on the fiduciary income tax return.

Although the rule against double deductions precludes overlapping estate tax and income tax deductions for the same item, the executor or trustee can elect to deduct a particular item on the estate tax return or the income tax return, whichever is more advantageous. The executor or trustee can pick and choose, claiming an estate tax deduction for some items and an income tax deduction for others; indeed, a particular item may be bifurcated and deducted in part on the estate tax return and in part on the income tax return. The election is made by filing a waiver, in connection with the income tax return for the taxable year in which an item is claimed as a deduction, stating that the item has not been allowed and will not be allowed as an estate tax deduction under § 2053 or § 2054. The regulations allow the waiver to be filed at any time within the applicable limitation period (generally three years after filing the income tax return), and specifically provide that claiming a deduction on the estate tax return does not preclude allowance of an income tax deduction, as long as the estate tax deduction is not finally allowed and the waiver is duly filed. Reg. § 1.642(g)–1. Thus, an executor or trustee may claim the same item as a deduction on both the estate tax return and the income tax return, with appropriate disclosure, wait to see which deduction appears more advantageous, and then file a waiver (or abandon the income tax deduction) accordingly. Of course, once a waiver is filed, the item cannot subsequently be allowed as an estate tax deduction because the waiver operates as a relinquishment of the right to a deduction under § 2053 or § 2054.

The rule against double deductions has no application to deductions in respect of a decedent. (See § 3.4, *supra*.) Nor does it apply to items that are deductible for estate tax purposes but not for income tax purposes. Thus, for example, the portion of an estate's administration expenses that is attributable to tax-exempt income and therefore disallowed as an income tax deduction may nevertheless be deducted on the estate tax return. Rev. Rul. 59–32, 1959–1 C.B. 245.

§ 5.10 QUALIFIED BUSINESS INCOME

Section 199A, enacted in 2017, allows noncorporate taxpayers (including individuals, estates, and trusts) to deduct up to 20% of their "qualified business income" for taxable years beginning after 2017 and before 2026. Although the deduction is allowed "below the line" (i.e., in computing taxable income but not adjusted gross income), it is not an itemized deduction and is not subject to the 2% floor. I.R.C. § 63(b)(3) and (d).

Qualified business income generally includes the taxpayer's share of net income from a domestic business conducted by a pass-through entity (i.e., a partnership, S corporation, estate, or trust) or a sole proprietorship; it does not include capital gains or other portfolio-type investment income, nor does it include wages or other compensation paid to the taxpayer for personal services. The deduction cannot exceed 20% of taxable income (excluding net capital gains and qualified dividend income). For taxpayers with taxable income above a threshold amount, the deduction is further restricted in two important respects: (1) the deductible amount is limited to specified percentages of amounts paid by the business as wages to employees or invested in tangible, depreciable property; and (2) the deduction is phased out or eliminated for income derived from most personal and professional service businesses (e.g., health, law, accounting, and performing arts). The threshold amount for a single individual, an estate, or a trust is $157,500 (indexed for inflation); for a married couple filing jointly, the threshold amount is $315,000 (indexed for inflation).

Regulations promulgated in 2019 clarify several issues concerning the availability of the § 199A deduction to estates and trusts. Notably, the regulations provide that in determining whether the taxable income of an estate or trust exceeds the $157,500 threshold amount, taxable income is computed after taking into account any distribution deduction under §§ 651 or 661. Reg. § 1.199A–6(d)(3)(iv). This provision prevents taxable distributions from being counted twice, since the entity's distribution deduction is matched by the beneficiaries' inclusion of an equivalent amount. The regulations also clarify that qualified business income must be allocated between an estate or trust and its beneficiaries based on their respective shares of distributable net income. Reg. § 1.199A–6(d)(3)(ii). In making this allocation, DNI is determined without regard to § 199A. If the estate or trust has no DNI, the qualified business income is allocated entirely to the entity. Furthermore, in applying the wage-and-property limitation, the regulations prescribe the same method for allocating items between the entity and the beneficiaries. Consequently, by making distributions that carry out DNI to one or more beneficiaries, an estate or trust may be able to increase the total amount allowable as a deduction under § 199A in the hands of the beneficiaries. Nevertheless, the regulations warn that a trust may be disregarded in determining the threshold amount under § 199A if the trust was "formed or funded with a principal purpose of avoiding, or of using more than one, threshold amount." Reg. § 1.199A–6(d)(3)(vii).

CHAPTER 6
DISTRIBUTABLE NET INCOME

§ 6.1 OVERVIEW

The concept of "distributable net income" (DNI) is the centerpiece of Subchapter J's mechanism for apportioning the taxable income of an estate or a trust between the entity and its beneficiaries. Before examining the details of how DNI is computed, it is helpful to consider briefly the role that DNI plays in regulating the amount and character of taxable distributions that an estate or a trust makes to its beneficiaries.

Recall that estates and trusts generally serve as intermediaries for gratuitous transfers of property (and of income) from the transferor who originally owned the property (i.e., the decedent or grantor) to the beneficiaries who will ultimately receive it. For income tax purposes, gifts and bequests of property are excluded from the beneficiary's gross income, but the exclusion does not extend to income from the property. I.R.C. § 102(a) and (b). Accordingly, while property is held in an estate or a trust, the income it generates is subject to tax, and the primary function of Subchapter J is to apportion the burden of the tax on such income between the entity and its beneficiaries. This is accomplished by treating the entity as a conduit to the extent that it makes taxable distributions to the beneficiaries: the entity is allowed a deduction for such distributions, and the recipients are required to include the same amount in gross income. The amount deducted by the entity on account of its taxable distributions matches the amount includible by the beneficiaries. To determine the extent to which a particular distribution carries out taxable income from the entity to the beneficiaries, some mechanism is necessary to distinguish taxable income from tax-free gifts of property. Stripped to its essentials, that is the primary function of DNI.

DNI serves two important purposes: it measures the amount of taxable income that can be carried out from an estate or a trust to its beneficiaries, imposing a ceiling on the amount of distributions that is deductible by the entity and includible by the beneficiaries; and it measures the character of those taxable distributions, preserving their tax attributes (e.g., taxable or tax-exempt income, capital or ordinary gain) in the hands of the beneficiaries. Broadly speaking, then, to the extent that income items enter into DNI and are included in taxable distributions made by an estate or a trust, they will be taxed to the beneficiaries rather than to the entity. Conversely, to the extent that income items do not enter into DNI or are not distributed, they will be taxed to the entity. Thus, neither the taxable income of an estate or a trust, nor that of the beneficiaries, can be computed without first determining (1) the items that enter into DNI and (2) the amounts distributed (or deemed distributed) for the entity's taxable year. The first inquiry is the subject of this chapter, and the second is the subject of Chapter 7, *infra*. Any distributions in excess of DNI have no effect on the taxable income of the entity or that of the beneficiaries; in effect, the excess amounts are treated as tax-free gifts or bequests. The concept of DNI, enacted in 1954, largely avoids difficult tracing problems which arose under prior law from the need to determine whether distributions were actually made from the entity's income for the current taxable year.

§ 6.2 GENERAL DEFINITION

The starting point for computing the DNI of an estate or a trust is the entity's taxable income for the taxable year, subject to several modifications enumerated in the statute. I.R.C. § 643(a). At first glance, this formulation may seem merely circular, since the amount of the entity's taxable income depends on the amount allowed as a deduction for distributions, which depends on DNI, which in turn is computed by reference to the entity's taxable income. On closer inspection, however, the circularity disappears because the very first enumerated modification states that in computing DNI no deduction shall be taken for distributions. I.R.C. § 643(a)(1). Once the distribution deduction is removed from the computation, the remaining items of gross income and deduction entering into the entity's taxable income are readily ascertained. In other words, the starting point for computing DNI is the sum of all items entering into the entity's gross income for the taxable year, reduced by the allowable deductions other than the distribution deduction. Conceptually, this makes good sense. Since DNI imposes a ceiling on the amount of the distribution deduction, the computation of DNI precedes that of the distribution deduction.

The second statutory modification requires that the deduction allowed under § 642(b) in lieu of a personal exemption (see § 5.3, *supra*) shall also be disregarded in computing DNI. I.R.C. § 643(a)(2). This too makes good sense, since the § 642(b) deduction operates solely to insulate the entity from paying tax on de minimis amounts of otherwise taxable income and has no bearing on the taxable amount passing through to the beneficiaries. Indeed, if the § 642(b) deduction were allowed in computing DNI, the beneficiaries might benefit from the entity's deduction in addition to their own personal exemptions.* The net effect of ignoring the § 642(b) deduction at this stage is not to deny the deduction altogether but merely to preserve it for the exclusive benefit of the estate or trust as a taxable entity.

§ 6.3   CAPITAL GAINS

Proceeds realized by an estate or a trust from the sale or exchange of property, including capital gains, are normally allocated to corpus rather than to income under general fiduciary accounting principles. (See § 7.2, *infra*.) For income tax purposes, however, net capital gains are included in the entity's gross income. To the extent that capital gains enter into DNI, the tax on those gains may be shifted from the entity to beneficiaries who receive taxable distributions. This result is entirely appropriate in the case of terminating distributions

---

* The personal exemption for individual taxpayers is set at zero for taxable years beginning after 2017 and before 2026. I.R.C. § 151(d)(5). The § 642(b) exemption for estates and trusts, however, remains unchanged.

made during the entity's final taxable year, but in other cases it might seem unfair for beneficiaries who receive no immediate benefit from appreciation in particular trust property to be taxed on the capital gain realized from a sale or exchange of the property.

The statute attempts to resolve the problem by providing that capital gains, to the extent allocated to corpus, shall generally be excluded from DNI unless they are (1) paid, credited, or required to be distributed to any beneficiary during the taxable year, or (2) paid, permanently set aside, or to be used for charitable purposes under § 642(c). I.R.C. § 643(a)(3). For this purpose, an allocation made by the executor or trustee pursuant to a discretionary power granted in the will or trust instrument (or under local law) will be respected as long as the fiduciary's exercise of discretion is "reasonable and impartial." Reg. § 1.643(a)–3(b).

Capital losses are excluded from DNI except to the extent that they are netted against capital gains that enter into DNI. When capital gains do enter into DNI, they are normally netted against capital losses unless the gain realized on sale or exchange of a particular asset is used in determining the amount of a distribution. Reg. § 1.643(a)–3(d). Net capital losses, other than those allowed as deductions upon termination, do not enter into DNI and therefore do not pass through to the beneficiaries.

The statute implicitly treats capital gains as entering into DNI to the extent that they are properly allocated to fiduciary accounting income, and the regulations expressly so provide. Reg. § 1.643(a)–

3(b)(1). Thus, a trust provision requiring that capital gains be allocated to income (rather than to corpus) will be respected for tax purposes and the gains will be included in DNI. Reg. § 1.643(a)–3(e) (Example 4). The result is the same if the allocation is made by the trustee pursuant to a reasonable and impartial exercise of discretionary power granted in the trust instrument (or under local law). Reg. § 1.643(a)–3(b)(1).

Even if capital gains are allocated to corpus on the books of the estate or trust, they may enter into DNI to the extent that they are "treated consistently by the fiduciary on the trust's books, records, and tax returns as part of a distribution to a beneficiary" or are "actually distributed to the beneficiary or utilized by the fiduciary in determining the amount that is distributed or required to be distributed to a beneficiary." Reg. § 1.643(a)–3(b)(2) and (b)(3). The regulations provide several examples of situations in which capital gains are "actually distributed to" (or utilized in determining the amount distributed to) a beneficiary: in one example, a trust instrument directs that specific property be sold and the proceeds be distributed to a beneficiary; a second example involves a trustee who sells property during the trust's final taxable year and makes a terminating distribution of all the trust property; in a third example, the trustee sells property to fund a required distribution of half the trust property to the beneficiary at age 35. In each case, the capital gains are included in DNI, even though they are allocated to corpus, because they are actually distributed to a beneficiary or are utilized in determining the amount of a distribution. Reg. § 1.643(a)–3(e) (Examples 6, 7, and 9). As noted above, an exercise of fiduciary discretion in allocating capital gains will be respected only if it is reasonable, impartial, and otherwise authorized by the governing instrument or local law. In addition, the regulations (as amended in 2003) allow an executor or trustee considerable discretion to treat capital gains as part of a distribution to a beneficiary or as an amount retained by the entity, as long as the treatment, once established, is followed "consistently." Thus, a trustee may consistently treat discretionary distributions of trust corpus as being made first from any capital gains realized during the taxable year, or from capital gains from the sale of certain assets; similarly, a trustee may consistently treat unitrust amounts in excess of the trust's ordinary and tax-exempt income as consisting either of capital gains or of trust corpus. Reg. § 1.643(a)–3(e) (Examples 2, 3, 12, and 13).

In sum, the question of whether a particular item of capital gain enters into DNI involves an element of tracing, since it must be determined whether the gain is properly allocated to income or to corpus and (if allocated to corpus) whether the gain is treated as part of a distribution to a beneficiary. The burden of tracing is considerably alleviated, however, by the regulations which generally give controlling effect to the fiduciary accounting treatment of the gain on the entity's books, including allocations made by the executor or trustee in a reasonable and impartial exercise of discretion.

§ 6.4 EXTRAORDINARY DIVIDENDS AND TAXABLE STOCK DIVIDENDS

If an estate or a trust owns stock in a corporation and receives a distribution of cash or other property that is treated as a dividend for tax purposes, the dividend is included in the entity's gross income and hence generally enters into DNI as well, regardless of whether it is allocated to income or to corpus for fiduciary accounting purposes.

Nevertheless, a special rule, applicable only to "simple" trusts, requires that extraordinary dividends and taxable stock dividends be excluded from DNI to the extent that the trustee, acting in good faith, determines that they are properly allocated to corpus under the trust instrument and applicable local law. I.R.C. § 643(a)(4); Reg. § 1.643(a)–4. A simple trust is one which is required to distribute all of its fiduciary accounting income currently and which makes no other distributions or deductible charitable payments during the taxable year. See § 7.3, *infra*. By definition, any extraordinary dividends and taxable stock dividends received by such a trust, if properly allocated to corpus, cannot be distributed to the current income beneficiaries and are instead held for future distribution. Therefore, it seems perfectly sensible that such items are excluded from DNI. Even if it is subsequently determined that the trustee erred in allocating an extraordinary dividend or a taxable stock dividend to corpus instead of including it in a required current income distribution, the erroneous allocation will not trigger a retroactive adjustment in the trust's DNI as long as the trustee acted in "good faith." This result is confirmed by a separate provision which states more generally that extraordinary dividends and taxable stock dividends allocated to corpus by a fiduciary acting in good faith shall not be considered as fiduciary accounting income. I.R.C. § 643(b); Reg. § 1.643(b)–2.

The special rule of § 643(a)(4) has no application to estates or to complex trusts, which include extraordinary dividends and taxable stock dividends in DNI regardless of whether they are allocated to income or to corpus for fiduciary accounting purposes. Similarly, even in the case of a simple trust, extraordinary dividends and taxable stock dividends enter into DNI if the trustee allocates those items to income (rather than to corpus) on the trust's books.

§ 6.5 TAX-EXEMPT INTEREST

For the most part, DNI consists of items entering into the gross income of an estate or a trust, reduced by deductions allowed in arriving at the entity's taxable income. Nevertheless, the statute requires that tax-exempt interest on state and local bonds, reduced by expenses allocable to such interest, must also be included in DNI. I.R.C. § 643(a)(5); Reg. § 1.643(a)–5(a). The reason for treating net tax-exempt interest as a component of DNI has nothing to do with the *amount* of taxable distributions that the entity can deduct or that the beneficiaries must include under the conduit rules. Instead, the significance of including net tax-exempt interest in

DNI stems solely from its effect on the *character* of the items passing through from the entity to the beneficiaries. Including net tax-exempt interest in DNI along with the taxable income items ensures that distributions made by an estate or a trust to its beneficiaries will be deemed to comprise a ratable share of each class of items included in DNI. In other words, distributions made by the entity will carry out both tax-exempt interest and taxable income items to the beneficiaries, even though the portion of the distributions consisting of net tax-exempt interest will be disregarded in determining the amounts deductible by the entity and includible by the beneficiaries. The allocation of expenses to tax-exempt interest is discussed in § 7.3, *infra*.

If an estate or a trust makes a deductible charitable contribution, the amount of net tax-exempt interest included in DNI under § 643(a)(5) must be reduced to the extent that the amount paid, permanently set aside, or to be used for charitable purposes is deemed to consist of net tax-exempt interest. Reg. § 1.643(a)–5(b). The portion of a deductible charitable contribution consisting of net tax-exempt interest is appropriately excluded from DNI because it is neither retained by the entity nor distributed to the beneficiaries. The regulations provide that a provision in a will or trust instrument specifically identifying the source of a charitable contribution will be respected "to the extent such provision has economic effect independent of income tax consequences," but otherwise presume that the contribution consists of a ratable share of each class

of items of income of the estate or the trust. Reg.
§ 1.643(a)–5(b).

§ 6.6   CHARITABLE CONTRIBUTIONS

In general, charitable contributions made by an
estate or a trust do not enter into DNI. This result
follows from the combined effect of the § 642(c)
deduction, which removes from taxable income, and
hence from DNI, the portion of the charitable
contributions consisting of gross income items, and a
separate adjustment which removes from DNI the
portion of the charitable contributions consisting of
net   tax-exempt   interest   (see   § 6.5,   *supra*).
Nevertheless, solely for the purpose of determining
the portion of required current income distributions
that is taxable to the beneficiaries, a special rule
requires that DNI be computed without regard to the
§ 642(c) deduction if the resulting amount is less than
the amount of required current income distributions.
I.R.C. § 662(a)(1). The effect of this rule is to prevent
the required current income beneficiaries from
enjoying any benefit from the § 642(c) deduction. See
§ 7.4, *infra*. Furthermore, in determining the
character   of   the   required   current   income
distributions in the hands of the beneficiaries, the
§ 642(c) deduction is taken into account only to the
extent that FAI for the current taxable year exceeds
the required current income distributions. I.R.C.
§ 662(b); Reg. § 1.662(b)–2.

§ 6.7 NET INVESTMENT INCOME

In addition to the regular income tax, estates and trusts are subject to a separate tax on net investment income under I.R.C. § 1411. The tax is imposed at a flat rate of 3.8% on the lesser of (1) the entity's undistributed net investment income for the taxable year or (2) the entity's adjusted gross income in excess of the dollar amount at which the top marginal income tax bracket begins. I.R.C. § 1411(a)(2). The top marginal income tax rate begins at a relatively low threshold, although it is indexed for inflation—in 2020 the threshold was $12,950. Consequently, an estate or a trust with relatively modest amounts of net investment income may be subject to the § 1411 tax unless the entity distributes the net investment income to the beneficiaries or contributes the net investment income to charity.

The § 1411 tax applies to net investment income, which is defined as the entity's "investment income" reduced by allowable deductions allocable to such income. Very broadly speaking, investment income includes interest, dividends, annuities, royalties and rents (not derived from a trade or business); business income from passive activities or financial trading; and net gains from the disposition of nonbusiness property. I.R.C. § 1411(c); Reg. § 1.1411–4. The statutory definition of investment income excludes compensation for personal services, distributions from qualified retirement plans and individual retirement accounts, and items excluded from gross income, as well as most active business income.

Net investment income comprises various items of gross income and deduction of an estate or a trust; therefore, net investment income enters into DNI. To the extent that the entity makes taxable distributions to its beneficiaries, those distributions will be deemed to consist of a ratable share of net investment income and of each other class of items entering into DNI, in the absence of specific provision for a different allocation in the governing instrument (or under local law). The portion of the distributions consisting of net investment income will retain its character in the hands of the beneficiaries for purposes of applying § 1411 at the beneficiary level. Reg. § 1.1411–3(e)(3). Similarly, if the entity makes deductible charitable contributions, the contributions will be deemed to consist of a ratable share of the entity's items of income unless the governing instrument (or local law) specifically provides a different allocation that has economic effect independent of the income tax consequences. Reg. § 1.1411–3(e)(4). In either case, to the extent that the amounts distributed to beneficiaries or contributed to charity consist of net investment income, they will reduce the amount of the entity's undistributed net investment income that is subject to the 3.8% tax.

To illustrate the operation of § 1411, suppose that a trust has $15,000 of dividend income, $10,000 of taxable interest, $5,000 of capital gain, and a $75,000 taxable distribution from an individual retirement account (IRA); the trust has no expenses. DNI is $100,000, comprising all of the items except for the capital gain. Net investment income is $30,000, comprising all of the items except for the IRA distribution. The trust distributes $10,000 of its current fiduciary accounting income to a beneficiary. The distribution is deemed to consist of $1,500 of dividends, $1,000 of interest, and $7,500 of IRA proceeds; these amounts reduce the trust's taxable income and are includible in gross income by the beneficiary. For purposes of the § 1411 tax, the trust's undistributed net investment income is $27,500 ($13,500 dividends, $9,000 interest, and $5,000 capital gain), and the beneficiary's net investment income is $2,500 ($1,500 dividends and $1,000 interest). Reg. § 1.1411–3(e)(5) (Example 1).

The tax on net investment income applies to estates and most trusts that are subject to Subchapter J. However, it has no application to tax-exempt trusts, charitable trusts, charitable remainder trusts, or foreign trusts. Reg. § 1.1411–3(b)(1).

CHAPTER 7

DISTRIBUTIONS

§ 7.1 OVERVIEW

When an estate or a trust distributes cash or other property to its beneficiaries, the distributions may be treated for income tax purposes as carrying out some or all of the entity's DNI for the taxable year. To the extent that the distributions consist of DNI, the entity functions as a conduit for income tax purposes. Broadly speaking, the entity is allowed to deduct taxable distributions up to the amount of DNI, and the beneficiaries are required to include the same amount in gross income. DNI measures both the amount and the character of taxable items passing through from the entity to the beneficiaries, and those items are apportioned among the beneficiaries based on their respective shares of DNI.

The deduction allowed to the entity is limited to the lesser of DNI or the amounts distributed. Similarly, the total amount includible by the beneficiaries cannot exceed DNI. Thus, DNI represents a ceiling on the taxable portion of the distributions. If the total amount distributed is less than DNI, the distributions are fully taxable to the beneficiaries, and the undistributed portion of DNI is taxed to the entity. If the total amount distributed exceeds DNI, the excess amount has no effect on the tax liability of the entity or the beneficiaries. In effect, DNI marks the boundary between taxable distributions of the entity's income and tax-free gifts of property. I.R.C. § 102(a) and (b).

To determine the amount of taxable distributions includible by the beneficiaries, the DNI carried out by the distributions must be apportioned among the beneficiaries. For this purpose, distributions are divided into two classes or tiers: the first tier consists of mandatory current income distributions, and the second tier consists of all other distributions (i.e., distributions of corpus or accumulated income, as well as discretionary distributions of current income). The main significance of the tier system is that distributions in the first tier receive a priority allocation of DNI up to the amount of such distributions; only DNI in excess of mandatory current income distributions (if any) is allocated to distributions in the second tier. Thus, mandatory current income distributions are fully taxable up to DNI, while other distributions are taxable only to the extent of any residual DNI left over after the first-tier allocation. For this purpose, "income" refers to fiduciary accounting income as determined under the governing instrument and local law, as discussed in § 7.2, *infra*.

By establishing a mechanical formula for allocating DNI, the tier system largely avoids the need to trace the actual source of distributions. DNI is apportioned among the distributions in each tier based on the amounts required to be distributed or actually distributed. Accordingly, beneficiaries who are entitled to receive current income must include a ratable share of the DNI allocable to first-tier distributions, while other beneficiaries include any residual DNI in proportion to the amounts of their respective distributions. DNI determines not only the taxable amount but also the character of the amounts distributed to each beneficiary. To the extent that a distribution carries out DNI, the tax characteristics of items entering into DNI at the entity level are preserved in the hands of the beneficiary.

Subchapter J provides a simplified statutory scheme for taxing distributions made by trusts that are required to distribute all income currently and make no other distributions or charitable payments during the taxable year. By definition, these trusts, referred to in the regulations as "simple" trusts, make distributions exclusively within the first tier. All other trusts are referred to as "complex" trusts and are governed by a more elaborate statutory scheme. (For the most part, estates are governed by the same rules as complex trusts.) The essential distinction between simple and complex trusts relates to the arrangement of the statutory provisions rather than their substantive content. Much of the complexity of the conduit rules stems from a handful of provisions concerning discretionary distributions, nontaxable distributions, and charitable payments, which apply exclusively to complex trusts. Apart from a few minor differences in operating rules, the basic statutory schemes governing simple and complex trusts are almost indistinguishable as a practical matter. Simple trusts are discussed in § 7.3, *infra*, and complex trusts are discussed in § 7.4, *infra*.

Although DNI generally must be apportioned ratably among all distributions within each separate tier, a strictly proportional allocation can produce inequitable results where an estate or a complex trust provides substantially separate and independent shares for different beneficiaries. To prevent unfairness in such cases, a special statutory rule requires that DNI be computed separately for the separate shares. The separate share rule is discussed in § 7.5, *infra*.

Not all distributions of cash or property made by an estate or a trust carry out DNI. Payments made to satisfy a gift or bequest of a specific sum of money or of specific property are expressly excluded from the rules governing taxable distributions, and are therefore treated as tax-free gifts or bequests. The scope of this exclusion is discussed in § 7.6, *infra*.

When an estate or a trust distributes property in kind, the entity generally recognizes no gain or loss. Moreover, the amount deductible by the entity and includible by the beneficiary is limited to the lesser of the property's fair market value or its basis in the entity's hands, and the entity's basis in the property carries over in the beneficiary's hands. In some cases, however, the entity may be permitted or required to realize gain or loss on the distribution, with corresponding adjustments in the amount of the distribution and the beneficiary's basis. The tax treatment of in-kind distributions is discussed in § 7.7, *infra*.

Distributions made by an estate or a trust during its taxable year are generally reportable by the beneficiary in the beneficiary's taxable year that includes the end of the entity's taxable year. In effect, the beneficiary reports the distributions as if they occurred on the last day of the entity's taxable year. This timing rule is subject to a few limitations and qualifications which are discussed in § 7.8, *infra*.

Subchapter J includes an elaborate set of "throwback" rules aimed at trusts that accumulate income in one or more taxable years and then distribute the accumulated income to beneficiaries in a subsequent taxable year. If the trust's marginal tax rate is lower than that of its beneficiaries, substantial tax savings may be achieved by accumulating taxable income for several years, paying tax at the trust level, and eventually distributing trust corpus or accumulated income with little or no additional tax burden to the beneficiaries. To prevent this sort of manipulation, the throwback provisions impose an additional tax on the beneficiaries who receive such "accumulation distributions." The additional tax is intended to approximate the incremental tax liability that the beneficiaries would have incurred if the income had been distributed currently instead of accumulated, subject to an offset for the taxes actually paid by the trust. The codification of the multiple trust rule in 1984, and the enactment of the compressed tax rate schedule for trusts in 1986, largely eliminated the tax advantages of accumulating income in trusts, and in 1997 Congress repealed the throwback rules for most domestic trusts. Nevertheless, those rules continue to apply to foreign trusts, to domestic trusts that once were foreign trusts, and to a few domestic trusts that were created before March 1, 1984. The throwback rules are discussed in Chapter 11, *infra.*

Note on terminology. The term "taxable distribution" is used throughout this book to refer to a distribution, made by an estate or a trust to one or more beneficiaries, which is or might be treated as carrying out DNI under the conduit rules of §§ 651–662, discussed in § 7.3 and § 7.4, *infra.* The term refers to the full amount of the distribution, including any tax-free portion in excess of DNI. In contrast, a "nontaxable distribution" refers to a distribution which is excluded from the conduit rules under the statutory safe harbor of § 663(a)(1), discussed in § 7.6, *infra.* Charitable payments are not treated as distributions to beneficiaries; they are discussed separately in § 5.6, *supra.*

§ 7.2 FIDUCIARY ACCOUNTING INCOME

The concept of "income required to be distributed currently" plays a key role in determining the amount and character of taxable distributions made by estates and trusts. In this context, and more generally for purposes of the conduit rules of Subchapter J, the term "income" in its unmodified form refers to the income of an estate or a trust "determined under the terms of the governing instrument and applicable local law"—in other words, to items allocated to income (as opposed to corpus or principal) under applicable principles of fiduciary accounting. I.R.C. § 643(b). Of course, "income" may have quite a different meaning when it is modified by specific tax terms (e.g., "gross income," "taxable income," or "distributable net income"), and it is important to distinguish carefully between the tax and fiduciary accounting concepts.

In administering an estate or a trust, a fiduciary is required to account for all receipts, payments, and distributions of cash or other property, and to allocate each item either to income or to principal. (The terms "principal" and "corpus" have the same meaning in trust accounting parlance and are used interchangeably.) The separate income and principal accounts reflect the different (and potentially conflicting) interests of the beneficiaries. Indeed, a beneficiary's right to receive current or future distributions is traditionally defined in terms of income and principal. For example, suppose that a trust instrument directs that net income be distributed currently to Alice and that the remaining property be distributed at her death to her issue then living. To the extent that the trustee allocates particular items of receipt or expense to income (rather than to principal), those items will directly affect the amount that Alice receives each year (as well as the amount and character of the distributions that she reports on her individual income tax return). Conversely, items allocated to principal (rather than to income) will constitute the trust property to be distributed at Alice's death to her surviving issue. If the trustee has discretion to accumulate income and add it to principal, or to invade the trust property and distribute it to Alice, the impact of fiduciary accounting allocations may be attenuated as far as the beneficiaries are concerned, but an allocation of certain items to income or to principal may still have significance for income tax purposes.

Under traditional fiduciary accounting principles, amounts representing current returns (e.g., dividends, interest, and rent) from property held by an estate or a trust are generally allocated to income, while the underlying property and proceeds from the sale or exchange thereof are generally allocated to principal. A different allocation may be permitted or required by the terms of a governing instrument, however, and the regulations (as amended in 2003) indicate that such an allocation will be respected for tax purposes if it is made pursuant to local law and provides for "a reasonable apportionment between the income and remainder beneficiaries of the total return of the trust for the year." Reg. § 1.643(b)–1.

For example, a trustee may be authorized by state statute to switch from a traditional definition of trust income to a "unitrust" approach under which income consists of a fixed percentage (e.g., between 3% and 5%) of the value of the trust property, determined annually. (For a more detailed discussion of the unitrust concept in connection with split-interest charitable trusts, see § 9.2, *infra*.) Alternatively, a trustee operating under a prudent investor standard may have a statutory power to make adjustments between income and principal in order to fulfill a duty of impartiality owed to the income beneficiaries. A switch between methods of determining income authorized by state statute will not be treated as a taxable event for income or gift tax purposes. Similarly, an allocation to income of gain from the sale or exchange of property will generally be respected for tax purposes if the allocation is either required by the terms of the governing instrument (or by local law) or made pursuant to a "reasonable and impartial" exercise of fiduciary discretion.

Nevertheless, the regulations warn that allocations may not be respected for tax purposes if they "depart fundamentally from traditional principles" of fiduciary accounting. Reg. § 1.643(b)–1. For example, if a trust instrument purports to provide for mandatory income distributions but expressly allocates all dividends and interest to principal, the trust will not be recognized as one that is required to distribute all of its income currently. See also Rev. Rul. 90–82, 1990–2 C.B. 44 (direction in trust instrument to charge principal payments on mortgage note against trust income).

Whether a particular receipt is credited to income or to principal for fiduciary accounting purposes has no bearing on whether it is includible in gross income. Thus, although many items of fiduciary accounting income are also includible in gross income (e.g., dividends, taxable interest, and rent), this is not invariably the case; an obvious example is tax-exempt interest. Moreover, realized capital gains are includible in gross income even though they are normally allocated to principal rather than to income on the books of an estate or a trust. By the same token, whether a particular expense is charged against income or against principal does not determine whether it is deductible in computing taxable income. Administration expenses (e.g., fiduciary commissions and attorney and accounting fees) may be deductible for income tax purposes even though they are charged in whole or in part against principal on the books of an estate or a trust. An income tax deduction may be disallowed for other payments (e.g., expenses attributable to tax-exempt interest) even though they are properly charged against fiduciary accounting income.

Allocations of particular items to income or to principal directly increase or reduce the amount of fiduciary accounting income (FAI), but such allocations affect DNI only in a few isolated cases. Two obvious examples have already been noted: capital gains, which enter into DNI under § 643(a)(3) only if they are allocated to FAI or in a few cases if they are allocated to corpus (see § 6.3, *supra*); and extraordinary dividends and taxable stock dividends, which enter into the DNI of a simple trust under § 643(a)(4) only if they are allocated to FAI (see § 6.4, *supra*). For the most part, however, DNI and FAI are separate and independent computations which serve different purposes under the conduit rules of Subchapter J. DNI represents a ceiling on the amounts of taxable distributions that are deductible by the entity and includible by the beneficiaries, while FAI represents a ceiling on the amount of DNI that can be allocated to income required to be distributed currently. FAI may be exactly equal to DNI, but this is a rare coincidence; ordinarily the two amounts are different, and FAI may be either larger or smaller than DNI in a particular case.

By way of illustration, suppose that a trust has $15,000 of taxable interest, $10,000 of tax-exempt interest, a $5,000 death benefit (an item of income in respect of a decedent, allocated to corpus), and a deductible $8,000 administration expense (charged to income). FAI is $17,000, comprising the taxable interest and the tax-exempt interest, reduced by the administration expense. DNI is $22,000, comprising the taxable interest, the tax-exempt interest, and the death benefit, reduced by the administration expense. Alternatively, assume the same facts except that the administration expense is charged to corpus. In that case, FAI (no longer reduced by the administration expense) would be $25,000, and DNI would still be $22,000.

As the preceding example suggests, most deductible expenses (e.g., administration expenses, interest, and taxes) automatically enter into DNI regardless of whether they are charged against income or principal for fiduciary accounting purposes. (A few items, however, such as a beneficiary's allocable share of depreciation, may be reported directly by the beneficiary without entering into DNI. See § 5.7, *supra*.) A deduction that reduces DNI has the incidental effect of limiting the amount of taxable distributions that are deductible by an estate or a trust and includible in the hands of the beneficiaries. Thus, the benefit of tax deductions frequently flows through to beneficiaries who currently receive distributions even though the items that gave rise to the deductions were actually paid from principal held for the remainder beneficiaries.

This mismatch may seem unfair to the remainder beneficiaries, but it is an inherent consequence of the conduit rules that use DNI to measure the amount and character of taxable distributions. The drafters of the conduit rules concluded that any potential unfairness was outweighed by the practical advantages of avoiding the need to trace the source of distributions, preventing deductions from being wasted in the hands of an estate or a trust, and minimizing the significance of differences in income and principal allocations under local law.

§ 7.3 SIMPLE TRUSTS

A "simple" trust is one which (1) by its terms is required to distribute all of its income currently, (2) does not make any other distributions during the taxable year, and (3) does not provide for any amounts to be paid, set aside, or used for charitable purposes. I.R.C. § 651(a). Whether all of the trust's income is required to be distributed currently depends on the terms of the trust and on local law. The "income" required to be distributed currently is the trust's fiduciary accounting income, net of any items properly charged to income. The trustee may make discretionary allocations of items to income or to principal, as long as the exercise of discretion is reasonable and impartial, without violating the requirement that all income must be distributed currently (see § 7.2, *supra*). Similarly, the trustee may set aside amounts of current income for a depreciation reserve pursuant to the terms of the trust. As long as the trustee is under a duty to distribute all of the trust income currently, the distributions need not actually be made before the end of the taxable year; as a practical matter, the trustee may make quarterly distributions of income shortly after the end of each quarter. Reg. § 1.651(a)–2(a).

As long as all of the trust income is required to be distributed currently, it is immaterial whether the trustee has discretion to sprinkle the income among several beneficiaries or whether their respective shares of income are fixed. However, a trust will not qualify as a simple trust if the trustee has discretion to distribute the trust income currently or to accumulate it, even if the trustee actually distributes all of the income. Reg. § 1.651(a)–2(b). A trust may qualify as a simple trust in some years and not in others. For example, if the trustee has discretion to accumulate income until a beneficiary reaches age 21 and thereafter must distribute all of the income currently, the trust will be a complex trust while the beneficiary is under age 21 but it may qualify as a simple trust (if no other amounts are distributed) beginning in the taxable year after the beneficiary reaches age 21. Reg. § 1.651(a)–2(c).

A trust will not qualify as a simple trust if it makes any distributions, other than the required distributions of current income, during the taxable year. The test is not whether the trustee has discretion to make such distributions, but whether they are actually made. Thus, for example, if all of the trust income is required to be distributed currently and the trustee also has discretion to invade trust corpus for the income beneficiary, the trust fails to qualify as a simple trust only in years when the trustee actually invades trust corpus. Reg. § 1.651(a)–3(b). By the same token, a trust is never a simple trust in the year of termination when it is required to distribute its remaining property. Reg. § 1.651(a)–3(a). More generally, a trust cannot qualify as a simple trust in any year in which current income is permitted to be accumulated (even if it is actually distributed) or in which the trustee makes mandatory or discretionary distributions of corpus or accumulated income.

The regulations interpret the prohibition on charitable payments to mean only that a simple trust must not actually be eligible for a charitable deduction under § 642(c) during the taxable year. The terms of the trust may provide for future, contingent, or discretionary payments to charitable organizations as long as no deduction is allowable under § 642(c) for amounts paid, set aside, or used for charitable purposes during the taxable year. Reg. § 1.651(a)–4.

Once it is determined that a trust qualifies as a simple trust, the tax treatment of distributions is relatively straightforward. The trust is allowed a deduction for the lesser of (1) the amount of income required to be distributed currently (which by definition is equal to FAI), or (2) DNI, reduced in either case by net tax-exempt income. I.R.C. § 651(a) and (b); Reg. § 1.651(b)–1. The same amount, whether actually distributed or not, is includible in gross income by the beneficiaries. I.R.C. § 652(a);

Reg. § 1.652(a)–1. If there is more than one beneficiary, the amount of taxable distributions is apportioned among the beneficiaries based on the amount of income that each is entitled to receive. The taxable amount is limited to the lesser of FAI or DNI, excluding net tax-exempt income. Thus, if FAI is less than or equal to DNI, each beneficiary is taxable on the full amount of his or her required distributions of FAI (other than tax-exempt income). If FAI is greater than DNI, each beneficiary is taxable on a share of DNI (other than tax-exempt income) in proportion to his or her required distributions of FAI. Reg. § 1.652(a)–2.

To illustrate, suppose that a simple trust is required to distribute its net income to a single beneficiary. The trust has $20,000 of taxable interest, a $3,000 death benefit (an item of income in respect of a decedent, allocated to corpus), and a deductible $5,000 administration expense (charged to income). FAI is $15,000, comprising the taxable interest reduced by the administration expense. DNI, which also includes the death benefit, is $18,000. The trust can deduct the full $15,000 income distribution, and the beneficiary must include the same amount in gross income. Alternatively, assume the same facts except that the administration expense is charged to corpus. In that case, FAI (no longer reduced by the administration expense) would be $20,000, and DNI would still be $18,000. Both the trust's distribution deduction and the beneficiary's includible amount would then be limited to $18,000, and the beneficiary would receive the remaining $2,000 tax-free.

Furthermore, each beneficiary's taxable distributions are deemed to consist of a ratable share of all items entering into DNI, unless the trust instrument specifically allocates different classes of income to different beneficiaries. I.R.C. § 652(b). Such an allocation will be respected only to the extent that it is required by the trust instrument and has "an economic effect independent of the income tax consequences of the allocation." Reg. § 1.652(b)–2(b). Thus, a provision in the trust instrument granting the trustee discretion to allocate taxable income to one beneficiary and tax-exempt income to another beneficiary will not be effective for tax purposes, nor will a provision that purports to affect the character but not the amount of income distributable to different beneficiaries. However, a direction to pay all of the trust's tax-exempt income to one beneficiary and all of the remaining income to another beneficiary would be valid.

Items of deduction entering into DNI must be allocated among the various classes of taxable and tax-exempt income, to reflect the amount and character of taxable distributions flowing through to the beneficiaries. The allocation also serves to identify the portion of otherwise deductible expenses that is attributable to tax-exempt income and therefore disallowed under I.R.C. § 265(a). The regulations provide three basic rules for allocating deductions. First, all deductible items that are directly attributable to one class of income must be allocated to that class. For example, deductible repairs, property taxes, and expenses of maintaining rental property reduce the net rental income included in DNI. Second, deductions that are not directly attributable to a specific class of income may be freely allocated to any class, as long as an appropriate portion is allocated to tax-exempt income. These "floating" deductions include, for example, administration expenses such as fiduciary, attorney, and accountant fees. Finally, to the extent that any deductible items exceed the amount of income to which they are directly attributable, they may be freely allocated to any other class in the same manner as other floating deductions, except that excess deductions attributable to tax-exempt income may not be offset against any other class of income. Reg. § 1.652(b)–3.

To illustrate the operation of these rules, suppose that a simple trust has two beneficiaries who are each entitled to receive half of the trust's current income. The trust has FAI of $100, consisting of $60 of rental income and $40 of tax-exempt interest. The trust also has $20 of deductible administration expenses which are charged to corpus. DNI is $80, consisting of the rental income and the tax-exempt interest, reduced by the deductible administration expenses. The trust is entitled to a distribution deduction of $48 ($80 DNI less $32 net tax-exempt interest, assuming a pro rata allocation of the administration expenses between the rental income [60%] and the tax-exempt interest [40%]). Since FAI exceeds DNI, each beneficiary must include $24 (half of DNI, excluding net tax-exempt interest) in gross income. Each beneficiary's distribution is deemed to consist of a ratable one-half share of each item entering into DNI (i.e., $24 of rental income and $16 of tax-exempt interest).

The regulations seem to contemplate that floating deductions will generally be apportioned ratably to tax-exempt income (step two, above) *after* deducting items directly attributable to each income class (step one, above). Reg. § 1.652(b)–3(b). In several examples, however, the computation is based on the ratio of tax-exempt income to total income *before* deducting items directly attributable to any income class. Reg. §§ 1.652(c)–4, 1.661(c)–2, and 1.662(c)–4. The portion of the distribution consisting of tax-exempt income may be greater under this alternative approach if expenses directly attributable to other classes of income are chargeable to income. In the preceding example, suppose that the trust has $10 of deductible expenses directly attributable to the rental income and $10 of floating deductions, and all of those items are charged to income (rather than corpus). If the rental income is reduced by direct expenses (step one) before apportioning the floating deductions (step two), the $10 of floating deductions will be allocated $5.56 to rental income ($10 × $50 rental income/$90 total income after direct expenses) and $4.44 to tax-exempt income ($10 × $40 tax-exempt income/$90 total income after direct expenses). As a result, the total amounts distributed will consist of $44.44 rental income ($60 − $10 − $5.56) and $35.56 tax-exempt income ($40 − $4.44). If the order of the steps is reversed, however, the $10 of floating deductions will be allocated $6 to rental income ($10 × $60 rental income/$100 total income before direct expenses) and only $4 to tax-exempt income ($10 × $40 tax-exempt income/$100 total income before direct expenses). Under this approach, the total amounts distributed will consist of $44 rental income ($60 − $10 − $6) and $36 tax-exempt income ($40 − $4).

In some cases, it may be inappropriate to allocate floating deductions based solely on the income of an estate or trust for the current year. For example, suppose that in its final taxable year a trust distributes all of its assets and pays a fiduciary termination fee which is based on asset values and taxable income during the full period of administration. Instead of allocating the termination fee based on the trust's income for the current year, the Service has ruled that "a reasonable and appropriate method of allocation would be one based on the ratio of tax-exempt income realized by the trust during its existence to the total of ordinary income (including tax-exempt income) realized by the trust during its existence plus the excess of capital gains realized over capital losses sustained over the life of the trust plus any net unrealized capital appreciation of the assets distributed." Rev. Rul. 77–466, 1977–2 C.B. 83. This ruling is consistent with judicial authority holding, on similar facts, that unrealized capital appreciation must be taken into account in determining the deductible portion of fiduciary termination fees. Fabens v. Commissioner, 519 F.2d 1310 (1st Cir. 1975).

§ 7.4   ESTATES AND COMPLEX TRUSTS

A complex trust is any trust other than a simple trust. The rules governing distributions from complex trusts are considerably more elaborate than the rules for simple trusts, mostly because of the need to distinguish taxable gifts of income from tax-free gifts of property and to allocate DNI among different classes of taxable distributions without tracing the actual source or character of particular distributions. Estates are generally subject to the same rules as complex trusts; they are never treated as simple trusts. (As noted elsewhere, estates enjoy a larger exemption than trusts, as well as more flexibility in electing a fiscal year. See § 5.2 and § 5.3, *supra.*)

Under the conduit rules for taxing distributions made by an estate or a complex trust, distributions are classified under a two-tier system. The first tier consists of amounts of fiduciary accounting income for the taxable year that are required to be distributed currently, and the second tier consists of all other amounts properly paid, credited, or required to be distributed currently. (Some distributions are expressly excluded from the conduit rules under § 663(a)(1), discussed in § 7.6, *infra.*) An estate or a complex trust is entitled to a deduction for the lesser of (1) the total amount of first-tier and second-tier distributions or (2) DNI, reduced in either case by net tax-exempt income. I.R.C. § 661(a) and (c). The beneficiaries, collectively, must include the same total amount in gross income. I.R.C. § 662(a). Thus, the amount of the entity's distribution deduction is exactly matched by the total amount includible in gross income by the beneficiaries.

The primary function of the tier system is to allocate DNI between different classes of beneficiaries, for purposes of determining the amount and character of the taxable portion of the distributions in the hands of the beneficiaries. DNI is allocated on a priority basis to first-tier distributions, and only thereafter to second-tier distributions. In other words, DNI is carried out first to beneficiaries who are entitled to receive current income distributions, and then to beneficiaries who receive other distributions. Any residual DNI not allocated to first-tier or second-tier distributions is taxed to the entity rather than to the beneficiaries, and any distributions in excess of DNI are neither deductible by the entity nor taxable to the beneficiaries. Thus, if DNI is less than or equal to the first-tier distributions, those distributions will absorb all of the DNI, which will be apportioned among the first-tier beneficiaries in proportion to their respective shares of income; the second-tier distributions will be completely tax-free. Only if DNI is greater than the first-tier distributions will there be any DNI to be carried out by the second-tier distributions. In that case, the second-tier distributions will carry out the remaining DNI (up to the amount of the second-tier distributions), which will be apportioned among the second-tier beneficiaries based on the amounts of their distributions. Thus, DNI is allocated on a priority basis to first-tier distributions and then to second-tier distributions, and DNI is apportioned ratably among the beneficiaries within each tier unless the trust instrument specifically allocates different classes of income to different beneficiaries. I.R.C. § 662(b); Reg. § 1.662(b)–1; see § 7.3, *supra*. In sum, the tier system provides mechanical rules for allocating and apportioning DNI which largely avoid the problems of tracing the source and character of distributions.

A simple example illustrates the basic operation of the tier system. Suppose that a testamentary trust requires that $10,000 of current income be distributed to Alice and authorizes the trustee in its discretion to distribute corpus to Alice or to Basil. In a year when the trust has $3,000 of taxable interest, $9,000 of dividends, $5,000 of capital gain (not included in DNI), and no expenses, the trustee distributes $10,000 to Alice and $10,000 to Basil. Because the total amount distributed to Alice and Basil ($20,000) is greater than DNI ($12,000), the trust's distribution deduction is limited to $12,000. (The capital gain is excluded from DNI and is therefore taxed to the trust.) The $10,000 mandatory current income distribution to Alice is a first-tier distribution which carries out $10,000 of DNI and is fully includible in her gross income. (Alice reports $2,500 of taxable interest and $7,500 of dividends, in proportion to her share of the items entering into DNI.) The $10,000 discretionary distribution to Basil is a second-tier distribution which carries out the remaining $2,000 of DNI; only $2,000 is includible in Basil's gross income. (Basil reports $500 of taxable interest and $1,500 of dividends, in proportion to his share of the items entering into DNI.) If the trust in the preceding example had a deductible administration expense of $2,000, DNI would be only $10,000. In that case, the first-tier distribution to Alice would still be fully taxable but the second-tier distribution to Basil would be entirely tax-free.

First tier. The first tier corresponds closely to the required current income distributions from a simple trust, and is determined in much the same way. Reg. § 1.661(a)–2(b). First-tier distributions also include "any amount required to be distributed which may be paid out of income or corpus to the extent such amount is paid out of income." I.R.C. §§ 661(a)(1) and 662(a)(1). For example, if a trust provides for annuity payments to be made from income or corpus, the annuity payment is treated as a first-tier distribution "to the extent there is income . . . not paid, credited, or required to be distributed to other beneficiaries for the taxable year," and as a second-tier distribution only after current income is exhausted. Reg. § 1.662(a)–2(c). The same is true of a court-ordered support allowance payable from income or corpus of an estate to the decedent's surviving spouse or dependent family members. Reg. §§ 1.661(a)–2(e), 1.662(a)–2(c), and 1.662(a)–3(b).

Beneficiaries who are presently entitled to receive the income of an estate or a trust are taxable as first-tier beneficiaries regardless of whether the income is actually distributed to them. This treatment accommodates the routine administrative practice of trustees who compute the trust's net income at the end of each year and shortly thereafter make a final "catch-up" payment of any amounts required to be distributed currently but not actually paid during the year in question.

Occasionally, there may be uncertainty concerning the identities of the beneficiaries or the amounts of income they are entitled to receive. For example, suppose that a trustee, acting in good faith, withholds an amount of income pending litigation concerning the validity or construction of the trust instrument. Should the disputed amount be taxed currently to the beneficiaries who are ultimately determined to be entitled to it, even if their rights are not vindicated or enforced until a subsequent year? Or should the amount be taxed to the trust on the ground that it is properly withheld and therefore not currently required to be distributed? The courts have held that the beneficiaries are currently taxable on the amounts that they are entitled to receive, regardless of any delay in determining their rights under the trust instrument. DeBrabant v. Commissioner, 90 F.2d 433 (2d Cir. 1937); United States v. Higginson, 238 F.2d 439 (1st Cir. 1956); Rev. Rul. 62–147, 1962–2 C.B. 151.

If an executor or a trustee is not required to distribute income currently but instead has discretion to distribute the income or accumulate it, any discretionary distributions of income (or other amounts) are treated as second-tier distributions. This point is especially relevant for estates, which are seldom required to distribute income currently. For example, suppose that a will leaves specific shares of stock to Andy and leaves the residuary estate in trust to pay income from the time of the testator's death to Beatrice. During the period of estate administration, the executor generally has discretion to withhold distributions of property and income until debts, taxes and administration expenses have been paid. Therefore, the estate is properly taxable on dividends that it accumulates for future distribution to Andy and on the residuary income that will eventually become payable to Beatrice upon funding of the testamentary trust.

If an estate or a trust makes deductible charitable payments, a special rule prevents the first-tier beneficiaries from enjoying any tax benefit from the entity's § 642(c) deduction. In determining the taxable portion of first-tier distributions, DNI must be computed without regard to the § 642(c) deduction. I.R.C. § 662(a)(1); Reg. § 1.662(a)–2(b). By its terms, the DNI "gross-up" applies only if the amount of required current income distributions is greater than DNI (computed without regard to the § 642(c) deduction), but this limitation makes no practical difference because the first-tier distributions will be fully taxable in any other case (i.e., where the amount of such distributions is less than or equal to modified DNI). The DNI gross-up affects only first-tier distributions; it does not apply to second-tier distributions. In effect, the entity's deductible charitable payments occupy an intermediate tier, carrying out DNI after the first-tier distributions and before the second tier distributions. Furthermore, in determining the character of first-tier distributions in the hands of the beneficiaries, the § 642(c) deduction is taken into account only to the extent that FAI for the current taxable year exceeds the first-tier distributions. I.R.C. § 662(b); Reg. § 1.662(b)–2. These adjustments ensure that deductible charitable payments have no effect on the amount or the character of the first-tier distributions reported by the beneficiaries.

To illustrate, suppose that a trust with DNI of $80 and FAI of $150 makes required current income distributions of $90 to Audrey and $60 to Ben, as well as a deductible $20 charitable payment from income accumulated in previous years. The ceiling on the taxable amount of first-tier distributions is $100 ($80 DNI, grossed up by the $20 charitable deduction). Accordingly, the required income distributions carry out $60 of DNI to Audrey ($100 × 90/150) and $40 to Ben ($100 × 60/150). If Audrey and Ben were second-tier beneficiaries (i.e., if their income distributions were discretionary rather than mandatory), the distributions would carry out only $48 to Audrey ($80 × 90/150) and $32 to Ben ($80 × 60/150). As a further variation, assume the facts are the same as in the original example, except that the $60 mandatory distribution of current income is made to the charity (rather than to Ben) and the $20 discretionary distribution of accumulated income is made to Ben (rather than to the charity). In that case, the ceiling on the taxable amount of first-tier distributions would be $140 ($80 DNI, grossed up by the $60 charitable deduction). Therefore, Audrey would be fully taxable on her $90 first-tier distribution, and

Ben would receive his $20 second-tier distribution tax-free.

Second tier. Distributions, other than required current income distributions, are classified as second-tier distributions if they are "properly paid, credited, or required to be distributed." I.R.C. §§ 661(a)(2) and 662(a)(2). (Charitable payments are not treated as distributions for this purpose, since they are already removed from DNI by the § 642(c) deduction. See § 5.8, *supra*.) Thus, all discretionary distributions, as well as all mandatory distributions of current or accumulated income and corpus, are classified as second-tier distributions. If there are no required current income distributions, all distributions made during the taxable year will be taxed as second-tier distributions and will carry out DNI (up to the amount distributed), to be apportioned among the beneficiaries based on their respective distributions. Amounts paid in error (e.g., to the wrong recipient or in the wrong amount) are neither deductible to the entity nor includible to the recipient because they are not "properly" paid; conversely, amounts erroneously withheld are treated as taxable distributions (even though not actually paid) to the extent that they are "required to be distributed." Amounts not actually paid may also be treated as taxable distributions if they are properly "credited" to a beneficiary. For this purpose, a mere bookkeeping entry is not sufficient; the credited amounts must be immediately available to the beneficiary and beyond recall by the fiduciary.

Estate of Johnson v. Commissioner, 88 T.C. 225, aff'd
mem., 838 F.2d 1202 (2d Cir. 1987).

In general, distributions are taken into account for
a taxable year only if they are properly paid, credited,
or required to be made during the year in question. A
special rule, however, provides that the executor of
an estate or the trustee of a complex trust may elect
to treat amounts "properly paid or credited" during
the first 65 days of the entity's taxable year as if
made on the last day of the preceding taxable year.
I.R.C. § 663(b). (This rule, which formerly applied
only to complex trusts, was amended in 1997 to apply
to estates as well.) The total amount eligible for the
election is limited to the greater of the entity's FAI or
DNI for the preceding taxable year, reduced in either
case by amounts already paid, credited, or required
to be distributed during that year. Reg. § 1.663(b)–
1(a)(2). Thus, the 65-day rule allows a fiduciary,
promptly after the end of each taxable year, to make
"catch-up" distributions of any amounts of FAI or
DNI that were not actually distributed during the
preceding year, but does not permit supplementary
tax-free distributions of corpus. The election may be
made for a particular distribution or even a portion
thereof. Any amount deemed distributed on the last
day of the preceding taxable year "shall be so treated
for all purposes," including determination of the
amount includible by the beneficiary. Reg.
§ 1.663(b)–1(a)(2).

Payments made to third parties may constitute
constructive distributions to the extent that the
payments indirectly confer economic benefits on the

beneficiaries. For example, payments to defray a beneficiary's living expenses or to maintain the beneficiary's residence may be treated as taxable distributions. If a trust holds residential property available for rent-free occupancy by the beneficiary, however, there is a risk that payments made by the trustee to maintain the property may be treated as nondeductible administration expenses. Commissioner v. Plant, 76 F.2d 8 (2d Cir. 1935); DuPont Testamentary Trust v. Commissioner, 514 F.2d 917 (5th Cir. 1975), on remand, 66 T.C. 761 (1976), aff'd, 574 F.2d 1332 (5th Cir. 1978).

Payments made to a beneficiary's creditors in satisfaction of the beneficiary's legal obligations may also constitute constructive distributions. For example, if a trustee pays a beneficiary's income tax liability or pays the beneficiary's mortgage debt, the payments are treated as additional amounts distributed to the beneficiary. In this context, the regulations provide that a beneficiary's legal obligation to support another person is taken into account "if, and only if, the obligation is not affected by the adequacy of the dependent's own resources." Reg. § 1.662(a)–4. For example, if a parent has a legal obligation to support a minor child without regard to the child's own resources (at least as long as the parent has adequate means), a trustee's payments for the child's support will be treated as constructive distributions to the parent. In contrast, if the parent is entitled to use the child's own resources to provide support, the amounts paid by the trustee are properly treated as distributions to the child (rather than to the parent, who in effect has no legal support obligation). In any event, the scope of a parent's legal support obligation depends on local law, and to the extent that the parent's obligation is measured by reference to the parent's resources or station in life, it is determined without considering the trust income in question. To forestall the possibility of inadvertent deemed distributions, a trust instrument may include an "Upjohn" clause that expressly prohibits the trustee from making any distributions that would have the effect of discharging a parent's legal support obligation. Cf. Upjohn v. United States, 72–2 U.S. Tax Cas. (CCH) ¶ 12,888 (W.D. Mich. 1972).

Character of distributions. Amounts distributed by an estate or a trust have the same character in the beneficiary's hands as in the entity's hands. Thus, to the extent that first-tier or second-tier distributions carry out DNI to the beneficiaries, each beneficiary is generally treated as receiving a ratable share of each class of items entering into DNI, unless the terms of the governing instrument "specifically allocate different classes of income to different beneficiaries." I.R.C. § 662(b); Reg. § 1.662(b)–1. The statutory language concerning specific allocations is identical to the parallel provision concerning simple trusts in § 652(b) and presumably will be interpreted in the same way. Thus, a specific allocation under the governing instrument will be respected for tax purposes only if it is mandatory and only to the extent that it has an economic effect independent of its income tax consequences. See Reg. § 1.652(b)–2(b), discussed in § 7.3, *supra.* Similarly, the rules for allocating deductible items among the various classes of income entering into DNI of an estate or a complex trust are presumably the same for an estate or a complex trust as for a simple trust. See Reg. § 1.652(b)–3, discussed in § 7.3, *supra.*

§ 7.5   SEPARATE SHARES

Under the tier system applicable to estates and complex trusts, distributions carry out DNI first to mandatory current income beneficiaries in the first tier and then to other beneficiaries in the second tier, and DNI generally must be apportioned ratably among the beneficiaries in each tier based on the amounts of their respective distributions. The mechanical rules for allocating DNI among various beneficiaries sometimes produce inequitable results which are ameliorated to some extent by the "separate share" rule of § 663(c). Under that provision, "substantially separate and independent shares of different beneficiaries" in a complex trust are treated as separate trusts for the sole purpose of determining the amount of DNI carried out by distributions to the beneficiaries. The separate share rule also applies to estates, as the result of a 1997 amendment, but it has no application to simple trusts. The effect of the separate share rule is limited to determining the amount of DNI allocable to the beneficiaries; it has no impact on the status of an estate or a trust as a single taxable entity for any other purpose (e.g., required returns, allowable exemptions, or unused loss carryovers or excess deductions on termination). Of course, a grantor who wishes to create separate trusts (rather than merely separate shares within a single trust) is generally free to do so, subject to the consolidation rule concerning multiple trusts (see § 5.4, *supra*).

To illustrate the operation of the separate share rule, suppose that a trust provides for two beneficiaries, Audrey and Basil, to share equally in distributions of income and corpus and gives the trustee discretion to determine the timing and amount of distributions. In a year when the trust has $600 of DNI, the trustee exercises its discretion to distribute $300 of current income and $300 of corpus to Audrey and nothing to Basil. In the absence of a separate share rule, the distribution would carry out $600 of DNI to Audrey, who would therefore be liable for tax on all of the trust's current income even though half of the income is actually accumulated for future distribution to Basil. The separate share rule of § 663(c) avoids this unfortunate result by requiring that DNI be computed separately for the beneficiaries' respective trust shares as if they were separate trusts. Accordingly, Audrey's share of DNI is limited to $300, corresponding to her one-half trust share, and she is taxed on only $300 of her $600 distribution; the rest of the distribution is neither deductible to the trust nor taxable to Audrey. Since the trustee made no distributions to Basil, the remaining $300 of DNI allocated to Basil's share is taxed to the trust, and the resulting tax liability should be charged against Basil's share. If the trustee distributes the accumulated amount to Basil in a subsequent year (in addition to his share of current income), the accumulated amount will be tax-free.

The separate share rule is mandatory, not elective. Reg. § 1.663(c)–1(d). The regulations offer some guidance concerning the scope of the rule. In general, separate shares exist if "the economic interests of the beneficiary or class of beneficiaries neither affect nor are affected by the economic interests accruing to another beneficiary or class of beneficiaries." Reg. § 1.663(c)–4(a). It is of no consequence that a share has multiple beneficiaries with indeterminate interests, that the share may ultimately merge with another share, or that the shares are not administered separately on the fiduciary's books. The key is that distributions or accumulations made with respect to each share have no effect on the other shares. For example, if a trust provides three equal shares for the grantor's three children and the trustee has discretion with respect to each share to distribute or accumulate income and to invade corpus for one child and the child's spouse or issue, the shares are considered to be "substantially separate and independent" within the meaning of § 663(c). The separate share rule would not apply, however, if the trustee had a power to make disproportionate distributions of income or corpus for any of the children without adjustments to preserve the interests of the other children in their respective shares. Reg. § 1.663(c)–3(a)–(c).

A bequest of specific property ordinarily includes any income generated by the property prior to distribution from the decedent's estate. Such income constitutes a separate share of the estate, even if the underlying property is excluded from the conduit rules under § 663(a)(1) (see § 7.6, *infra*). For example, if Claire is entitled to receive specific shares of stock (including the income thereon) under her deceased parent's will, the post-death dividends on the stock will be allocated exclusively to Claire and will not be included in any other beneficiary's share of DNI. The residuary estate also constitutes a separate share of the estate, and if the residuary estate is divided into fractional portions for two or more beneficiaries, each portion is treated as a separate share. Reg. §§ 1.663(c)–4(a) and 1.663(c)–5 (Example 8).

The regulations also treat a surviving spouse's elective share and (in most cases) a pecuniary formula bequest as separate shares, with the result that amounts distributed in satisfaction of the elective share or the pecuniary bequest do not carry out DNI attributable to other beneficiaries' shares. Reg. §§ 1.663(c)–4(a) and (b), and 1.663(c)–5 (Examples 4 and 7).

If an election is made under § 645 to treat a qualified revocable trust as part of an estate (see § 4.4, *supra*), the electing trust and its income constitute a separate share of the estate. Reg. § 1.663(c)–4(a).

The effect of the separate share rule, where it applies, is simply to require that DNI be determined separately for each separate share of the estate or trust in computing the amount of DNI carried out by distributions from each share to its beneficiaries. The total amount of DNI for all of the separate shares is taken into account in computing the entity's distribution deduction under § 661, and the DNI allocated to each separate share is used to determine the amount and character of the taxable distributions made to the beneficiaries of the share.

§ 7.6   NONTAXABLE DISTRIBUTIONS

The conduit rules of §§ 661 and 662 generally treat amounts distributed by an estate or a complex trust to its beneficiaries as taxable distributions to the extent of DNI. To the extent that distributions carry out DNI, they are treated as taxable gifts of income rather than tax-free gifts of property. I.R.C. § 102(a) and (b). Nevertheless, amounts described in § 663(a)(1) are expressly excluded from the conduit rules and therefore do not carry out DNI to the beneficiaries. The function of this statutory exclusion is to allow such amounts to be treated as tax-free gifts of property which are neither deductible by the entity nor taxable to the beneficiaries.

The statutory exclusion applies to "[a]ny amount which, under the terms of the governing instrument, is properly paid or credited as a gift or bequest of a specific sum of money or of specific property and which is paid or credited all at once or in not more than 3 installments," but it does not apply to "an amount which can be paid or credited only from the income of the estate or trust." I.R.C. § 663(a)(1). The regulations add that in order to qualify for the exclusion "the amount of money or the identity of the specific property must be ascertainable under the terms of a testator's will as of the date of his death, or under the terms of an inter vivos trust instrument as of the date of the inception of the trust." Reg. § 1.663(a)–1(b)(1). For example, bequests of $5,000 cash, 100 shares of Nifty stock, or the decedent's vintage sports car all clearly qualify, as do bequests of all of the decedent's bank accounts or personal effects. A specific devise of real property also qualifies if the property is subject to administration and therefore part of the estate, but if title passes directly from the decedent to the devisee under local law (and the property is not needed to pay debts, taxes or administration expenses), the exclusion may be superfluous. Reg. §§ 1.661(a)–2(e) and 1.663(a)–1(c)(1).

In contrast, a residuary bequest or a comparable gift of trust corpus does not come within the exclusion because the identity of the specific property cannot be ascertained from the terms of the will or the trust instrument, and the same is true of an intestate share. Reg. § 1.663(a)–1(b)(2). As a practical matter, it may be desirable to provide in a will or trust instrument for specific gifts of real property, motor vehicles, household items and personal effects, to remove them from the residuary estate and prevent them from being treated as taxable distributions when they are delivered to the beneficiaries.

The regulations state that a pecuniary formula bequest (routinely used to take advantage of the marital deduction or the unified credit for estate tax

purposes*) does not qualify for the exclusion because
neither the identity of the property nor the amount
of money is ascertainable from the governing
instrument as of the time of the decedent's death;
instead, the amount and composition of such a
bequest depend on the executor's exercise of
discretion and payment of administration expenses
and other charges during the period of
administration following the decedent's death. Reg.
§ 1.663(a)–1(b). Similarly, a fractional formula
bequest is a form of residuary bequest which
comprises neither a specific sum of money nor
specifically identifiable property. The same
reasoning also lends support to the conclusion that a
surviving spouse's elective share does not qualify for
the exclusion, although the decisions are not
unanimous on this point. Brigham v. United States,
160 F.3d 759 (1st Cir. 1998); but cf. Deutsch v.
Commissioner, 74 T.C.M. (CCH) 935 (1997). As a
practical matter, the significance of treating a
pecuniary formula bequest, a fractional formula
bequest, or an elective share as a taxable distribution
is mitigated by the separate share rule, which applies
to estates by virtue of a 1997 statutory amendment
and limits the amount of DNI allocable to such
distributions (see § 7.5, *supra*). The regulations
provide illustrative examples. Reg. § 1.663(c)–5
(Examples 2, 4, and 7).

---

*   For a more detailed discussion of marital deduction
planning, see McNulty & McCouch, Federal Estate and Gift
Taxation § 78 (9th ed. 2020).

The Service has ruled that a bequest of a specific dollar amount, payable in cash or in other property (to be valued at the date of distribution), qualifies for the exclusion because the amount of the bequest is ascertainable at death even though the medium of payment is not. Rev. Rul. 86–105, 1986–2 C.B. 82. In contrast, a bequest of shares of Nifty stock owned by the testator at death and worth no more than $100 at the date of distribution does not qualify because the amount of the bequest is not ascertainable at death even though the medium of payment is. Rev. Rul. 72–295, 1972–1 C.B. 197. A testamentary direction to sell Blackacre and distribute the proceeds also fails to qualify for the exclusion because the amount of the proceeds cannot be ascertained until after the testator's death.

A distribution qualifies for the § 663(a)(1) exclusion only if it is payable all at once or in not more than three installments. This requirement is intended to distinguish tax-free gifts and bequests from annuities and similar periodic payments which carry out DNI to the beneficiaries. The regulations sensibly focus on the terms of the will or trust instrument rather than on the actual number of payments, and deny the exclusion only if the governing instrument requires payment in more than three installments. Reg. § 1.663(a)–1(b)(2). If the governing instrument is silent, all gifts and bequests which are to be paid in the ordinary course of administration are considered to be payable in a single installment. Moreover, gifts and bequests of articles for personal use (e.g., personal and household effects, automobiles, and the like) are disregarded for purposes of the three-installment rule. Reg. § 1.663(a)–1(c)(1). Thus, for example, an outright bequest of an automobile, $10,000 cash, 500 shares of Nifty stock and Blackacre is treated as payable all at once. If a testator leaves a specific sum of money or specific property to be held in trust, the funding of the testamentary trust with estate assets qualifies as a nontaxable distribution (assuming the will does not require funding in more than three installments); the estate and the trust are treated as separate taxable entities. If the trust beneficiary is entitled to receive distributions of corpus upon reaching age 25, 30, and 35, the distributions from the trust are also nontaxable. If the terms of the trust provide for a fourth distribution of corpus upon reaching age 40, however, the exclusion does not apply and all four distributions from the trust will carry out DNI to the beneficiary.

The § 663(a)(1) exclusion is expressly inapplicable to any amount which can be paid "only from the income of the estate or trust." The regulations interpret this to mean that the exclusion does not apply to a gift or bequest which is required to be paid from the current year's income or from income accumulated in previous years. However, if the governing instrument allows payment from income or corpus, or is silent concerning the source of payment, and the other statutory requirements are met, the exclusion is available. Reg. § 1.663(a)–1(b)(2) and (b)(3).

Under local law, if payment of a pecuniary legacy is delayed by more than one year, the beneficiary may be entitled to interest on the delayed payment. Regardless of whether the legacy itself qualifies for the § 663(a)(1) exclusion, the amount of interest paid by the estate arguably should be treated as a taxable distribution that carries out DNI to the beneficiary under the conduit rules of §§ 661 and 662. Davidson v. United States, 149 F. Supp. 208 (Ct. Cl. 1957) (interest on delayed legacy treated as distribution of current income under pre-1954 law). The Service, however, takes the position that the interest on a delayed legacy represents an amount payable with regard to an indebtedness incurred by the estate rather than a distribution of estate income. Consequently, the estate's payment of interest does not carry out DNI under the normal conduit rules; instead, the interest payment is treated as a nondeductible personal interest expense of the estate under § 163(h) and is includible in the beneficiary's gross income under § 61(a)(4). Rev. Rul. 73–322, 73–2 C.B. 44 (specific legacy); Reg. § 1.663(c)–5 (Example 7) (surviving spouse's elective share). Despite its questionable conceptual premise, this analysis finds some support in the case law. United States v. Folckemer, 307 F.2d 171 (5th Cir. 1962).

§ 7.7 DISTRIBUTIONS IN KIND

An estate or a trust generally realizes no gain or loss when it distributes property other than cash to a beneficiary. The basis of the distributed property in the beneficiary's hands is equal to its adjusted basis in the entity's hands immediately before the distribution, adjusted for any gain or loss recognized by the entity on the distribution. In the case of a second-tier distribution in kind, the amount of the distribution taken into account under the conduit rules of §§ 661 and 662 is the lesser of the property's adjusted basis in the hands of the estate or the trust or its fair market value. I.R.C. § 643(e)(1) and (e)(2). For example, suppose that Blake receives a distribution from his deceased mother's residuary estate of securities with a fair market value of $230 and a basis of $200 (equal to fair market value at the mother's death). In computing the amounts deductible by the estate under § 661 and includible by Blake under § 662, the amount of the distribution is $200, and Blake takes a carryover basis of $200 in the distributed securities. If property is distributed in a nontaxable distribution under § 663(a)(1), the basis of the property in the beneficiary's hands carries over directly from the estate or the trust, adjusted for any gain or loss recognized by the entity.

The basic rules concerning distributions in kind are subject to several important exceptions and qualifications. Under the regulations, an estate or a trust which distributes any property other than cash in satisfaction of a required current income distribution (i.e., a first-tier distribution from an estate or a complex trust, or any distribution from a simple trust) must realize gain or loss as if the property were sold for its fair market value on the date of distribution. Reg. §§ 1.651(a)–2(d) and 1.661(a)–2(f). Accordingly, the entity will realize gain or loss equal to the difference between the property's fair market value and its adjusted basis; the amount of the distribution taken into account under the conduit rules will be the fair market value of the property, and the basis of the property in the beneficiary's hands will be equal to its fair market value. (The entity may not be allowed to deduct any loss on the deemed sale, but in that case the loss will be preserved in the beneficiary's hands to offset gain on a subsequent disposition of the property. I.R.C. § 267(b)(6), (b)(13), and (d).)

More generally, an estate or a trust realizes gain or loss whenever it distributes property other than cash in satisfaction of a beneficiary's entitlement to a specific dollar amount (or to specific property other than the distributed property). Reg. § 1.661(a)–2(f). This result follows directly from a longstanding judicial doctrine dating back to the 1930s. In the leading case of Kenan v. Commissioner, 114 F.2d 217 (2d Cir. 1940), the beneficiary of a testamentary trust was entitled upon reaching age 40 to receive a $5 million distribution which was payable in cash or in kind at the discretion of the trustees. The trustees chose to distribute appreciated securities in partial satisfaction of the required distribution, and the court held that the distribution constituted a deemed sale or exchange in which the trust realized capital gain as if it had sold the securities and distributed the proceeds in cash. The court noted that the beneficiary was entitled to a fixed amount which was a charge against all of the trust property, and contrasted the situation with that of a beneficiary entitled to receive the specific property under the terms of the will or the trust. Note that in both cases—a gift of a specific sum of money and a gift of specific property—the distribution itself may qualify as a nontaxable distribution under § 663(a)(1), but only in the former case does the estate or the trust realize "*Kenan* gain" on a deemed sale or exchange. Rev. Rul. 66–207, 1966–2 C.B. 243. Of course, the estate or the trust will also realize gain or loss if it distributes property different from the specific property to which the beneficiary is entitled under the terms of the will or the trust instrument.

The *Kenan* doctrine also has implications for distributions made by an estate or a trust in satisfaction of pecuniary formula gifts. A common estate planning technique provides for the division of a decedent's residuary estate into two portions, a marital share which qualifies for the estate tax marital deduction and a nonmarital share which absorbs the decedent's available unified credit. If the marital share is defined as a pecuniary amount (e.g., the amount of the minimum marital deduction necessary to eliminate or minimize estate tax liability, taking into account other deductible transfers and the unified credit), the funding of the marital share will carry out DNI from the estate to the recipient (i.e., the spouse or a trust for the spouse's benefit); the distribution is not excluded from the conduit rules by § 663(a)(1) because the pecuniary formula amount is not ascertainable as of the decedent's death. (See § 7.6, *supra*.) Nevertheless, the formula does yield a specific dollar amount (after taking account of the executor's exercise of discretion and payment of administration expenses and other charges after death), and the estate will realize gain or loss if it distributes property other than cash to fund the marital share. Rev. Rul. 60–87, 1960–1 C.B. 286. The distribution of the rest of the estate assets to fund the nonmarital share will also carry out DNI, but because a residuary bequest is not a specific dollar amount the estate will not realize gain or loss on the distribution. If the marital and nonmarital shares were defined by formula as fractional shares of the residuary estate (instead of a pecuniary amount and a residuary share), both shares could be funded without causing the estate to realize gain or loss on the distributions. Rev. Rul. 55–117, 1955–1 C.B. 233. An estate may deduct a loss recognized on a distribution of property in satisfaction of a pecuniary bequest, but no deduction is allowed for a similar loss recognized by a trust. I.R.C. § 267(b)(6) and (b)(13).

The *Kenan* doctrine is not elective. If an estate or a trust distributes property other than cash in satisfaction of a beneficiary's entitlement to a specific dollar amount (or to different specific property), the entity is required to realize gain or loss. In other cases, however, the executor or trustee may elect to treat a distribution as a deemed sale or exchange and report gain or loss "as if [the distributed] property had been sold to the distributee at its fair market value." I.R.C. § 643(e)(3). A § 643(e)(3) election may be especially useful when the estate or trust makes distributions in kind to several different beneficiaries and the distributed assets have significantly different basis-to-value ratios. The § 643(e)(3) election allows the executor or trustee to recognize any built-in gain or loss on all of the assets distributed in kind and thereby avoid potential unfairness to the beneficiaries who would have received low-basis assets if the election were not made. The § 643(e)(3) election is made on the entity's fiduciary income tax return and applies to all of the entity's distributions made during the taxable year. If the fiduciary elects to recognize gain or loss, the amount of the distribution taken into account under §§ 661 and 662 is the fair market value of the property, and the beneficiary takes the property with a basis equal to its fair market value (i.e., the entity's pre-distribution basis adjusted for gain or loss recognized by the entity on the distribution).

For example, suppose that Carol receives a distribution from her deceased father's residuary estate of securities with a fair market value of $200 and an adjusted basis of $150 (equal to fair market value at the father's death). If the executor makes a § 643(e)(3) election, the estate will recognize $50 of capital gain, which presumably should be included in DNI on the ground that it is actually distributed to Carol or used in determining the amount of her distribution (see § 6.3, *supra*). The amount of the distribution is $200, for purposes of determining the amounts deductible by the estate and includible by Carol under the conduit rules, and the basis of the securities in Carol's hands will be $200. The election applies only to distributions that are subject to the conduit rules; it does not apply to distributions excluded from those rules by § 663(a)(1).

§ 7.8 TIMING OF BENEFICIARY'S INCLUSION

If an estate or a trust and its beneficiaries have identical taxable years, the amount allowed as a distribution deduction to the entity for its taxable year must be included in gross income by the beneficiaries for the same taxable year. Most individuals report income on a calendar-year basis and most trusts are required to do so, but estates are permitted to use a fiscal year. (See § 5.2, *supra*.) Therefore, discrepancies between the timing of the entity's deduction and a beneficiary's inclusion of distributions arise primarily in connection with distributions made by an estate that reports income on a fiscal-year basis or distributions made to a beneficiary in the year of his or her death.

Under the conduit rules governing taxable distributions made by an estate or a trust, the beneficiary's inclusion, like the entity's deduction, depends on the entity's DNI and the amounts distributed by it during its taxable year. As a practical matter, the amount includible by the beneficiary cannot be determined until the end of the entity's taxable year. Accordingly, if the beneficiary's taxable year is different from that of the estate or the trust, the beneficiary generally includes distributions in his or her taxable year which includes the end of the entity's taxable year. I.R.C. §§ 652(c) and 662(c); Reg. §§ 1.651(c)–1 and 1.661(c)–1. In the case of an estate that elects a fiscal year, this provision offers opportunities for deferral of up to one year.

To illustrate, suppose that a decedent dies on November 30, 2020 and the estate elects a fiscal year ending January 31. Any distributions made by the estate during its first, short taxable year (beginning at death and ending two months later) will carry out DNI for that period and will be reported by the beneficiaries on their returns for 2021. Distributions for the estate's second taxable year (beginning February 1, 2021 and ending January 31, 2022) will be reported by the beneficiaries on their returns for 2022.

Although the estate's fiscal year election offers a limited deferral opportunity, it may also result in "bunching" of income for the beneficiaries when the estate terminates. Continuing the previous example, suppose that the estate makes a terminating distribution on July 31, 2023. On their returns for 2023, the beneficiaries will have to report distributions for the estate's full taxable year ending January 31, 2023 as well as its final, short taxable year ending six months later. Rev. Rul. 71–180, 1971–1 C.B. 204. The incremental tax burden to the beneficiaries of including distributions for two taxable years will be alleviated by any excess deductions or unused loss carryovers that flow through to the beneficiaries in the entity's final taxable year. See § 5.6, *supra*.

A special problem arises when a beneficiary of an estate or a trust dies during the entity's taxable year.

If the beneficiary receives a distribution from the entity but dies before the end of the entity's taxable year, the statutory provision requiring the beneficiary to report distributions for the entity's taxable year "ending within or with his taxable year" cannot be applied literally. Because the beneficiary's final taxable year ends at death, the beneficiary cannot report the distributions on a return for any year that includes the end of the entity's taxable year. The regulations adopt a pragmatic approach which requires a cash-basis beneficiary to report on his or her final return only amounts actually distributed to the beneficiary before death. The amount and character of the includible amounts, however, are still determined by reference to DNI for the entity's taxable year that includes the date of the beneficiary's death. Reg. §§ 1.652(c)–2 and 1.662(c)–2. Any distributions made after death will be taxed to the beneficiary's estate (or other successor). To the extent that the beneficiary was entitled during life to amounts that are not actually paid until after death, such amounts are taxed to the recipients as income in respect of a decedent (IRD). See § 3.2, *supra*.

To illustrate, suppose that a testamentary trust is required to distribute all of its income currently to Colin during his life and then to his children during their lives. Colin, a cash-basis taxpayer, dies on April 30, having received one quarterly distribution of income for the year of his death. The trust, which qualifies as a simple trust and reports on a calendar-year basis, makes a distribution to Colin's estate of the "stub income" that was accrued but unpaid at

Colin's death; the remaining income for the period after Colin's death is distributed to his children. The income distributed to Colin before his death will be reported on his final return, and the stub income distributed to his estate will be taxed to the estate as IRD. The amount and character of items includible in gross income by Colin and his estate will be determined based on their respective shares of DNI and amounts distributed for the trust's taxable year. The distributions of income to the children will be taxed to them under the normal conduit rules of § 652. Suppose instead that Colin died before receiving any quarterly income distributions. In that case, the entire amount of income accrued but unpaid at Colin's death would be distributed to his estate and would be taxed to the estate as IRD; none of the trust income for the year of Colin's death would be reported on his final return.

A similar rule applies to distributions made by an estate or a trust to a beneficiary other than an individual (e.g., an estate, trust, partnership or corporation) which ceases to exist during the distributing entity's taxable year. The amount of taxable distributions included by the beneficiary for its final taxable year is computed in the same manner as in the case of a deceased individual, except that amounts required to be distributed before the beneficiary's termination must be included on the beneficiary's final return even if they are actually distributed to the beneficiary's successor in interest. Reg. §§ 1.652(c)–3 and 1.662(c)–3. In effect, this rule puts a beneficiary other than an individual on an accrual method for its final year with respect to required distributions from the estate or the trust.

§ 7.9 ILLUSTRATIVE COMPUTATIONS

This chapter concludes with two examples which provide an opportunity to review basic concepts of fiduciary accounting income (FAI), distributable net income (DNI), and fiduciary taxable income discussed in previous chapters. The computations are designed to illustrate the operation of the conduit rules.

Example 1: Simple Trust

A testamentary trust is required to distribute its net income currently to two beneficiaries, Fred and Ginger, in equal shares. The trustee is authorized to invade corpus but does not do so during the current taxable year. Accordingly, the trust is a simple trust for the taxable year, and it has the following cash receipts and expenditures:

Receipts:	
Dividends	$60,000
Taxable interest	25,000
Tax-exempt interest	15,000
Rent	50,000
Expenditures:	
Realty maintenance	$10,000
Real property tax	5,000

Mortgage payments	15,000
Trustee fee	8,000
State income tax	2,000
Federal income tax	8,000

The realty maintenance and real property tax are directly related to the rental income. The mortgage payments, also directly related to the rental income, consist of $12,000 interest (charged to income) and $3,000 principal (charged to corpus). The rental property is eligible for a tax depreciation deduction of $6,000, and the trustee transfers an equivalent amount from income to corpus as a depreciation reserve pursuant to the governing instrument. The trustee fee is fully deductible for tax purposes, and is charged half to income and half to corpus. The trust has no net capital gain or loss for the current taxable year. The state and federal income taxes are attributable to the previous year's net capital gain and are charged to corpus.

(a)   *Fiduciary accounting income.* The trust's FAI is $113,000, computed as follows:

Income:

Dividends	$60,000	
Taxable interest	25,000	
Tax-exempt interest	15,000	
Rent	<u>50,000</u>	
Total income		$150,000

Expenses:

Realty maintenance	$10,000	
Real property tax	5,000	
Mortgage interest	12,000	
Depreciation reserve	6,000	
Trustee fee	4,000	
Total expenses		− 37,000
Net fiduciary accounting income		$113,000

Fred and Ginger are each entitled to half of the trust's net FAI, or $56,500.

(b)   *Distributable net income.* The trust's DNI is $107,000, computed as follows:

Gross Income:

Dividends	$60,000	
Taxable interest	25,000	
Rent	50,000	
Total gross income		$135,000

Deductions:

Realty maintenance	$10,000
Real property tax	5,000
Mortgage interest	12,000
Depreciation	6,000
Trustee fee	7,200
State income tax	2,000

Total deductions		− 42,200
Tentative taxable income		$ 92,800
Gross tax-exempt interest	$15,000	
Less allocable trustee fee	− 800	
Net tax-exempt interest		14,200
Distributable net income		$107,000

The expenses directly related to rental income (i.e., realty maintenance, real property tax, mortgage interest, and depreciation) are allocated to that income. The remaining deductible items (trustee fee and state income tax) are allocated to taxable interest.

A portion of the trustee fee must be allocated to tax-exempt interest, and that portion is disallowed as a deduction. Here, the nondeductible portion of the trustee fee is $800 ($8,000 × 15,000/150,000), based on the ratio of tax-exempt interest to total income included in DNI on a gross basis (i.e., before deducting direct expenses). See Reg. §§ 1.652(c)–4, 1.661(c)–2, and 1.662(c)–4. (The regulations also authorize a different allocation method, based on the net amounts of income included in DNI after deducting direct expenses. See Reg. § 1.652(b)–3(b). Under this method, the nondeductible portion of the trustee fee would be $1,026 ($8,000 × 15,000/117,000). The amount of DNI would remain unchanged, but the amount of taxable income flowing through to the beneficiaries would be correspondingly larger.)

Note that in computing the trust's tentative taxable income and DNI, the distribution deduction and the $300 personal exemption are not taken into account. (The personal exemption could be deducted in computing tentative taxable income and then added back in computing DNI, reaching the same end result.) Note also that the full amount allowable as a tax deduction for depreciation is set aside as a reserve (i.e., transferred from income to corpus), and so the depreciation deduction is allocated entirely to the trust. The retention of $6,000 as a depreciation reserve does not affect the trust's status as a simple trust. Reg. § 1.651(a)–2(a).

The $6,000 difference between FAI ($113,000) and DNI ($107,000) is attributable to two items—the $2,000 state income tax and $4,000 of the trustee fee—which are charged to corpus on the trust's books but are allowed as deductions in computing the trust's taxable income.

The items of income and expense entering into DNI are summarized as follows:

	Dividends	Taxable interest	Tax-exempt interest	Rent	Total
Gross amount	$60,000	$25,000	$15,000	$50,000	$150,000
Realty maintenance				10,000	10,000
Real property tax				5,000	5,000
Mortgage interest				12,000	12,000
Depreciation				6,000	6,000
Trustee fee		7,200	800		8,000
State income tax		2,000			2,000
Net DNI	$60,000	$15,800	$14,200	$17,000	$107,000

(c)   *Distribution   deduction.*   The   trust   is
required to distribute its net FAI of $113,000. The
distribution deduction is limited to the lesser of that
amount or the trust's DNI (adjusted to exclude net
tax-exempt   interest).   Thus,   the   distribution
deduction is $92,800 ($107,000 DNI less $14,200 net
tax-exempt interest).

(d)   *Trust's taxable income.* The trust's taxable
income is deemed to be zero; it cannot be a negative
number. The computation is as follows:

Tentative taxable income (see (b), *supra*)	$92,800
Less distribution deduction	−92,800
Less personal exemption	− 300
Taxable income	− $300

Note that the trust's $300 personal exemption is
wasted here because the mandatory distribution of
net FAI carries out all of the trust's DNI and the trust
has no other taxable income. If the trust had a capital
gain that was allocated to corpus and therefore did
not flow through to the beneficiaries, the exemption
would reduce the trust's taxable income.

(e)   *Inclusion by beneficiaries.* The total amount
includible by the beneficiaries in gross income is
equal to the trust's distribution deduction of $92,800
(see (c), *supra*). Since Fred and Ginger each received
half of the trust's net FAI, they must each include a
ratable one-half share of the net taxable items
entering into DNI, viz., dividends ($30,000), taxable
interest ($7,900), and rent ($8,500). In addition, they

are each treated as receiving half of the net tax-exempt interest ($7,100). The dividends, taxable interest, and rent also constitute net investment income which may be subject to a 3.8% tax if a beneficiary's adjusted gross income exceeds the taxable threshold under § 1411. (The trust is not taxable under § 1411 because all of its net investment income passes through to the beneficiaries.)

Because the full amount of tax depreciation was set aside as a reserve on the trust's books, the entire deduction is allocated to the trust. However, if the amount of tax depreciation exceeded the amount set aside as a reserve (or if there were no reserve), the excess would be allocated equally to the beneficiaries. For example, if tax depreciation was $7,000 and the trustee set aside a reserve of $6,000, Fred and Ginger would each be entitled to deduct $500 of depreciation directly on their personal tax returns.

Example 2: Complex Trust

The facts are the same as in Example 1, with three material differences. First, the trust is a complex trust. The governing instrument does not require any distributions of net income, but instead authorizes the trustee to make discretionary distributions of net income or corpus to Fred and Ginger and to a designated charity. The trustee properly pays $45,000 to the charity and also distributes $20,000 to Fred and $60,000 to Ginger during the current taxable year. Second, the trust has a capital gain of $10,000, which is allocated to corpus on the trust's books. Third, no amount is set aside as a depreciation reserve.

(a)   *Fiduciary accounting income.* The trust's FAI is $119,000, computed as follows:

Income:

Dividends	$60,000	
Taxable interest	25,000	
Tax-exempt interest	15,000	
Rent	50,000	
Total income		$150,000

Expenses:

Realty maintenance	$10,000	
Real property tax	5,000	
Mortgage interest	12,000	
Trustee fee	4,000	
Total expenses		− 31,000
Net fiduciary accounting income		$119,000

The $45,000 charitable payment is deemed to come from net income, and the $80,000 distributions to Fred and Ginger are deemed to carry out the rest of the net income ($74,000) as well as a residual amount of corpus ($6,000).

(b)   *Distributable net income.* The trust's DNI is $107,000, computed as follows:

Gross Income:

Dividends	$60,000	
Taxable interest	25,000	
Rent	50,000	
Long-term capital gain	10,000	
Total gross income		$145,000

Deductions:

Charitable deduction	$40,500	
Realty maintenance	10,000	
Real property tax	5,000	
Mortgage interest	12,000	
Trustee fee	7,200	
State income tax	2,000	
Total deductions		− 76,700
Tentative taxable income		$ 68,300
Long-term capital gain		− 10,000
Gross tax-exempt interest	$15,000	
Less charitable portion	− 4,500	
Less allocable trustee fee	− 800	
Net tax-exempt interest		+ 9,700
Distributable net income		$ 68,000

The $10,000 capital gain is allocable to corpus and is not deemed distributed. Therefore, it is excluded from DNI and is includible in the trust's taxable income.

As in Example 1, a portion of the trustee fee must be allocated to tax-exempt interest. The allocation method is the same as in the earlier example, and the deductible portion of the trustee fee is $7,200 ($8,000 − $800). Furthermore, a portion of the charitable payment must be allocated to tax-exempt interest, and that portion is disallowed as a charitable deduction. The charitable payment is deemed to consist of a ratable portion of each item of income entering into DNI, and the nondeductible portion of the charitable payment is therefore $4,500 ($45,000 × 15,000/150,000). See Reg. §§ 1.643(a)–5(b), 1.661(c)–2, and 1.662(c)–4. Thus, the charitable deduction is $40,500 ($45,000 − $4,500). The DNI remaining after subtracting the charitable payment and other deductible items flows through to the beneficiaries.

Because no amount is set aside as a depreciation reserve, the $6,000 depreciation deduction is allocated to Fred, Ginger, and the charity in proportion to their shares of FAI. None of the depreciation deduction is allocated to the trust, and the deduction does not enter into DNI.

The $51,000 difference between FAI ($119,000) and DNI ($68,000) is attributable to the $45,000 charitable payment and the $6,000 of deductible items charged to corpus on the trust's books ($2,000 state income tax and $4,000 trustee fee).

The items of income and expense entering into DNI are summarized as follows:

	Dividends	Taxable interest	Tax-exempt interest	Rent	Total
Gross amount	$60,000	$25,000	$15,000	$50,000	$150,000
Charitable payment	18,000	7,500	4,500	15,000	45,000
Realty maintenance				10,000	10,000
Real property tax				5,000	5,000
Mortgage interest				12,000	12,000
Trustee fee		7,200	800		8,000
State income tax		2,000			2,000
Net DNI	$42,000	$8,300	$9,700	$8,000	$68,000

(c) *Distribution deduction.* The charitable payment (reduced by the portion allocable to tax-exempt interest) is made from gross income pursuant to the governing instrument and is deductible under § 642(c). The distribution deduction is limited to the lesser of the amount distributed to Fred and Ginger ($80,000) or DNI (adjusted to exclude net tax-exempt interest). Thus, the distribution deduction is $58,300 ($68,000 − $9,700).

(d) *Trust's taxable income.* The trust's taxable income is $9,900, determined as follows:

Tentative taxable income (see (b), *supra*)	$68,300
Less distribution deduction	−58,300
Less personal exemption	− 100
Taxable income	$ 9,900

The trust's $100 personal exemption offsets an equal amount of taxable income, leaving the trust with $9,900 of taxable income (consisting of long-term capital gain). The rest of the trust's income is paid to charity or carried out to the beneficiaries. The capital gain is net investment income subject to a 3.8% tax under § 1411. Because the trust's adjusted gross income exceeds the taxable threshold amount by more than $10,000, the full amount of undistributed capital gain ($10,000) is subject to tax at the trust level under § 1411.

(e)   *Inclusion by beneficiaries.* The distributions to Fred and Ginger are second-tier distributions which carry out ratable shares of DNI. (The trust does not require any current income distributions, nor does it provide for separate shares.) Because Fred received $20,000 and Ginger received $60,000, each beneficiary is accountable for a ratable share of the items entering into DNI:

	Fred	Ginger	Total
Dividends	$10,500	$31,500	$42,000
Taxable interest	2,075	6,225	8,300
Tax-exempt interest	2,425	7,275	9,700
Rent	2,000	6,000	8,000
Total	$17,000	$51,000	$68,000

Thus, the distributions to Fred and Ginger carry out all of the trust's $68,000 of DNI (including net tax-exempt interest). They receive the balance of their distributions tax-free ($3,000 to Fred and $9,000 to Ginger). Fred and Ginger may be subject to a 3.8% tax on net investment income (dividends, taxable interest, and rent) if their adjusted gross income exceeds the taxable threshold under § 1411.

Because there is no depreciation reserve, the $6,000 depreciation deduction is allocated to Fred, Ginger, and the charity in proportion to their shares of FAI: $960 to Fred ($6,000 × 20,000/125,000), $2,880 to Ginger ($6,000 × 60,000/125,000), and $2,160 ($6,000 × 45,000/125,000) to the charity. See Reg. § 1.662(c)–4. Fred and Ginger report their allocable shares of depreciation directly on their personal tax returns.

CHAPTER 8
GRANTOR TRUSTS

§ 8.1 OVERVIEW

Under the "grantor trust" provisions of I.R.C. §§ 671–679, a grantor or other person who holds specified powers or interests with respect to a trust (or a portion thereof) may be treated as the owner of the trust (or portion) for federal income tax purposes. To the extent that the grantor trust rules apply, they supersede the regular provisions of Subchapter J. A grantor trust is generally ignored as a separate taxable entity for substantive income tax purposes, and the trust's items of income, deduction, and credit are reported directly by the deemed owner on his or her personal income tax return.

The basic structure of the grantor trust rules has not changed greatly since those rules were codified in 1954, and the volume of litigated cases decided since then has remained relatively low. Thus, one might infer that the statutory drafters have achieved their goal of providing clear guidelines which allow drafters and taxpayers to carry out their legitimate planning objectives without interference, or perhaps merely that enforcement has not been especially rigorous in this area.

In any event, the statutory scheme reflects a partial response to a broader problem of income shifting which has posed challenges for the government and for taxpayers (and their advisers) since the early days of the federal income tax. Long before 1954, taxpayers sought to reallocate taxable income, derived from personal services or capital assets, among their immediate family members without relinquishing dominion and control. The entities of choice in this endeavor were trusts as well as family partnerships. As early as 1924, Congress responded by enacting specific statutory provisions aimed at trusts in which the grantor retained a power to revoke or a right to receive present or future distributions of income. These provisions, the predecessors of §§ 676 and 677, survived a constitutional challenge when the Supreme Court held in Corliss v. Bowers, 281 U.S. 376 (1930), that a grantor who created a trust for his wife and children was properly taxable on the trust's income (which was distributed to his wife) because his retained power of revocation, though unexercised, gave him substantial control over the trust. Speaking for the Court, Mr. Justice Holmes observed that "taxation is not so much concerned with the refinements of title as it is with actual command over the property taxed—the actual benefit for which tax is paid."

Because of their narrow focus, the early grantor trust statutes were easily circumvented, and grantors soon began to create trusts which allowed them to retain substantial beneficial interests and powers while skirting the existing statutory prohibitions. The famous case of Helvering v. Clifford, 309 U.S. 331 (1940), involved an irrevocable trust created by a grantor for the "exclusive benefit" of his wife. The trust was to last for five years (or until the earlier death of the grantor or his wife), and upon termination the trust corpus was payable to the grantor and any accrued or undistributed income was payable to his wife. The grantor, as sole trustee, retained "absolute discretion" to distribute or accumulate the annual trust income during the trust term, as well as broad administrative powers. The Supreme Court accepted the government's argument that the trust's income was properly taxable to the grantor based on his dominion and control under the predecessor of § 61. "So far as his dominion and control were concerned it seems clear that the trust did not effect any substantial change. In substance his control over the corpus was in all essential respects the same after the trust was created, as before." The Court found that the arrangement represented nothing more than "a temporary reallocation of income within an intimate family group," as indicated by "the short duration of the trust, the fact that the wife was the beneficiary, and the retention of control over the corpus."

Perhaps the most troubling aspect of the *Clifford* decision was the Court's open-ended rationale which provided little guidance for lower courts but invited an inquiry into the facts and circumstances of each case. The decision prompted Judge Learned Hand to lament that the *Clifford* test, "impalpable enough at best," would, if "continually refined by successive distinctions, each trifling in itself," lead the courts into "a morass from which there will be no escape" and end in "utter confusion." Kohnstamm v. Pedrick, 153 F.2d 506 (2d Cir. 1945). The Treasury responded in 1945 by promulgating the so-called "*Clifford* regulations" which sought to translate the Court's vague multi-factor test into a series of discrete and reasonably clear grantor trust rules. The *Clifford* regulations dealt separately with the questions of trust duration, retained control over beneficial interests, and administrative powers, and provided the doctrinal foundation for the grantor trust provisions enacted in 1954.

The codified version of the grantor trust rules specifies in elaborate detail the types of retained interests and powers that can cause all or part of a trust's income to be attributed to the grantor for federal income tax purposes. In effect, those rules supply a statutory definition of "dominion and control" which completely supersedes the doctrine announced by the Supreme Court in *Clifford*. To remove any possible doubt on this point, the statute announces that, except as specified in §§ 671–679, "[n]o items of a trust shall be included in computing the taxable income and credits of the grantor or of any other person solely on the grounds of his dominion and control over the trust under section 61 (relating to definition of gross income) or any other provision of [the Code]." I.R.C. § 671. The clear message is that the statutory grantor trust rules now provide the exclusive basis for attributing a trust's income to the grantor based on the grantor's retained interests or powers with respect to the trust property. Consequently, if a grantor successfully navigates the statutory maze of §§ 671–679 without triggering any of its provisions, the grantor cannot be treated as the owner of the trust under § 61 based on the *Clifford* theory of dominion and control.

Nevertheless, even if the grantor fully complies with the grantor trust provisions, the regulations point out that trust income may still be attributed to the grantor under general tax principles for reasons other than dominion and control. For example, an employee who assigns his right to future salary payments remains taxable on the salary even if the assignee is an irrevocable, nongrantor trust. The anticipatory assignment of income doctrine applies to the same extent as if no trust were involved, and it operates without regard to the assignor's retention of dominion or control. Likewise, a bondholder who assigns the right to future interest payments may continue to be taxed on the interest even if it is paid to a nongrantor trust. Reg. § 1.671–1(c). Furthermore, compliance with the grantor trust rules does not prevent the income of a trust from being attributed to the grantor under rules concerning family partnerships and transfer-leaseback arrangements. Thus, for example, under § 704(e), a grantor and a nongrantor trust may be recognized as partners in a family partnership, but their distributive shares of partnership income may nevertheless have to be adjusted to reflect reasonable compensation for the grantor's services and to ensure proportionate returns on their respective capital investments. Of course, if a trust lacks economic reality, it may also be disregarded as a sham for federal tax purposes, regardless of any purported compliance with the grantor trust rules. See Markosian v. Commissioner, 73 T.C. 1235 (1980) ("pure" trust); Zmuda v. Commissioner, 79 T.C. 714 (1982) ("common law business trust").

The grantor trust provisions, §§ 671–679, comprise Subpart E of Subchapter J. The central operative provision is § 671, which attributes a trust's items of income, deduction, and credit directly to a grantor (or another person) to the extent that the grantor (or other person) is treated as the owner of any portion of the trust. Accordingly, the portion of the trust's income that is attributed to the grantor (or other person) is treated for income tax purposes as if it were received by the deemed owner, and is includible in computing taxable income by the deemed owner, not by the trust. Moreover, § 671 is generally interpreted to mean that in applying substantive income tax rules to transactions between a wholly owned grantor trust and the deemed owner, the grantor trust is disregarded as a separate taxable entity. If only part of the trust's income is attributed to the grantor (or other person), the remaining portion is taxed to the trust under the normal rules of Subchapter J. The questions of who qualifies as a "grantor," what constitutes a "portion" of a trust, and how the attributed items affect the deemed owner's income tax liability under § 671 are examined in more detail in §§ 8.2–8.4, *infra*.

For reporting purposes, a grantor trust may be required to file a skeleton income tax return with an attached statement indicating the items of income, deduction, and credit which are attributed to the deemed owner. The filing requirements for grantor trusts are discussed in § 8.5, *infra*.

In applying the grantor trust rules, certain powers or interests held by the grantor's spouse, or by a "nonadverse party" or a "related or subordinate party," are attributed to the grantor. These attribution rules, which appear in § 672, rest on the theory that by keeping these powers and interests within the specified group of close family members and associates, the grantor has indirectly retained dominion and control over the trust and should therefore continue to be treated as a deemed owner for income tax purposes. The attribution rules of § 672 are discussed in § 8.6, *infra*.

An important limitation appears in § 672(f), which generally prevents a foreign grantor, in all but a few cases, from being treated as the owner of a trust under the grantor trust rules. As a result, in most cases the deemed owner of a grantor trust will be a U.S. citizen or resident (or a domestic corporation). This provision is discussed in connection with foreign trusts in § 10.4, *infra*.

The remaining grantor trust provisions identify specific powers or interests which may, if held by the grantor (or another person), cause the holder to be treated as the owner of all or part of a trust's income under § 671. These taxable triggers, which are discussed in §§ 8.7–8.12, *infra*, include: a reversionary interest in trust corpus or income which is worth more than 5% of the initial value of corpus or income (§ 673); a power affecting beneficial enjoyment of trust corpus or income (§ 674); certain administrative powers affecting the disposition, borrowing, or investment of trust property (§ 675); a power to revoke (§ 676); a right to receive current or future distributions of trust income (§ 677); and a power held by a person other than the grantor to withdraw property from the trust (§ 678). Thus, §§ 673–677 identify the powers or interests which, if held by a grantor, will cause trust income to be attributed to the grantor; in contrast, the holder of a power of withdrawal described in § 678 is by definition a person other than the grantor, who will nevertheless qualify as a deemed owner of the portion of the trust that is subject to the power.

Finally, under § 679, a U.S. grantor who transfers property to a foreign trust is generally treated as the owner of a ratable portion of the trust for any taxable year in which the trust has one or more U.S. beneficiaries. This provision, which applies even if the U.S. grantor retains no powers or interests in the foreign trust, is discussed in connection with foreign trusts in § 10.3, *infra*.

It should be emphasized that the grantor trust rules apply only for federal income tax purposes. The tests of whether a grantor has relinquished sufficient dominion and control over the trust property so that the transfer will be treated as a completed gift for gift tax purposes, or whether the grantor has retained a power or interest which will cause the trust property to be included in the grantor's gross estate for estate tax purposes, operate independently of these income tax rules. Thus, it is possible for a particular transfer to be treated as incomplete for income tax purposes yet complete for gift and estate tax purposes, with the result that the grantor may continue to be subject to income tax until his or her death on trust property that is held exclusively for other beneficiaries and is not includible in the grantor's gross estate for estate tax purposes. Indeed, estate planners expend considerable amounts of energy and ingenuity in designing such "intentional grantor trusts," which are widely used despite lingering uncertainty about their tax consequences.

When the grantor trust rules were codified in 1954, they represented a statutory gauntlet through which grantors were obliged to run in order to avoid an unwelcome prospect of continuing tax liability on the income from property held in trust. In the intervening years, the income tax rate structure has been largely flattened, and the income tax brackets applicable to trusts have become so compressed that the overall tax burden is often lower if a trust is classified as a grantor trust than if it is taxed as a separate taxable entity under the normal rules of Subchapter J. Consequently, many grantors no longer view grantor trust status as a trap to be avoided but instead embrace it as a tax planning opportunity.

§ 8.2   GRANTOR OR OTHER DEEMED OWNER

Under § 671, the grantor or another person who is treated as the owner of any portion of a trust may be required to include all or part of the trust's income in computing his or her taxable income. Before examining the income tax consequences of deemed ownership, it is important to understand who qualifies as a grantor and who may be treated as owning a portion of a trust.

In traditional usage, a grantor is a person who creates a trust or furnishes property to fund a trust— in other words, a settlor or a trustor, terms which are often used interchangeably as synonyms for a grantor. The identity of the grantor or settlor may be material for various purposes, such as interpreting the terms of the trust instrument, satisfying creditors' claims, or determining marital property rights on death or divorce. Ordinarily there is little difficulty in identifying the grantor when a trust is created and funded by the same person. The situation may be more complicated, however, if a trust is funded indirectly by someone other than the person who nominally created it, or if more than one person contributes property to the same trust.

For purposes of the grantor trust rules, the regulations define a grantor as "any person to the extent that such person either creates a trust, or directly or indirectly makes a gratuitous transfer . . . of property to a trust." Reg. § 1.671–2(e)(1). For example, if a person creates or funds a trust on behalf of another person, both persons are treated as grantors of the trust. However, the regulations go on to state that "a person who creates a trust but makes no gratuitous transfers to the trust is not treated as an owner of any portion of the trust" under §§ 671– 677 or 679. Thus, a grantor will be treated as the owner of all or part of a trust for income tax purposes only if he or she makes a gratuitous transfer to the trust. (In contrast, a person who holds a power of withdrawal described in § 678 will qualify as a deemed owner for income tax purposes even though the power holder did not create the trust or contribute any property to it and therefore by definition cannot be a grantor.) In sum, the income attribution rules of § 671 come into play only if a person is (1) a grantor who makes a gratuitous transfer to the trust and holds (directly or by attribution) a power or an interest described in §§ 673–677, (2) a U.S. grantor who transfers property to a foreign trust with U.S. beneficiaries described in § 679, or (3) a person other than a grantor who holds a power of withdrawal described in § 678.

The distinction between the status of a grantor and that of a deemed owner under the grantor trust rules may be significant if the nominal creator of a trust does not transfer any property to the trust. Such a person will qualify as a grantor and may incur reporting obligations even though he or she is not a deemed owner of any part of the trust. For example, a U.S. grantor who creates a foreign trust is required to report the creation of the trust, even if the trust is not immediately funded and therefore has no deemed owner. I.R.C. § 6048(a)(3)(A)(i) and (a)(4)(A).

To illustrate the income tax definition of a trust grantor, consider the following examples, which are drawn from Reg. § 1.671–2(e)(6):

1.   Amanda creates and funds a trust for her children, and Brian subsequently contributes additional property to the trust. Both Amanda and Brian are grantors of the trust, and if each of them retains a proscribed power or interest they will each be treated as owning part of the trust's income in proportion to their respective contributions.

2. Gary creates a discretionary trust at Hazel's request, contributing $10,000 of Gary's own funds which are promptly reimbursed by Hazel. Both Gary and Hazel are grantors, but even if both of them are also permissible beneficiaries, the trust's income will be attributed only to Hazel, not to Gary, because in substance the trust is funded exclusively with Hazel's gratuitous transfer.

3. Rose creates and funds a trust in which she retains no powers or interests that would cause her to be a deemed owner, but under the trust instrument Silas has an unrestricted power to withdraw $10,000 from the trust. Rose is the sole grantor of the trust. Silas is not a grantor, but he is treated as the owner of part of the trust's income under § 678 based on his withdrawal power. To the extent that the trust's income is not attributed to Silas, it is taxed to the trust or its beneficiaries under the normal rules of Subchapter J.

In determining whether a grantor makes a gratuitous transfer to a trust, contributions of cash or other property are taken into account to the extent that the grantor does not receive property (or services or the right to use property) from the trust in exchange. Reg. § 1.671–2(e)(2). For this purpose, a beneficial interest in the trust does not constitute property received from the trust. Thus, for example, if Ralph, through a broker, contributes cash to an investment trust in exchange for units of beneficial interest in the trust, Ralph is treated as a grantor and as a deemed owner of a portion of the trust; for this purpose, his contribution qualifies as a gratuitous transfer because the units he purchased are not treated as property received from the trust. If Ralph subsequently sells his units to Sylvia, Sylvia may also be treated as a grantor. Reg. § 1.671–2(e)(3).

A corporation or a partnership may be treated as a grantor if it makes a gratuitous transfer of property to a trust for its own business purposes. However, if the transfer is made for the personal purposes of one or more shareholders or partners, the transaction will be recast as a constructive distribution to those shareholders or partners, followed by another transfer to the trust. As a result, the shareholders or partners (instead of the corporation or the partnership) will be treated as the grantors of the trust. Reg. § 1.671–2(e)(4).

When one trust makes a gratuitous transfer to another trust, the grantor of the first trust is also generally treated as the grantor of the second trust, unless the transfer is made pursuant to another person's exercise of a general power of appointment. For example, suppose that the trustee of an existing trust, of which Phyllis is the sole grantor, exercises a discretionary power to distribute all of the trust property to a new trust with slightly different terms. (This process is often referred to as "decanting" the trust property.) Phyllis will generally be treated as the grantor of the new trust as well. However, if the original trust granted a general power of appointment to Roger, and Roger exercised that power by directing the trustee to create the new trust, then Roger would be treated as the grantor of the new trust. Reg. § 1.671–2(e)(5).

Even before the detailed definition of a grantor was added to the regulations in 1999, it was clear that trust income may be attributed to a person who indirectly contributes property to a trust and retains powers or interests described in the grantor trust rules, even if the trust is nominally created by another person or by a court. For example, if a personal injury action filed on behalf of a minor child results in a damage award, a court may order that the damages be paid into a trust established by the court for the child's benefit. Since the trust is funded entirely with the child's property and has the child as its sole beneficiary, the child is treated as the grantor and the deemed owner of the entire trust for income tax purposes. Rev. Rul. 83–25, 1983–1 C.B. 116; see also Moore v. Commissioner, 23 T.C. 534 (1954).

A further example involves the use of "reciprocal trusts." Suppose that as part of a common plan, Joseph and Janet, a married couple, create a pair of separate and substantially similar trusts, with each spouse named as the primary beneficiary of the trust created by the other spouse. The net result, of course, is that Joseph and Janet each end up holding powers and interests which would, if held by the grantor of the trust, cause the grantor to be treated as the owner of the trust for tax purposes. Nevertheless, they may insist that neither the grantor trust provisions nor their estate tax counterparts are applicable because the arrangement has been structured precisely so that neither spouse holds any tax-sensitive powers or interests in the trust that he or she created.

At one time, it was thought that this gambit might achieve the desired result, but the Supreme Court effectively dashed such hopes in United States v. Estate of Grace, 395 U.S. 316 (1969). In *Grace*, the Court had no difficulty in "uncrossing" the two trusts and treating each spouse as the grantor of the trust established for that spouse's benefit, in accordance with the substance of the transaction. Moreover, the Court made it clear that the result did not require a finding that the trusts were created in exchange for each other or with a tax-avoidance motive. Instead, "the reciprocal trust doctrine requires only that the trusts be interrelated, and that the arrangement, to the extent of mutual value, leaves the settlors in approximately the same economic position as they would have been in had they created trusts naming themselves as life beneficiaries."

Although the issue in *Grace* involved inclusion of the trust property in the gross estate of a deceased spouse under § 2036, its rationale is equally applicable in the income tax context. Thus, for example, if Joseph and Janet create two trusts for their grandchildren, with Janet named as trustee of the trust created by Joseph and Joseph named as trustee of the trust created by Janet, the trusts may be uncrossed if this will result in each spouse being treated as both the grantor and the deemed owner of the trust that was nominally created by the other spouse. Krause v. Commissioner, 57 T.C. 890 (1972), aff'd, 497 F.2d 1109 (6th Cir. 1974), cert. denied, 419 U.S. 1108 (1975).

§ 8.3   PORTION OF A TRUST

Once a grantor (or another person) is identified as the deemed owner of all or part of a trust under the grantor trust rules, the next step is to ascertain which "portion" of the trust the grantor (or other person) is treated as owning. The relevant portion of the trust, of course, will depend on the particular powers or interests held by the grantor (or other person) and on the application of specific grantor trust rules. Nevertheless, it is useful at this point to describe in general terms the various types of partial ownership that may be involved and how they are measured.

By definition, the grantor trust rules treat a grantor (or another person) as the owner of a portion of a trust, with the result that the deemed owner must include on his or her income tax return the items of the trust's income, deductions, and credits that are attributable to that portion. Depending on the nature and extent of the powers and interests involved, the grantor (or other person) may be treated as owning the entire trust, a fractional share of the entire trust, a dollar amount, an interest in the "ordinary income" of the trust, an interest in trust corpus, items attributable to specific trust assets, or some combination thereof.

Undoubtedly the simplest situation involves a grantor who is treated as the owner of the entire trust. This typically happens when the grantor contributed all of the property in the trust and retained an unrestricted power of revocation under § 676. The same result can also occur if the grantor retained a reversionary interest described in § 673, a dispositive or administrative power described in §§ 674 and 675, or a right to income described in § 677. A person other than the grantor is treated as the owner of the entire trust if that person holds an unrestricted power of withdrawal described in § 678. In each of these cases, if the power or interest extends to the entire trust, there is no need to apportion items of income, deduction, or credit between the grantor (or other person) and the trust. All of those items are attributed to the deemed owner and reported on his or her income tax return as if they were received or paid directly by the deemed owner. Reg. § 1.671–3(a)(1). In effect, the grantor trust is disregarded for substantive income tax purposes.

If the deemed owner is treated as owning an undivided fractional share of the trust or an interest expressed as a dollar amount, a ratable share of each item of the trust's income, deduction, and credit is normally allocated to the owned portion. In the case of a pecuniary amount, the allocable share of each item normally consists of a fraction with a numerator equal to the pecuniary amount and a denominator equal to the fair market value of the trust corpus at the beginning of the taxable year. Reg. § 1.671–3(a)(3). For example, suppose that Larry has a right to withdraw $20,000 from income or corpus of a trust created by his grandparents. The trust corpus was worth $100,000 at the beginning of the taxable year, and the trust's gross income for the year consists of

$3,000 of dividends and $5,000 of capital gain; the trust also paid a deductible expense of $500. Larry is treated as owning one fifth of each item ($20,000 power of withdrawal/$100,000 trust corpus); accordingly, he will include $600 of dividends and $1,000 of capital gain in his gross income and will deduct $100 of the expense in computing his taxable income.

Sometimes the deemed owner holds a power or interest that extends only to the income or corpus of a trust. For example, if a grantor creates an irrevocable trust for his or her children, subject to a retained right to receive the income for life or a retained power to sprinkle income among the children, the grantor will be treated as the owner of the trust's income under § 674 or § 677. In this context, the regulations refer to the trust's fiduciary accounting income (borrowing the statutory definition of income from § 643(b), discussed in § 7.2, *supra*) as "ordinary income." Reg. § 1.671–2(b). If the deemed owner's power or interest is limited to the trust's ordinary income, the regulations require the deemed owner to take into account "those items which would be included in computing the tax liability of a current income beneficiary, including expenses allocable to corpus which enter into the computation of distributable net income." Reg. § 1.671–3(c). Suppose, for example, that Ellen creates an irrevocable trust to pay all of the trust's net income to herself during her lifetime, and at her death to distribute the remaining trust property to her children. She is treated as owning the ordinary income of the trust under § 677. The trust's gross income for the taxable year consists of $6,000 of dividends (allocated to income) and $4,000 of capital gain (allocated to corpus); the trust also has a deductible expense of $2,000 (allocated half to income and half to corpus). In reporting her taxable income, Ellen will take account of the $6,000 of dividends as well as the $2,000 deductible expense, since both of these items would enter into DNI and pass through to a current income beneficiary if the trust were a nongrantor trust. (Note that the full amount of the expense, including the portion charged to corpus, is allocated to her, just as if she were a current income beneficiary.) The capital gain, which was allocated to corpus, does not enter into DNI and is therefore taxable entirely to the trust on its fiduciary income tax return.

If the deemed owner's power or interest is limited to a fractional share of the trust's ordinary income, a ratable share of each item entering into DNI is attributable to the owned portion and must be included in computing the deemed owner's taxable income.

If the owned portion of the trust is limited to a fixed dollar amount of ordinary income, the regulations prescribe a subtly different method of computation. First, the deemed owner must take into account "a portion of those items of income and expense entering into the computation of ordinary income . . . sufficient to produce income of the dollar amount required." Then there will be attributed to the deemed owner "a pro rata portion of other items entering into the computation of distributable net income . . . such as expenses allocable to corpus, and a pro rata portion of credits of the trust." Reg. § 1.671–3(c). In the preceding example, suppose that instead of retaining a right to all of the trust's net income, Ellen is entitled to receive a fixed annual amount of $2,000 payable solely from trust income. In that case, her fixed payment ($2,000) represents 40% of the trust's net ordinary income ($6,000 dividends less $1,000 expense allocable to income). Therefore, in computing her taxable income Ellen must report 40% of the ordinary income items entering into DNI as well as the other items entering into DNI, resulting in a net amount of $1,600:

Dividends (40% × $6,000)	$2,400
Deductible expense allocable to income (40% × $1,000)	− 400
Dollar amount of ordinary income	$2,000
Deductible expense allocable to corpus (40% × $1,000)	− 400
Net inclusion	$1,600

The rest of the trust's items, including the capital gain, are allocated to the trust. Reg. § 1.677(a)–1(g) (Example 2).

If the deemed owner's power or interest is limited to trust corpus, the owned portion of the trust includes only items of income, deduction, and credit that do not enter into DNI. Reg. § 1.671–3(c). In effect, the deemed owner of an interest in corpus reports the items of income, deduction, and credit that would be taxed to a nongrantor trust which distributed all of its current ordinary income. For example, suppose that Martin creates an irrevocable trust for his minor child, retaining only a reversionary interest in trust corpus in the event of the child's death before reaching age 21. Martin is treated as the owner of the trust corpus under § 677. The trust's gross income for the taxable year consists of $6,000 of dividends (allocated to income) and $4,000 of capital gain (allocated to corpus); the trust also has a deductible expense of $2,000 (allocated half to income and half to corpus). In reporting his taxable income, Martin will include the $4,000 of capital gain, without any reduction for the portion of the deductible expense charged to corpus. The trust's remaining items of income, deduction, and credit are attributable to the ordinary income portion of the trust and will be taxed to the trust or to Martin's child under the normal conduit rules. Reg. § 1.677(a)–1(g) (Example 2).

One final possibility, encountered less frequently, involves a power or interest relating to specific trust property. In that case, the regulations provide that "all items directly related to that property are attributable to the [deemed owner's] portion." Items directly related to other trust property are allocated to the trust, and "[i]tems that relate both to the portion treated as owned by the grantor and to the balance of the trust must be apportioned in a manner that is reasonable in the light of all the circumstances of each case, including the terms of the governing instrument, local law, and the practice of the trustee if it is reasonable and consistent." Reg. § 1.671–

3(a)(2). For example, suppose that Greg created an irrevocable trust for other beneficiaries and funded it with income-producing securities and Blackacre. Greg's only retained power or interest in the trust is a right to receive all income from Blackacre, including any proceeds from a sale or exchange of the property. The trust's income for the taxable year consists of rent from Blackacre, investment income, and capital gain from other trust property; the trust also paid local property tax on Blackacre as well as deductible administration expenses. The rental income and the deductible property tax are directly related to Blackacre and are therefore allocated entirely to Greg. The general administration expenses should be apportioned between Greg and the trust in a reasonable manner (e.g., based on the portion of the trust's total income attributable to Blackacre, or perhaps on the value of Blackacre as a portion of the total value of the trust property at the beginning of the taxable year). The investment income and capital gain from other property are allocated to the trust and taxed under the normal conduit rules.

Although S corporations are generally not permitted to have trusts as shareholders, several exceptions for specific types of trusts are provided by statute. One important exception involves a trust that is deemed to be wholly owned by an individual U.S. citizen or resident under the grantor trust rules. This exception applies during the deemed owner's life and for up to two years after death. I.R.C. § 1361(c)(2)(A)(i) and (c)(2)(A)(ii). (Some relief from the two-year limit may be available if a § 645 election

is made to treat a "qualified revocable trust" as part
of the deceased grantor's estate, as discussed in § 4.4,
supra.) In such cases, the deemed owner or the
deemed owner's estate is treated as the eligible S
shareholder. I.R.C. § 1361(c)(2)(B)(i) and (c)(2)(B)(ii).

Another type of trust that is permitted to hold
stock in an S corporation is a "qualified subchapter S
trust" (QSST). By its terms, a QSST must have only
one current beneficiary who actually receives (or is
entitled to receive) all of the trust's current income as
well as any distributions of corpus that occur during
the beneficiary's life and all of the trust property if
the trust terminates during the beneficiary's life; the
beneficiary must also be a U.S. citizen or resident.
I.R.C. § 1361(d). If the beneficiary makes an election
under § 1361(d), the QSST qualifies as an eligible S
shareholder, and for purposes of § 678 the beneficiary
is "treated as the owner of that portion of the trust
which consists of stock in an S corporation." I.R.C.
§ 1361(d)(1)(A) and (d)(1)(B). Thus, the attribution
rule for specific trust property generally applies to S
corporation stock held by an electing QSST, and the
rest of the trust's income is taxed to the trust and the
beneficiary under the normal conduit rules.

To illustrate, suppose that Tiffany, the sole current
beneficiary of a QSST, makes an election under
§ 1361(d) to be treated as the deemed owner of S
corporation stock held by the trust. Tiffany will be
taxed directly on all of the trust's items of income,
deduction, and credit that relate directly to the S
corporation stock (including items passed through
from the S corporation to the QSST), as well as a

reasonable portion of other items not directly related to any particular trust property. If the trust terminates during Tiffany's life, she will receive all of the trust property, including the S stock. As a direct owner, rather than a deemed owner, she will continue to qualify as an eligible S shareholder. However, the distribution of the S corporation stock to Tiffany will terminate the QSST election, and the tax consequences of the distribution will be determined under the normal distribution rules, without regard to Tiffany's status as a deemed owner of the stock under § 678. Similarly, if the trust disposes of the S corporation stock during Tiffany's life, the QSST election will terminate and any gain on the sale will be taxed to the trust rather than to Tiffany. Reg. § 1.1361–1(j)(8).

§ 8.4 CONSEQUENCES OF DEEMED OWNERSHIP

When the grantor or another person is treated as the owner of any portion of a trust under the grantor trust rules, § 671 provides that "there shall . . . be included in computing the taxable income and credits of the grantor or the other person those items of income, deductions, and credits against tax of the trust which are attributable to that portion of the trust to the extent that such items would be taken into account . . . in computing taxable income or credits against the tax of an individual." The regulations amplify this provision with the statement that each item so included "is treated as if it had been received or paid directly by the grantor or other person (whether or not an individual)." Reg. § 1.671–

2(c). Thus, a grantor trust is generally treated as an alter ego of the deemed owner for substantive income tax purposes.

In many cases, a grantor trust is simply disregarded, and the deemed owner is treated as if he or she owned the trust property directly. For example, if the trustee of a revocable trust holds state or local bonds that yield tax-exempt income or realizes long-term capital gain on a sale or exchange of trust property, the bond interest and the capital gain have the same character in the grantor's hands as if the trust did not exist. Similarly, charitable contributions made by the trust are aggregated with the grantor's other contributions in applying the percentage limitations on the grantor's charitable deduction under § 170, and dividends received by the trust from sources in a particular foreign country are aggregated with the grantor's other income from sources in the same country in computing the limitation on the grantor's foreign tax credit under § 904. Reg. § 1.671–2(c). If the trust engages in business activity, the deduction allowed to the grantor for qualified business income under § 199A is computed as if the grantor "directly conducted the activities of the trust." Reg. § 1.199A–6(d)(2). Deductible items paid by the trust are taken into account in computing the 2% floor on the grantor's miscellaneous itemized deductions under § 67.* Reg. § 1.67–2T(b)(1).

---

*   Miscellaneous itemized deductions are not allowed to individual taxpayers (or to estates and trusts) for taxable years beginning after 2017 and before 2026. I.R.C. § 67(g).

A grantor trust is also routinely disregarded in determining whether gain realized by the trust qualifies for nonrecognition in the grantor's hands. For example, if a revocable trust purchases property to replace property that was involuntarily converted into money, the grantor may elect not to recognize gain on the involuntary conversion under § 1033, regardless of whether the original property was held by the trust or directly by the grantor. Rev. Rul. 88–103, 1988–2 C.B. 304. Likewise, a grantor who exchanges real property for an interest in a grantor trust that holds other real property of like kind may elect not to recognize gain on the exchange under § 1031; the grantor is treated as acquiring an interest in the trust's real property rather than a certificate of trust or a beneficial interest. Rev. Rul. 2004–86, 2004–2 C.B. 191 (Delaware statutory trust). By the same token, if a grantor trust realizes gain on a sale of the grantor's principal residence, the grantor is entitled to exclude the gain under § 121 to the same extent as if the grantor owned the residence directly. Rev. Rul. 85–45, 1985–1 C.B. 183.

The Service takes the position, and most courts agree, that a wholly owned grantor trust is generally disregarded for income tax purposes; it is not recognized as a taxable entity separate from the grantor. Because the grantor is treated as owning the trust property, a transaction between the grantor and the trust is not recognized as a sale or exchange for income tax purposes. Rev. Rul. 85–13, 1985–1 C.B. 184. The implications are often favorable for the taxpayer. For example, a grantor who sells property in exchange for an installment note may transfer the note to a revocable trust, and the trust may transfer the note back to the grantor, without triggering gain recognition; neither transfer is treated as a taxable "disposition" under § 453B. Rev. Rul. 74–613, 1974–2 C.B. 153; Rev. Rul. 76–100, 1976–1 C.B. 123. Similarly, if two grantor trusts are wholly owned by the same grantor, the purchase of a life insurance policy on the grantor's life by one trust from the other is not treated as a "transfer" under § 101(a)(2); even if the policy is purchased from a nongrantor trust, the "transfer for value" is not taxable because the grantor is treated as the owner of the policy purchased by the grantor trust. Rev. Rul. 2007–13, 2007–1 C.B. 684.

Nevertheless, there is some authority for a narrower interpretation of § 671. In one case, an irrevocable trust held as its only asset stock of a closely held corporation with a cost basis of $30,000. Several years later, the grantor purchased the stock from the trust in exchange for the grantor's unsecured $320,000 promissory note, and shortly afterward received a liquidating distribution of the corporation's assets. The grantor deducted the interest he paid on the promissory note as well as a capital loss computed using a $320,000 cost basis in the stock (i.e., the face amount of the promissory note). Judge Friendly, writing for the Second Circuit, concluded that (1) the grantor was the deemed owner of the trust under § 675(3) because the sale of the stock in exchange for the grantor's promissory note amounted to an indirect loan without adequate security; and (2) the trust should be respected as "a fully independent tax-paying entity" even though its items of income, deduction, and credit were reported by the grantor and not the trust. "[Section] 671 dictates that, when the grantor is regarded as 'owner,' the trust's income shall be attributed to him—nothing more." Accordingly, the court allowed the deductions for the interest expense and the capital loss. Rothstein v. United States, 735 F.2d 704 (2d Cir. 1984). Judge Friendly relied on the separate concurring opinion of Judge Oakes for the first proposition and on that of Judge Feinberg for the second, but neither of the other judges agreed on both points. In particular, Judge Friendly's interpretation of § 671 has not been followed by other courts, and the Service has flatly rejected that interpretation in a revenue ruling involving substantially identical facts, arguing that it would be "anomalous" to ignore the existence of a trust for purposes of income attribution while respecting it as "a separate entity capable of entering into a sales transaction with the grantor." Instead, the Service treats the deemed owner of a wholly owned grantor trust as "the owner of the trust's assets" for substantive income tax purposes. Rev. Rul. 85–13, 1985–1 C.B. 184. Under the Service's approach, the grantor in *Rothstein* would realize a capital gain on the liquidating distribution, computed using his original $30,000 basis in his stock. The grantor's purchase of the stock from his wholly owned grantor trust would be disregarded for income tax purposes, as would his payments of interest on the promissory note.

A trust may lose its status as a grantor trust, either during the deemed owner's lifetime or at death, as a consequence of the termination of the powers or interests described in the grantor trust rules. If a trust ceases to be a grantor trust during the deemed owner's lifetime, but remains in existence as a nongrantor trust, the deemed owner may recognize gain on a constructive transfer of the property held in the trust. For example, suppose that Bernard creates an irrevocable trust and retains powers which cause him to be treated as the deemed owner of the entire trust. The trust holds a limited partnership interest and Bernard, as the deemed owner, deducts losses attributable to the partnership interest for several years. At the crossover point when the partnership begins to generate gains, however, Bernard relinquishes his retained powers; the trust ceases to be a grantor trust, and Bernard simultaneously ceases to be the deemed owner of the partnership interest. When the trust ceases to be a grantor trust, the regulations treat Bernard as making a constructive transfer of the partnership interest to the trust, which now exists as a separate taxable entity. Bernard's recognized gain on the transfer is equal to the excess (if any) of the trust's share of partnership liabilities over the basis of the partnership interest. Reg. § 1.1001–2(c) (Example 5). On closely similar facts, the Tax Court upheld the validity of the regulations and reached the same result in Madorin v. Commissioner, 84 T.C. 667 (1985). (The Tax Court expressly distinguished *Rothstein* without commenting on the Second Circuit's holding or its rationale.)

Along the same lines, suppose that Clara, a U.S. citizen, creates a foreign trust for nonresident alien beneficiaries and retains powers which cause Clara to be the deemed owner of the entire trust. If Clara subsequently releases her retained powers, the trust will cease to be a grantor trust and will remain in existence as a nongrantor foreign trust. At that time, according to a revenue ruling, Clara will be treated as making a constructive transfer to the trust of the property it already holds, and she will recognize any built-in gain on the trust property under § 684. Rev. Rul. 87–61, 1987–2 C.B. 219. (See § 10.6, *infra*.)

The ability of a deemed owner to switch a trust from grantor trust status to nongrantor trust status and back again is sometimes described as "toggling." For example, if a trust initially qualifies as a grantor trust under § 675(4) solely because the grantor retains a nonfiduciary power to substitute trust property for other property of equivalent value (see § 8.11, *infra*), a compliant third party may be given a power to eliminate or reinstate the grantor's power, thereby terminating or restoring grantor trust status. The Service has identified the selective use of toggling, when combined with a complex series of transactions intended to generate artificial tax losses or to avoid recognizing gain, as a "transaction of interest" which may give rise to reporting requirements and accuracy-related penalties. I.R.S. Notice 2007–73, 2007–2 C.B. 545. However, a simple termination of grantor trust status, without toggling back to grantor trust status, falls outside the transaction of interest described in the notice.

A trust qualifies as a grantor trust only during the deemed owner's lifetime. At the deemed owner's death, the trust automatically loses its grantor trust status (unless there is another living deemed owner), since the trust's income cannot be attributed to a deceased owner. Upon the deemed owner's death, the trust itself generally continues in existence as a nongrantor trust for some period of time. Even if the terms of the trust require that it terminate and distribute all of the trust property to beneficiaries upon the deemed owner's death, the trust may be required to file fiduciary income tax returns— normally as a complex trust, except in the case of a qualified revocable trust that elects to be treated as part of the deceased owner's estate (see § 4.4, *supra*)—for the period necessary to wind up the administration of the trust and complete the required distribution.

When a trust loses its grantor trust status by reason of the grantor's death, the income tax consequences are not entirely clear. Presumably neither the deceased grantor nor the trust itself recognizes gain, even if the trust property is encumbered by liabilities which exceeded the basis of the property in the grantor's hands immediately before death. As a general matter, if the trust property is "acquired from the decedent," it should receive a fresh-start basis equal to its unencumbered fair market value under § 1014(a), just as if the property had been owned directly by the deceased grantor. However, the powers and interests which may cause a grantor to be treated as the deemed owner of a trust during lifetime are not necessarily the same as those which cause the property to be "acquired from the decedent" under § 1014(b). For example, a grantor may be treated as the deemed owner of a trust under § 675(4) by reason of a nonfiduciary power to substitute property of equivalent value, but such a power does not cause the trust property to be included in the grantor's gross estate at death, nor does the trust property clearly come within any of the categories of property acquired from a decedent enumerated in § 1014(b). The prospect of achieving a stepped-up income tax basis for appreciated property without even the prospect of an offsetting estate tax liability presents an intriguing but untested planning possibility. Unfortunately, there is no authority directly on point, and the Service has given notice that it will no longer issue letter rulings on the issue of "[w]hether the assets in a grantor trust receive a § 1014 basis adjustment at the death of the deemed owner of the trust for income tax purposes when those assets are not includible in the gross estate of that owner under [the federal estate tax]." Rev. Proc. 2020–3, § 5.01(9), 2020–1 I.R.B. 131.

§ 8.5 REPORTING

A trust is required to obtain a tax identification number (TIN) and file a fiduciary income tax return (Form 1041) if it has at least $600 of gross income or any amount of taxable income (or if any beneficiary is a nonresident alien). I.R.C. §§ 6109(a) and (b), and 6012(a)(4) and (a)(5). These requirements apply to wholly owned grantor trusts as well as to trusts that are partly or wholly nongrantor trusts. Rev. Rul. 75–278, 1975–2 C.B. 461. Thus, even if a wholly owned grantor trust is disregarded for substantive income tax purposes, it may nevertheless be required to file a return. Unlike most nongrantor trusts, a wholly owned grantor trust is not required to use a calendar year (see § 5.2, *supra*); instead, "the taxable year of the trust is disregarded and the grantor must report the gross income from the trust property as if the trust does not exist." Rev. Rul. 90–55, 1990–2 C.B. 161.

To the extent that items of a trust's income, deduction, and credit are attributed to a deemed owner, those items are not reported on the trust's return but instead are shown on a separate statement attached to the trust's return. Reg. § 1.671–4(a). Therefore, in the case of a wholly owned grantor trust, the return may be a skeleton document indicating the trust's grantor trust status, identifying the deemed owner, and referring to an attached statement listing the items that appear on the deemed owner's income tax return. This is the traditional method of reporting which applies by default to most grantor trusts.

The regulations provide two alternative reporting methods which can be used by most domestic grantor trusts that have only one deemed owner. (For this purpose, a married couple filing jointly is treated as one person.) Under the first alternative method, the deemed owner must complete a Form W-9 showing the deemed owner's name and TIN, and the trustee must furnish this information, along with the trust's address, to all payors. The trustee must also furnish the deemed owner (unless the deemed owner is also a trustee) with a statement showing the trust's items of income, deduction, and credit, identifying the payor of each item, and providing information necessary to take account of the items on the deemed owner's income tax return. Reg. § 1.671–4(b)(2)(i)(A) and (b)(2)(ii). The principal advantage of this method is that the trustee is not required to obtain a TIN for the trust or to file any return with the Service.

Under the second alternative method, the trustee must furnish each payor with the trust's name, TIN, and address, and must file a Form 1099 with the Service reporting the trust's income and showing the trust as the payor and the deemed owner as the payee. (The reported items do not include pass-through items from a partnership or an S corporation shown on Schedule K-1.) In addition, the trustee must furnish the deemed owner (unless the deemed owner is also a trustee) with a statement showing the trust's items of income, deduction, and credit, identifying the payor of each item, and providing information necessary to take account of the items on the deemed owner's income tax return. Reg. § 1.671–4(b)(2)(i)(B) and (b)(2)(iii). A wholly owned grantor trust that has more than one deemed owner may use the second alternative method, but not the first. Reg. § 1.671–4(b)(3).

Special reporting requirements apply to a "widely held fixed investment trust." An investment trust functions as a pooled investment vehicle for investors who hold certificates of beneficial interest representing undivided ownership of the trust assets; the investors are treated as grantors and deemed owners of the trust under the grantor trust rules. See § 4.3 and § 8.2, *supra*. The trustee is generally required to file a Form 1099 with the Service and to provide tax information to the beneficial owners who hold their interests directly. Frequently, however, the interests are held in "street name" by a financial intermediary (e.g., a brokerage firm, a bank or another "middleman") on behalf of or for the account of another beneficial owner, making it difficult or impossible for the trustee to identify the ultimate beneficial owner. In this situation, the "middleman" is required to file a Form 1099 with the Service and to provide tax information to the ultimate beneficial owner. Reg. § 1.671–5.

§ 8.6 ADVERSE, RELATED, AND SUBORDINATE PARTIES

A grantor who retains any one or more of various enumerated powers over the trust or its income is treated as owning a corresponding portion of the trust. The tax-sensitive powers include a power to revoke (§ 676), a power to control beneficial enjoyment, whether exercisable in favor of the grantor or other beneficiaries (§§ 674 and 677), and certain administrative powers (§ 675). However, the grantor trust rules could easily be circumvented if they applied only to powers actually held by the grantor. A competent drafter would need only to grant the same powers to a close relative or friend who could be counted on to comply with the grantor's instructions, wishes, or suggestions. Or the powers could be exercisable by the grantor with the consent of the relative or friend.

Accordingly, the grantor trust rules repeatedly refer to powers "exercisable by the grantor or a nonadverse party, or both, without the approval or consent of an adverse party." (In two places the statute refers simply to powers "exercisable by the grantor or a nonadverse party, or both," without mentioning the approval or consent of an adverse party, but the difference in phrasing appears to be purely stylistic.) In effect, powers held by a "nonadverse party," either alone or in conjunction with the grantor, are generally attributed to the grantor, reflecting a realistic assumption that in selecting another person to hold such powers the grantor is likely to choose someone who will be responsive to the grantor's wishes. Thus, the distinction between "adverse" and "nonadverse" parties has central importance in applying the grantor trust rules. The distinction is equally important for drafters of trust instruments who wish either to avoid grantor trust status or perhaps to achieve intentional grantor trust status for all or part of a trust. As noted below, the statute also contains a special attribution rule for the grantor's spouse, as well as a safe harbor for independent trustees.

An adverse party, for purposes of the grantor trust rules, is "any person having a substantial beneficial interest in the trust which would be adversely affected by the exercise or nonexercise of the power which he possesses respecting the trust." I.R.C. § 672(a). Thus, to qualify as an adverse party, a person must have a substantial beneficial interest and must also hold a power, either alone or in conjunction with the grantor, which can be exercised (or not exercised) in a manner that would diminish the holder's beneficial interest. A nonadverse party is "any person who is not an adverse party." I.R.C. § 672(b). The rationale is that a person who stands to lose a substantial benefit under the trust by exercising a power or consenting to its exercise will resist doing so—in other words, that the beneficiary will seek to preserve his or her benefits under the trust, and that the grantor's control over the trust will be correspondingly constrained. For example, if Sheila creates an irrevocable trust for the primary benefit of her brother Toby, and gives Toby an unrestricted power to invade trust corpus for himself or Sheila, Toby is an adverse party. To the extent that he exercises the power in favor of Sheila (or refuses to exercise it in favor of himself), his own share of future trust distributions will be diminished. As a result, Toby's power of appointment will not be attributed to Sheila and she will not be treated as the owner of the trust under § 676 or § 677. (Toby, however, will be a deemed owner under § 678.) The consequences for Sheila would be the same if she retained a power of revocation that could be exercised only with Toby's consent. (In that case, however, Toby would not be a deemed owner.) In contrast, if the power of appointment were held by a nonadverse party—e.g., Sheila's daughter, or an unrelated trustee—the power would be attributed to Sheila and she would be treated as the owner of the trust.

A beneficiary's interest may be mandatory or discretionary, present or future, vested or contingent, and it may extend to trust income, corpus or both. For this purpose, a general power of appointment over the trust property is treated as a beneficial interest in the trust. The regulations also state, not very helpfully, that a beneficial interest is considered to be "substantial" if its value in relation to the total value of the property subject to the power is "not insignificant." Reg. § 1.672(a)–1(a). It may be relatively obvious whether an interest is substantial if its value can be estimated by actuarial methods (e.g., a remainder interest contingent on surviving one or more specified lives in being, or survival for a fixed term of years). It may even be possible to estimate the likelihood of a contingency such as marriage, remarriage, or birth of issue. However, if the interest is subject to an unascertainable contingency such as a beneficiary's happiness or another person's exercise of unfettered discretion, it may be difficult to predict whether the interest will be considered substantial.

For example, suppose that Henry, age 80, creates a trust to pay income to his 40-year-old daughter Imelda for life, with remainder at her death to her 16-year-old daughter Jeanne if Jeanne is then living, and Henry retains a power to revoke the trust with the consent of either Imelda or Jeanne. Imelda and Jeanne each have a substantial beneficial interest which would be adversely affected by a revocation of the trust. Consequently, Henry is not a deemed owner, and the trust is not a grantor trust. In contrast, if Jeanne creates a trust to pay income to other beneficiaries during her own life, with remainder at her death to Henry if he is then living, a power of revocation exercisable by Jeanne with Henry's consent would probably not prevent Jeanne from being treated as the owner of the trust. The actuarial probability of Henry's surviving her is less than 3%, and so his remainder interest would almost certainly not be considered substantial.

Whether a beneficiary is considered to be "adverse" to the grantor depends not on the parties' subjective intentions or relationship but on the objective effect that an exercise of the power would have on the beneficiary's interest. A beneficiary may be an adverse party, even though it may be highly unlikely as a practical matter that the beneficiary would object to the grantor's exercise of the power. Indeed, since most beneficiaries are bound to a grantor by strong ties of personal affection or family relationship, they can ordinarily be expected to be cooperative or obedient. Nevertheless, the case law unequivocally supports the conclusion that close relatives and family friends can qualify as adverse parties.

A beneficiary is an adverse party only if the beneficiary's interest will be diminished by an exercise (or nonexercise) of the power in question. Moreover, if the beneficiary's interest in income or corpus is limited to only a part of the trust, the beneficiary is adverse only as to that part. For example, if Beryl creates a trust to pay income in equal shares to Clyde, Dale, and Ethan, and retains a power to revoke the trust with Clyde's consent, Clyde is adverse only as to one-third of the trust, and Beryl will be treated as owning the remaining two-thirds of the trust by reason of her power of revocation. Reg. § 1.672(a)–1(b). The interest of an ordinary income beneficiary may or may not be adverse to the exercise of a power over corpus.

Suppose that Daphne creates a trust to pay income to Edmund for life, with remainder at Edmund's death to Frances. If Edmund has a power to appoint the corpus to Daphne, exercisable either during life or by will, Edmund's interest is adverse to the exercise of the power during his life but not after his death. Therefore, Daphne would not be treated as the owner of the ordinary income portion of the trust during Edmund's life, but she would be taxable under § 677 on items allocable to corpus (e.g., capital gain) which might in the discretion of a nonadverse party be accumulated for future distribution to her. Reg. § 1.672(a)–1(c). Conversely, the interest of a remainder beneficiary is adverse to the exercise of a power over corpus but not to the exercise of a power that affects only the preceding income interest. In the preceding example, if Frances had a power to sprinkle the trust's ordinary income each year between Daphne and Edmund, the exercise of her power would have no effect on her remainder interest. Accordingly, Frances would be a nonadverse party with respect to her power, and Daphne, the grantor of the trust, would be taxable under § 677 on the ordinary income portion of the trust. Reg. § 1.672(a)–1(d).

Some powers are expressly permitted to be held by an "independent" trustee, even though the same powers in the hands of the grantor or any other nonadverse party would cause the grantor to be treated as a deemed owner. I.R.C. §§ 674(c) and 675(3). For this purpose, an independent trustee is one other than a "related or subordinate party" who is "subservient to the grantor." Thus, if these specific powers are to be created at all, it is important that they be held by independent trustees and not by related or subordinate parties who are subservient to the grantor. The prohibited group of related or subordinate parties includes any nonadverse party who falls into any of the following categories: (1) the grantor's spouse, if living with the grantor; (2) the grantor's parents, issue, or siblings; (3) any employee of the grantor; (4) any corporation, or its employees, in which the stock holdings of the grantor and the trust are "significant from the viewpoint of voting control"; and (5) any subordinate employee in a corporation of which the grantor is an executive. I.R.C. § 672(c). According to the legislative history, the common feature of these persons and entities is that the nature of their relationship with the grantor supports an inference that a power held by any of them is tantamount to a power in the grantor. Indeed, a related or subordinate party is expressly presumed to be subservient to the grantor's wishes, "unless such party is shown not to be subservient by a preponderance of the evidence." In view of the party's relationship with the grantor (and the fact that the grantor selected the party to act as trustee), it may be difficult to overcome the presumption of subservience, at least in the absence of direct conflict with the grantor or open defiance of the grantor's wishes. Accordingly, it is common practice to select trustees who are not related or subordinate parties to hold the powers in question. Fortunately, there is normally a broad range of available trustees, including lawyers, trust officers, accountants, and relatives outside the prohibited group (e.g., nieces and nephews, aunts and uncles, and in-laws).

A grantor or other person is considered to have a power "even though the exercise of the power is subject to a precedent giving of notice or takes effect only on the expiration of a certain period after the exercise of the power." I.R.C. § 672(d). This provision is intended to prevent trivial limitations from being used to circumvent the rules concerning presently exercisable powers. For example, if the terms of a revocable trust require that the grantor give 30 days' advance notice to the trustee before exercising the power to revoke, or provide that the revocation will take effect 30 days after the power is exercised, the grantor will be treated as holding a presently exercisable power of revocation and will be the deemed owner of the trust from its inception under § 676. Under an early version of the statute, a grantor who created a "year and a day" trust, retaining a power of revocation that would take effect one year and one day after the date of exercise, escaped being treated as the owner of the trust. Section 672(d) effectively forecloses this gambit.

Nevertheless, a substantial delay in the effective date of a power may insulate the grantor from being treated as a deemed owner, even if the power is presently exercisable. In a few places, the grantor trust rules provide a safe harbor for "a power the exercise of which can only affect the beneficial enjoyment of the income for a period commencing after the occurrence of an event such that the grantor would not be treated as the owner under section 673 if the power were a reversionary interest." I.R.C. §§ 674(b)(2), 676(b), and 677(a); Reg. § 1.672(d)–1. This safe harbor, which puts discretionary powers on a par with reversionary interests under § 673, will generally apply only if beneficial enjoyment of the interests subject to the power is delayed for so long that the interests are worth no more than 5% of the value of the underlying trust property. For example, suppose that Hazel creates a trust and reserves a power to revoke at the end of a specified period of years. Assuming a 6% interest rate, Hazel will be treated as the owner of the trust unless the power cannot take effect for at least 52 years after the inception of the trust. If Hazel instead reserves a power to revoke at the death of a specified income beneficiary, the safe harbor will apply only if the beneficiary is no more than 17 years old at the inception of the trust. For a more detailed explanation of the 5% test, see the discussion of reversionary interests in § 8.7, *infra*.

For purposes of the grantor trust rules, a grantor is treated as holding any power or interest held by the grantor's spouse. I.R.C. § 672(e). This provision was added in 1986 primarily to curb the use of a "spousal remainder trust" to circumvent the reversionary interest rule of § 673. To illustrate the technique, suppose that Adele creates an irrevocable trust to pay income to her son Ben for 8 years, and instead of retaining a reversionary interest (which would almost certainly cause her to be a deemed owner under § 673), Adele gives the remainder interest to her husband Charles, presumably with an implicit understanding that he will eventually return the property to her upon request. Under § 672(e), Adele is treated as owning Charles's remainder interest, and she is therefore a deemed owner under § 673 to the same extent as if she had retained a reversionary interest. More generally, since all of the spouse's powers or interests in a trust are automatically attributed to the grantor, it no longer matters whether the spouse would otherwise qualify as an adverse party. If Adele creates an irrevocable trust for Charles and gives him a power to invade corpus for Adele, Adele will be the deemed owner of the entire trust notwithstanding Charles's status as an adverse party.

The spousal attribution rule of § 672(e) applies to any person who was the grantor's spouse at the time the power or interest was created, unless the grantor and the spouse were legally separated under a decree of divorce or separate maintenance. Once the rule comes into play, it continues to apply even if the grantor and the spouse subsequently divorce. However, if the grantor marries the spouse after the creation of the power or interest, the spousal attribution rule applies only from the beginning of the marriage.

§ 8.7   REVERSIONARY INTERESTS

Section 673 treats the grantor as the owner of any portion of a trust in which the grantor retains a substantial reversionary interest. Under the current version of the statute, a reversionary interest is considered to be substantial if it is worth more than 5% of the value of the underlying property at the inception of the trust. Because the value of the reversion depends on the time period during which the grantor's possession and enjoyment are postponed and on the assumed interest rate, the statute bears directly on the use of short-term trusts to shift trust income from the grantor to other beneficiaries for income tax purposes. If a grantor wishes to shift income to other beneficiaries for a limited time while retaining ultimate ownership of the underlying property, § 673 specifies how long the grantor must forego possession and enjoyment of the transferred property in order to avoid being treated as the owner for income tax purposes. In effect, this provision represents a limited statutory exception to the judicial assignment of income doctrine.

From 1954 until 1986, § 673 treated the grantor as the owner of the trust only if the grantor's reversionary interest would take effect (or was reasonably expected to do so) within 10 years from the date of the transfer. This provision gave rise to widespread use of so-called "*Clifford* trusts" which paid income to the grantor's children or other beneficiaries for "ten years and a day" before returning the underlying property to the grantor on termination. An even shorter period was permitted if the trust term was measured by the life of the income beneficiary. In the nature of things, most of the *Clifford* trusts established before 1986 have run their course, though a few trusts with terms longer than the statutory 10-year minimum may still be in existence. The current 5% test was enacted in 1986 and applies to transfers in trust (including additions to preexisting trusts) made after March 1, 1986.

Under the general rule of § 673(a), the grantor is treated as the owner of a trust if the grantor retains a reversionary interest in the trust property, unless the value of the reversionary interest is no more than 5% of the value of the trust property at the time of the transfer. If the value of the reversionary interest exceeds the 5% threshold, the statute operates by treating the grantor as the owner of both the ordinary income and the corpus of the portion of the trust in which the grantor retains a reversionary interest. As a result, the grantor is generally treated as owning the entire trust. For example, if Mark creates an irrevocable trust to pay income to Nell for five years and then to return the property to Mark, and if the reversion is worth more than 5% of the value of the trust property (as is almost certainly the case), Mark will be the deemed owner of the entire trust for income tax purposes. The result will be the same if Mark names his wife Olivia as remainder beneficiary to receive the trust property at the end of the five-year term, since her interest will be attributed to Mark under § 672(e) (see § 8.6, *supra*) and treated as a retained reversion under § 673(a). If Mark's reversionary interest extends to only half of the trust property and the other half is given to another beneficiary (other than Olivia), Mark will be taxed on only half of the trust's income.

The 5% test is far more stringent than the 10-year rule set forth in the pre-1986 version of § 673(a). Under any plausible assumed rate of interest, a reversionary interest will normally be worth more than 5% of the underlying property unless the trust is expected to last for several decades. For example, assuming a 6% interest rate, a reversion following a 51-year term is worth 5.1215% of the underlying property; if the term is 52 years, the reversion is worth 4.8316%. Thus, unless the expected duration of the trust is at least 52 years, the reversionary interest will not comply with the 5% rule. The outcome is not materially different if the trust term is measured by the life of the income beneficiary. For example, assuming a 6% interest rate, a reversion following a life income interest in an 18-year-old beneficiary is worth 5.111% of the underlying property, but if the beneficiary is only 17 years old, the reversion is worth 4.886%. Accordingly, the reversionary interest will comply with the 5% rule only if the beneficiary is no more than 17 years old at the inception of the trust. In valuing a reversionary interest, it is assumed that any discretionary power will be exercised for the maximum benefit of the grantor, even if the power is held by a trustee or a third person (including an adverse party). I.R.C. § 673(c). However, the possibility that the property will return to the grantor or the grantor's spouse by intestacy is ignored. The 5% test ensures that virtually any reversionary interest retained by the grantor (and any remainder interest given to the grantor's spouse) will cause the grantor to be treated as the owner of the trust, unless the interest is so remote as to be negligible from its inception. As a practical matter, the 5% test has put an end to short-term trusts as a viable income-shifting technique.

In determining whether the 5% test is met, both the reversionary interest and the underlying property are valued as of the time the property is transferred to the trust. If a reversion is worth no more than 5% of the underlying property at the inception of the trust, a subsequent contribution of additional property to the trust must be tested at the time it is made. For example, suppose that Violet creates an irrevocable trust to pay income to Wilbur for 60 years, followed by a reversion in Violet which is worth less than 5% of the value of the trust property at the inception of the trust. Twenty years later, when the trust has a remaining term of 40 years, Violet contributes additional property to the trust. If Violet's reversion in the additional property is worth more than 5% of the value of that property when it is contributed to the trust, Violet will be treated as the owner of the additional property (but not the original trust property) under § 673.

Similarly, if the term of the original trust is extended, resulting in a postponement of the time for possession and enjoyment of the reversion, the grantor is deemed to make a new transfer in trust for the period from the effective date of the postponement until the new time for possession and enjoyment; to the extent that the grantor was not treated as owning the trust's income under the original trust, however, the deemed transfer does not impair that treatment during the original trust term. I.R.C. § 673(d). In the preceding example, suppose that 30 years after the creation of Violet's trust, when the original trust has a remaining term of 30 years, the trustee exercises a power to extend the trust term by an additional 10 years, thereby postponing Violet's possession and enjoyment of the underlying property. Under § 673(d), Violet is deemed to make a new transfer of the existing trust property, retaining a reversion which will take effect 40 years in the future (counting the 30-year remaining trust term and the 10-year extension). To the extent that the original trust complied with the 5% test at inception, the ordinary income portion of the trust will not be attributed to Violet during the remaining 30 years of the trust's original term. At the end of the original trust term, however, her immunity will expire and she will be treated as owning the ordinary income portion of the trust during the 10-year extension, unless her reversion is worth no more than 5% of the trust property at the time of the deemed transfer.

Section 673(b) provides a safe harbor for a reversion that will take effect at the death of the income beneficiary before age 21, if the beneficiary is a lineal descendant of the grantor who holds all of the present interests in the portion of the trust subject to the grantor's reversionary interest. This provision operates independently of the 5% test. For example, suppose that Lydia creates a trust to pay income to her 15-year-old son Matthew and to distribute the corpus to Matthew when he reaches age 35, subject to a reversion in Lydia if Matthew dies before reaching age 21. Lydia will not be treated as the owner of the trust under § 673, even if her remainder is worth more than 5% of the underlying property. A reversionary interest that comes within the safe harbor of § 673(b) will nearly always qualify independently under the 5% test of § 673(a). For example, assuming a 6% interest rate, a reversion at the death of a 15-year-old life income beneficiary is worth only 4.445% of the underlying property; the value of a reversion conditioned on the beneficiary's death before age 21 would be negligible. The practical significance of the § 673(b) safe harbor is correspondingly limited.

Compliance with § 673 does not insulate the grantor from being treated as a deemed owner under another provision of the grantor trust rules. Specifically, a grantor who retains a reversionary interest in a trust is taxable on items of income attributable to trust corpus (e.g., capital gain) regardless of whether the retained interest satisfies the 5% test of § 673(a) or the safe harbor of § 673(b). This result flows not from § 673 but from § 677(a)(2), which treats the grantor as the owner of any portion of the trust if income attributable to that portion is or may be held or accumulated for future distribution to the grantor without the consent of an adverse party. Reg. §§ 1.673(a)–1(a) and 1.677(a)–1(g) (Example 2); see § 8.9, *infra*. Thus, if the grantor retains a reversionary interest (or gives a remainder interest to a spouse), the grantor is generally treated as the owner of the trust corpus, even if the retained interest is highly unlikely to take effect in possession or enjoyment. If the 5% test of § 673(a) or the safe harbor of § 673(b) is met, the ordinary income portion of the trust which is not treated as owned by the grantor will be taxed to the trust and its beneficiaries under the normal conduit rules.

To avoid being treated as the owner of the trust's ordinary income under § 673, a grantor must give up possession and enjoyment of trust property for at least the minimum time period determined under the

5% test of § 673(a) or the safe harbor of § 673(b). That time period is relevant not only in applying § 673, but also in applying other grantor trust provisions concerning postponed powers affecting beneficial enjoyment. Certain provisions which cause the grantor to be treated as owning trust income by reason of a presently exercisable power do not apply if an exercise of the power can affect beneficial enjoyment of the income only for "a period commencing after the occurrence of an event such that the grantor would not be treated as the owner under section 673 if the power were a reversionary interest." I.R.C. §§ 674(b)(2), 676(b), and 677(a); see § 8.6, *supra*. For example, a grantor's retained power to revoke a trust does not cause the grantor to be treated as the owner of the trust if the beneficial interests subject to change by exercise of the power are so remote that they would satisfy the 5% test of § 673(a) if they were retained directly by the grantor.

§ 8.8 POWER TO REVOKE

A grantor is treated as owning any portion of a trust if "at any time the power to revest in the grantor title to such portion is exercisable by the grantor or a nonadverse party, or both." I.R.C. § 676(a). This provision, which has remained largely unchanged since it was first enacted in 1924, clearly applies to a grantor's unrestricted power to revoke a trust and reacquire the trust property. Thus, the grantor of a typical inter vivos revocable trust is treated as owning the entire trust for income tax purposes. It does not matter whether the power of revocation is retained expressly or by implication under the terms of the trust or by operation of law (e.g., where the grantor of an inter vivos trust is presumed under local law to retain such a power unless the trust is expressly made irrevocable). It is also immaterial whether the power is described as "a power to revoke, to terminate, to alter or amend, or to appoint." Reg. § 1.676(a)–1. Section 676 applies only to powers that can be exercised for the benefit of the grantor, but powers exercisable exclusively in favor of beneficiaries other than the grantor may cause the grantor to be treated as the owner of the trust under § 674 (see § 8.10, *infra*).

A power of revocation is normally exercisable by the grantor alone, but § 676(a) applies equally to such a power if it is exercisable by any nonadverse party, either alone or in conjunction with the grantor. Although the statutory language does not provide an express exception for a power held by an adverse party, this gap is filled by the regulations, which state that § 676(a) applies if the power is exercisable "by the grantor or a nonadverse party, or both, without the approval or consent of an adverse party." Reg. § 1.676(a)–1. Thus, although a grantor who retains an unrestricted power of revocation is treated as the owner of the entire trust, the power is disregarded if it can be exercised only with the consent of an adverse party (e.g., a life income beneficiary or a remainder beneficiary). By the same token, if a third person holds an unrestricted power to return the trust property to the grantor, the power is attributed to the grantor if the holder is a nonadverse party but not if the holder is an adverse party. For example, suppose that Julie creates a trust to pay income to Kate for life with remainder to Larry. Julie will be treated as the owner of the entire trust if she retains a power of revocation, even if the power can be exercised only with the consent of a nonadverse party (i.e., any person other than Kate or Larry). The result is the same if the power to return the trust property is exercisable solely by a nonadverse party, as in the case of a trustee's discretionary power to distribute income or corpus to the grantor. Rev. Rul. 57–8, 1957–1 C.B. 204. However, if the power is held solely by Kate or Larry, or if it can be exercised only with their consent, Julie will not be treated as the owner. Because the grantor is treated as holding any power held by the grantor's spouse under § 672(e) (see § 8.6, *supra*), the statute cannot be circumvented by requiring the consent of the grantor's spouse, even if the spouse qualifies as an adverse party. Thus, in the preceding example, if Julie is married to Larry, she will be treated as the owner of the trust if any person holds a power of revocation, unless the power is held solely by Kate (an adverse party other than Julie's spouse) or can be exercised only with Kate's consent.

If only a portion of the trust is subject to a power of revocation, the grantor is treated as owning only a corresponding portion of the trust for income tax purposes. In the preceding example, if the trust is irrevocable but Julie (who is unmarried) has a right to require that the trust's ordinary income for the current year be distributed to herself (instead of to Kate), Julie will be taxed only on the ordinary income portion of the trust (i.e., the items of income, deduction, and credit which would enter into DNI if the trust were a nongrantor trust). Alternatively, if Julie retains a power to withdraw the trust corpus at Kate's death if Julie is then living, Julie will be taxed on capital gains and other items attributable to the corpus portion of the trust. If two grantors make equal contributions to a trust and reserve a power of revocation which can be exercised by either grantor only with the other grantor's consent, each grantor will be treated as owning one half of the trust. Although each grantor has a substantial beneficial interest in the trust, neither grantor's interest would be adversely affected by exercise of the joint power. Accordingly, each grantor is treated as having an unrestricted power to revoke one half of the trust without the consent of an adverse party. DeAmodio v. Commissioner, 299 F.2d 623 (3d Cir. 1962).

The statute provides a safe harbor for "a power the exercise of which can only affect the beneficial enjoyment of the income for a period commencing after the occurrence of an event such that a grantor would not be treated as the owner under section 673 if the power were a reversionary interest." I.R.C. § 676(b). This provision ensures that a grantor who retains a power of revocation that will take effect only upon the occurrence of a remote event will not be treated as the owner of the trust if a similar reversionary interest taking effect upon the same event would not cause the grantor to be a deemed owner under § 673. Reg. § 1.676(b)–1. For example, suppose that Gretchen creates an irrevocable trust to pay income to her grandson Henry for life, and at Henry's death to distribute the corpus to Gretchen if she is then living. If the age difference between

Gretchen and Henry is sufficiently large that Gretchen's reversion is worth no more than 5% of the trust property at the inception of the trust, she will not be treated as owning the ordinary income portion of the trust under § 673 (see § 8.7, *supra*). Alternatively, suppose that instead of retaining a reversionary interest, Gretchen retains a power to revoke the trust at Henry's death if she is still alive. In the absence of § 676(b), Gretchen's power would cause her to be treated as owning the entire trust under the general rule of § 676(a), which applies if a power of revocation is exercisable "at any time." To prevent this anomalous result, § 676(b) ensures that a power of revocation is exempt under § 676 to the same extent as a comparable reversionary interest under § 673. However, the exemption lasts only until the power becomes presently exercisable. Thus, in the preceding example, if Gretchen in fact survives Henry, she will be treated as owning the entire trust from the date of Henry's death unless she has previously relinquished her power of revocation. In the meantime, she may be taxed on the trust's capital gains and other items attributable to corpus under § 677 (see § 8.9, *infra*), just as she would be if she had retained a reversionary interest.

§ 8.9   INCOME FOR GRANTOR'S BENEFIT

A grantor is treated as the owner of any portion of a trust if the income of that portion "is, or, in the discretion of the grantor or a nonadverse party, or both, may be (1) distributed to the grantor or the grantor's spouse; (2) held or accumulated for future distribution to the grantor or the grantor's spouse; or

(3) applied to the payment of premiums on policies of insurance on the life of the grantor or the grantor's spouse [except for policies irrevocably payable for charitable purposes]." I.R.C. § 677(a). This provision, like its counterpart in § 676 relating to powers of revocation, can be traced back to a provision originally enacted in 1924. The rationale of § 677 is that a grantor who is entitled or permitted to receive distributions of income or corpus has retained a substantial degree of beneficial enjoyment which justifies attributing ownership of a corresponding portion of the trust income or corpus to the grantor for income tax purposes. Thus, § 677 operates in conjunction with §§ 673 and 676 to treat the grantor as the owner of the trust based on the grantor's continuing present or possible future beneficial enjoyment of income or corpus. To some extent, the three provisions overlap, but the primary function of § 677 is to identify the extent of the grantor's retained beneficial interests in ordinary income or corpus, while § 673 focuses on whether a reversionary interest is sufficiently remote to exempt the grantor from deemed ownership of the preceding ordinary income interests, and § 676 focuses on powers which may be exercised for the grantor's benefit (as distinguished from retained beneficial interests).

The most obvious target of § 677 is an irrevocable trust under which the grantor (or the grantor's spouse) is required or permitted to receive distributions of income or corpus without the consent of an adverse party. Consider the following examples:

Example 1:   Ophelia creates an irrevocable trust to pay income to herself for life, with remainder to her son Philip. Ophelia will be treated under § 677(a)(1) as owning the ordinary income portion of the trust because she is entitled to receive all of the trust's current income. She has no interest in the trust corpus, however, and any capital gains or other items attributable to the corpus portion of the trust will be taxed under the normal conduit rules.

Example 2:   Same facts as Example 1, except that Ophelia's husband Ralph is named as the income beneficiary. The result is the same; Ophelia is the deemed owner of the ordinary income portion of the trust. Note that this outcome flows directly from § 677(a)(1), even without invoking the spousal attribution rule of § 672(e).

Example 3:   Same facts as Example 1, except that the trust instrument authorizes an independent corporate trustee in its sole discretion to accumulate current income and add it to corpus. Although Ophelia is not entitled to receive the trust's current income, the income may be distributed to her in the discretion of the trustee, who is a nonadverse party, without the consent of an adverse party. Therefore, Ophelia is treated under § 677(a)(1) as owning the ordinary income portion of the trust.

Example 4:   Ophelia creates an irrevocable trust to pay income to her son Philip for life, and at Philip's death to distribute the remaining trust property to herself if she is then living. (Assume that the age difference between Ophelia and Philip is sufficiently large that Ophelia's reversion is worth no more than 5% of the value of the underlying property at the inception of the trust, and Ophelia is therefore not treated under § 673 as owning the ordinary income portion of the trust.) Since she is not eligible to receive any of the trust's ordinary income currently or in the future, Ophelia will not be treated under § 677 as owning the ordinary income portion of the trust. (If her reversion did not come within the 5% safe harbor of § 673, however, the ordinary income portion would be attributed to her under § 673(a).) Nevertheless, her reversion will cause her to be treated as owning the corpus portion of the trust. It makes no difference that her reversion is unlikely ever to take effect in possession or enjoyment. The possibility that she may outlive her son is sufficient to bring § 677(a)(2) into play (even though that possibility is so remote that it is disregarded under § 673). Consequently, Ophelia will be treated as owning any capital gains, as well as any other items attributable to trust corpus. Reg. § 1.677(a)–1(f) and (g) (Example 2).

Example 5: Same facts as Example 4, except that the remaining trust property is payable at Philip's death to Ophelia's husband Ralph if he is then living. This is a spousal remainder trust, and the result is the same as in Example 4. Ophelia is treated under § 677(a)(2) as owning the corpus portion of the trust, even without invoking the spousal attribution rule of § 672(e).

Example 6: Same facts as Example 4, except that the trust instrument authorizes an independent trustee in its sole discretion to accumulate current trust income and add it to corpus. Although Ophelia is not assured of receiving any trust income currently or in the future, she is treated under § 677(a)(2) as owning the entire trust because the trustee, a nonadverse party, has discretion, without the consent of an adverse party, to accumulate the trust's current income and add it to the corpus in which Ophelia has a reversionary interest. Rev. Rul. 57–363, 1957–2 C.B. 326.

Example 7: Ophelia creates an irrevocable trust to pay income to her husband Ralph for life, with remainder at his death to Ophelia's son Philip. The trust instrument authorizes an independent corporate trustee in its sole discretion, and only with Ralph's consent, to distribute income or corpus to Ophelia. Although Ralph is technically an adverse party with respect to any discretionary distributions to Ophelia, his power to consent to such distributions is attributed to Ophelia under § 672(e) and is therefore ineffective to block the application of § 677(a)(1). Accordingly, Ophelia is treated as owning the entire trust because the trustee, a nonadverse party, has discretion to distribute income or corpus to Ophelia without the consent of any third party.

> *Example 8:*   Ophelia creates an irrevocable trust to pay income to her son Philip for life, with remainder at Philip's death to his issue then living. The trust instrument authorizes an independent corporate trustee in its sole discretion, and only with Philip's consent, to distribute trust income or corpus to Ophelia. Philip is an adverse party with respect to any discretionary distributions to Ophelia. Because the trustee can make such distributions only with Philip's consent, Ophelia is not treated under § 677(a)(2) as owning any portion of the trust.

Under § 677(a)(2), the grantor is treated as owning a portion of the trust if the income "may be" held or accumulated for future distribution to the grantor (or the grantor's spouse). On its face, this language appears to be broad enough to apply even if the possibility of future beneficial enjoyment is remote or speculative. The regulations confirm that the grantor will be treated as the owner of a portion of the trust "if he has retained any interest which might, without the approval or consent of an adverse party, enable him to have the income from that portion distributed to him at some time," but grantor trust status can be avoided if the grantor and the grantor's spouse are "divested permanently and completely" of their beneficial interests. Reg. § 1.677(a)–1(c).

Under § 677(a)(3), the grantor may be treated as owning a trust if the trust's income may be used to pay premiums on an insurance policy on the life of the grantor (or the grantor's spouse). This provision reflects a view of life insurance as a desirable and valuable, if not indispensable, component of a family savings plan. Under this view, the use of trust income to pay the costs of maintaining a policy represents an indirect benefit to the insured grantor, even if the policy itself is not owned or controlled by the grantor. While the rationale for singling out life insurance premiums for special treatment may be open to question, § 677(a)(3) has withstood constitutional challenge and has remained largely unchanged since 1924. On its face, the provision might be read to trigger grantor trust status based on the mere possibility that trust income might be used, without the consent of an adverse party, to pay premiums on a policy insuring the life of the grantor (or the grantor's spouse), subject only to a narrow exception for policies irrevocably payable for charitable purposes. The courts, however, have taken a much narrower view, applying § 677(a)(3) only if there is a policy in existence on which premiums might be paid during the taxable year. The Service has also ruled that the grantor of a trust is treated as owning "the amount of trust income which is used to pay the premiums" on policies of insurance on the grantor's life. Rev. Rul. 66–313, 1966–2 C.B. 245. To forestall the possibility of unintended grantor trust status under § 677(a)(3), many trust instruments expressly prohibit the trustee from using trust income to pay premiums on policies insuring the life of the grantor (or the grantor's spouse).

Section 677(a) provides a safe harbor for a power that can only affect trust income upon a remote event which would not cause a comparable reversionary interest to trigger grantor trust status under § 673. The statutory language is identical to its counterpart in § 676(b), and the rationale and effect of the two provisions are virtually interchangeable. (See § 8.8, *supra.*) The regulations provide that the grantor is not treated as the owner "when a discretionary right can only affect the beneficial enjoyment of the income of a trust received after a period of time during which a grantor would not be treated as an owner under section 673 if the power were a reversionary interest." Reg. § 1.677(a)–1(e). Note that the safe harbor in § 677(a) applies only to a discretionary power affecting trust income to be realized at some remote future time; it does not exempt a power to accumulate current income for possible distribution at some remote future time to the grantor (or the grantor's spouse) by reason of a reversion (or a remainder interest). Reg. § 1.677(a)–1(f).

For example, suppose that June creates an irrevocable trust, with an independent corporate trustee, to pay income to her grandson Keith for life, then to pay income in the trustee's sole discretion to June or any of Keith's issue then living until Keith's youngest child reaches age 21, and then to distribute any remaining trust property to Keith's issue then living. (Assume that the actuarial probability of June surviving Keith is no more than 5% at the inception of the trust, so that a comparable reversionary interest would not trigger grantor trust status under § 673.) As long as none of the trust's income for the current taxable year, whether attributable to income or to corpus, can be distributed currently or held for future distribution to June, the trustee's discretionary power to distribute ordinary income earned after Keith's death comes within the safe harbor of § 677(a), and June is not treated as owning any portion of the trust. If she actually does survive Keith and becomes eligible to receive current income in the trustee's discretion, then she will be treated as owning the ordinary income portion of the trust.

Nevertheless, the regulations warn that the safe harbor of § 677(a) does not apply "merely because the grantor [or the grantor's spouse] must await the expiration of a period of time before he or she can receive or exercise discretion over previously accumulated income of the trust, even though the period is such that the grantor would not be treated as an owner under section 673 if a reversionary interest were involved." Reg. § 1.677(a)–1(f). Thus, in the preceding example, if June held a reversionary interest in trust corpus, or if the trustee had discretion to distribute trust corpus to her after Keith's death, she would be treated as owning the corpus portion of the trust for the current taxable year.

A grantor is generally treated as the owner of a trust under § 677(a) to the extent that the trust income is or may be used, without the consent of an adverse party, to discharge a legal obligation of the grantor (or the grantor's spouse). Reg. § 1.677(a)–1(d). The rationale is that the grantor derives the same economic benefit from a trustee's application of

trust income to pay an obligation of the grantor (or
the grantor's spouse) as if the grantor received the
same amount from the trust and paid the obligation
personally. Accordingly, a power to apply trust
income for the benefit of the grantor by paying rent
or living expenses, interest or principal on a
mortgage debt, or any other legally enforceable
obligation of the grantor (or the grantor's spouse) will
cause the grantor to be treated as an owner,
"regardless of whether the income is actually so
applied." Reg. § 1.677(b)–1(d). Similarly, a grantor
who makes a "net gift" to a trust may be treated as
the owner of any trust income that might be used to
satisfy the grantor's gift tax liability. Krause v.
Commissioner, 56 T.C. 1242 (1971). The economic
benefit doctrine may have unexpected consequences
if a trust holds property encumbered by a debt for
which the grantor remains liable. There is some
judicial authority for treating the grantor as owning
any trust income that is or might be used to pay the
debt, even though the grantor also realizes gain on
the contribution of property encumbered by liabilities
in excess of the grantor's adjusted basis. To minimize
uncertainty, the grantor may be well advised to have
the trust assume the debt at the time of the
contribution, thereby terminating the grantor's
liability and avoiding the possibility of unwanted
grantor trust status.

Among the legal obligations which may be
discharged by distributions of trust income are the
obligations of the grantor (or the grantor's spouse) to
provide support for minor children or other
dependents. In the absence of a statutory exception

to the general rule of § 677(a), a trust might be treated as a grantor trust if the trustee had a discretionary power to use trust income for the support of the grantor's minor child, whether or not the power was exercised. Indeed, this was the outcome of the Supreme Court's decision in Helvering v. Stuart, 317 U.S. 154 (1942). Section 677(b) was added to the Code in 1944 to overrule the *Stuart* decision. It provides that a grantor is not taxable on trust income "merely because such income in the discretion of another person, the trustee, or the grantor acting as trustee or co-trustee, may be applied or distributed for the support or maintenance of a beneficiary (other than the grantor's spouse) whom the grantor is legally obligated to support or maintain, except to the extent that such income is so applied or distributed." Thus, under § 677(b), a grantor remains taxable on the trust's income to the extent that it is in fact used to discharge the grantor's support obligations, but the statute expressly prohibits attribution of ownership based on an unexercised discretionary power.

The § 677(b) safe harbor is subject to several important limitations. It applies only to discretionary powers, not to provisions requiring that trust income be used for the support of the grantor's dependents. Reg. § 1.677(b)–1(f). This makes sense, since a mandatory provision for the support of dependents amounts to a beneficial interest indirectly retained by the grantor and the safe harbor is intended to prevent the grantor from being taxed only on amounts that are not actually used for the grantor's benefit. Moreover, to the extent that a power might be exercised to use trust income for the support of the grantor's spouse, the safe harbor does not apply. Such a power is attributed to the grantor under § 677(a) and is expressly excluded from the safe harbor in § 677(b). The safe harbor relates solely to the satisfaction of the grantor's legal support obligations; a discretionary power that might be exercised to satisfy the grantor's other obligations (e.g., to pay rent or personal expenses) is subject to the general rule of § 677(a). Furthermore, although a discretionary power may be held by the grantor or by any other person, and may generally be held in a fiduciary or nonfiduciary capacity, a power held by the grantor (or the grantor's spouse) qualifies for the safe harbor only if it is held "as trustee," thereby providing some protection against abuse of discretion. Reg. § 1.677(b)–1(e). To illustrate the scope of the safe harbor, consider the following examples:

Example 1: Jack creates an irrevocable trust, with an independent corporate trustee, for his minor daughter Kim. The trustee is required to distribute income and corpus as needed for Kim's support, and has a discretionary power to accumulate the rest of the income or distribute it currently to Kim. Jack will be taxed on the trust income to the extent that it is required to be used for Kim's support; the discharge of Jack's legal support obligation represents a retained beneficial interest under § 677(a). The trustee's discretionary power to accumulate or distribute income not needed for Kim's support falls outside the § 677(b) safe harbor, but because that power cannot be exercised for Jack's benefit it does not cause him to be treated as owning any additional portion of the trust under § 677(a).

Example 2: Jack creates an irrevocable trust, with an independent corporate trustee, to accumulate income for his minor daughter Kim until she reaches age 30 and then to distribute the corpus and accumulated income to her. The trustee has a discretionary power to distribute income and corpus as needed for Kim's support. Jack will be taxed on the trust income under § 677(a) only to the extent that the trustee actually makes distributions that relieve him of his legal obligation to support Kim. To the extent that the trustee withholds distributions, Jack is not relieved of his support obligation and is shielded from deemed ownership under § 677(b).

Example 3: Same facts as Example 2, except that Jack is the sole trustee. The result is the same as in Example 2.

Example 4: Same facts as Example 2, except that the trustee also has a discretionary power to distribute income and corpus as needed for the support of Jack's wife Linda. Jack will be taxed on the trust income under § 677(a) to the extent that the trustee could have exercised its power for Linda's benefit, regardless of whether the power is actually exercised. Section 677(b) does not apply to a power that can be exercised in favor of the grantor's spouse.

Example 5: Jack creates an irrevocable trust, with an independent corporate trustee, to pay income to his minor daughter Kim until she reaches age 30 and then to distribute the corpus to her. Jack, in his individual capacity, retains a nonfiduciary power to direct the trustee to distribute income and corpus as needed for Kim's support. Jack will be taxed on the trust income under § 677(a) to the extent that he could have exercised his power to discharge his support obligation, whether or not he actually does so. His power falls outside the § 677(b) safe harbor because it is not held in a fiduciary capacity.

Example 6: Same facts as Example 5, except that the nonfiduciary power is held by Jack's brother John. Jack will be taxed on the trust income under § 677 only to the extent that John actually exercises the nonfiduciary power to relieve Jack of his legal support obligation; the power comes within the § 677(b) safe harbor.

If amounts distributed from a trust are actually used to discharge the grantor's support obligations, the regulations provide that the amounts so used are deemed to be paid first from ordinary income for the taxable year and then, to the extent that those amounts exceed the available ordinary income, from corpus or accumulated income. Reg. § 1.677(b)–1(c). The grantor is treated under § 677(a) as owning the ordinary income portion of the trust to the extent that the amounts used to discharge the support obligation are deemed paid from ordinary income. To the extent that those amounts are deemed paid from corpus or accumulated income, they are treated as distributions to the grantor and are taxed under the normal conduit rules. I.R.C. § 677(b); Reg. § 1.677(b)–1(b).

The scope of a grantor's legal support obligation is generally determined under applicable local law. According to the regulations, a support obligation is taken into account if the grantor is required to provide support without regard to the dependent's own resources, but not if the grantor is allowed to use the dependent's own resources and therefore becomes liable only as a last resort. Reg. § 1.662(a)–4. A judicial decree (e.g., a final divorce decree) may fix the amount of a particular grantor's obligation, but in the absence of such a decree the standard of support is often so indefinite that it may be difficult to determine whether trust distributions to pay for items such as a child's private school or college tuition, dancing or music lessons, or recreational activities will be taxable to the grantor under § 677 or to the child as a trust beneficiary under the normal conduit rules. Presumably, the grantor can minimize the risk of being treated as an owner under § 677 if the trust instrument expressly prohibits distributions that would discharge the grantor's support obligation or permits distributions only for items in excess of the applicable legal standard, or if the grantor's support obligation is fully satisfied by the creation of the trust itself.

If the grantor and the grantor's spouse are divorced or legally separated, the grantor will be treated under § 677(a) as owning any portion of the trust income which is or may be used to satisfy the grantor's continuing obligation to support the former spouse. As noted above, the same is true of any portion of the trust income which is required to be used to discharge the grantor's child support obligations. Until 2018, § 682 provided a special rule for amounts of trust income which were payable to the grantor's former spouse (and were not designated as child support payments) after divorce or legal separation. Such amounts were expressly excluded from the grantor trust rules and were treated instead as taxable distributions to the former spouse under the normal conduit rules. I.R.C. § 682(a) and (b); Reg. §§ 1.671–1(b) and 1.677(a)–1(a)(1). Section 682 was repealed in 2017, along with the alimony provisions of §§ 71 and 215, but those provisions remain in force for divorce or separation instruments that were executed before 2019. See § 12.2, *infra*.

§ 8.10   POWERS TO CONTROL BENEFICIAL ENJOYMENT

Section 674 addresses discretionary powers to control beneficial enjoyment of trust income and corpus. Unlike §§ 676 and 677, § 674 is not limited to powers that may be exercised primarily for the benefit of the grantor. Indeed, the main focus of § 674 is on powers that give the holder discretion to determine the timing and amount of distributions to other beneficiaries, reflecting the notion that such powers represent a substantial aspect of dominion and control, especially for grantors who have already made ample provision for their own immediate and expected future needs. The general rule of § 674(a) provides that the grantor is treated as the owner of "any portion of a trust in respect of which the beneficial enjoyment of the corpus or the income therefrom is subject to a power of disposition, exercisable by the grantor or a nonadverse party, or both, without the approval or consent of any adverse party." Viewed in isolation, this provision appears broad enough to reach any discretionary power that a trustee or another person might exercise over the beneficial enjoyment of income or corpus without the consent of an adverse party. The broad sweep of § 674(a) is immediately qualified, however, by detailed exceptions set forth in § 674(b) through (d), which function as a virtual road map of permitted powers. The exceptions are divided into three categories: the narrowest powers may be held by any person, including the grantor (§ 674(b)); somewhat broader powers, limited by a reasonably definite external standard, may be held by trustees other than the grantor or the grantor's spouse (§ 674(d)); and powers conferring broad discretion over income or corpus must be held by "independent" trustees (§ 674(c)). Very generally, the statutory categories reflect a sliding scale in which the flexibility of the permitted power varies inversely with the closeness of the relationship between the power holder and the grantor. Since the exceptions are not mutually exclusive, various powers can be given to different holders. The cumulative result is that most powers affecting beneficial enjoyment that are customarily used by estate planners for nontax purposes, other than an open-ended power to add beneficiaries, can be held with impunity either by the grantor or by another person as trustee.

Section 674(b) enumerates eight powers which may be held by any person, including the grantor, without causing the grantor to be treated as the owner of any portion of the trust. The first two provisions mirror safe harbors that already appear in other grantor trust rules, and their function is therefore merely to correlate § 674 with the other rules. One safe harbor involves an unexercised discretionary power to apply trust income for the support of a beneficiary whom the grantor is legally obligated to support. If the power does not cause the grantor to be treated as an owner under § 677 (see § 8.9, *supra*), it is similarly innocuous under § 674. I.R.C. § 674(b)(1). Moreover, if the trust income is in fact used for the beneficiary's support, the grantor will be taxed on the income so used under § 677 and § 674 will have no operative effect.

The second safe harbor refers to "a power, the exercise of which can only affect the beneficial enjoyment of the income for a period commencing after the occurrence of an event such that a grantor would not be treated as the owner under section 673 if the power were a reversionary interest." I.R.C. § 674(b)(2). This provision ensures that the grantor will not be treated as an owner under § 674 on the basis of a power that takes effect only upon some future event if a reversion taking effect at the same time would not cause the grantor to be a deemed owner under § 673. In other words, a postponed power will be disregarded under § 674 if the beneficial interests affected by its exercise are so remote that a comparable reversionary interest would be considered de minimis under § 673.

For example, suppose that Greta creates a trust to pay income to her three minor children for life, and retains a power to invade corpus or accumulate income only if she survives all three children. Had she retained a reversion to take effect in the event she survives all three children, she would avoid being taxed on the ordinary income portion of the trust under § 673 only if the reversion was worth no more than 5% of the underlying property at the inception of the trust (see § 8.7, *supra*). Similarly, her retained power will be ignored under § 674(b)(2) only if the present value of the interests subject to the power is no more than 5% of the value of the underlying property at the inception of the trust. Even supposing that the power comes within the safe harbor, if Greta in fact survives all of her children and she has not previously relinquished her power, the power will take effect at the death of the last child and she will be taxable on the trust income thereafter.

A power that is "exercisable only by will" generally escapes the reach of § 674. I.R.C. § 674(b)(3). However, this safe harbor does not apply to a power held by the grantor (or the grantor's spouse) over trust income if the income is accumulated for such disposition or may be so accumulated in the discretion of the grantor, the grantor's spouse, or a nonadverse party, without the consent of an adverse party. Thus, a grantor may retain a testamentary power over trust corpus, but not a power over income that is or might be accumulated without the consent of an adverse party. In effect, the safe harbor applies only if all of the trust's ordinary income is required to be distributed currently or can be accumulated only with the consent of the income beneficiary (or if the accumulated income is not subject to the power). Furthermore, even if the trust distributes all of its ordinary income currently, the grantor may still be taxed on capital gains and other items attributable to corpus if those items are accumulated or may be accumulated without the consent of an adverse party. Reg. § 1.674(b)–1(b)(3).

For example, suppose that Mike is the grantor of a trust which is required to distribute all of its ordinary income currently to his daughter Nina. Mike retains a testamentary power to appoint income earned after his death to his issue then living. This power comes within the § 674(b)(3) exemption for testamentary powers, and Mike will not be treated as owning any portion of the trust. However, if Mike's testamentary power of appointment applies to trust corpus, he would be treated as the owner of any capital gains realized by the trust to the extent that those gains are allocated to corpus and accumulated for future distribution subject to Mike's retained power. If the trust permitted discretionary accumulations of the trust's ordinary income by any person without Nina's consent, Mike would also be treated as the owner of the ordinary income portion of the trust. Accordingly, the practical significance of the § 674(b)(3) exemption is severely limited.

A power to determine the beneficial enjoyment of trust corpus or income is exempt from § 674 if "the corpus or income is irrevocably payable for a purpose specified in section 170(c)." I.R.C. § 674(b)(4). This exemption allows the grantor or any other person to hold a power to sprinkle income and corpus among several charitable beneficiaries, or to determine the time and manner of distributions to a single charitable beneficiary, without causing any portion of the trust to be treated as a grantor trust.

Among the most useful powers that can be held by a grantor or any other person without adverse income tax consequences is a power to distribute trust corpus to any one or more beneficiaries if "the power is limited by a reasonably definite standard which is set forth in the trust instrument." I.R.C. § 674(b)(5)(A). The power may be exercised in favor of beneficiaries who may become eligible to receive future distributions of income or corpus as well as those who are permitted or entitled to receive current distributions of income. The safe harbor does not apply, however, if any person has a power to add beneficiaries to those designated in the trust instrument (except to provide for after-born or after-adopted children).

According to the regulations, a standard is sufficiently definite if it is "clearly measurable" and the holder is "legally accountable" for its proper exercise. For example, powers to invade corpus for a beneficiary's "education, support, maintenance, or health," for the beneficiary's "reasonable support and comfort," or to enable the beneficiary to maintain an "accustomed standard of living" or meet an "emergency," are all sufficiently definite. In contrast, a power to invade for the beneficiary's "pleasure, desire, or happiness" is not. Reg. § 1.674(b)–1(b)(5). To illustrate, suppose that Martha creates a trust to pay income equally to her two brothers for life, with remainder at each brother's death to his issue then living. Martha can retain a power to invade corpus to pay the medical expenses of her brothers or any of their issue without being treated as the owner of the trust under § 674. However, if Martha can exercise her power to pay the medical expenses of a person who is not otherwise a beneficiary of the trust (e.g., a sister), the power falls outside the safe harbor. Reg. § 1.674(b)–1(b)(5)(iii) (Example 1).

Even if the power to distribute corpus is not limited by a definite standard, it qualifies under an alternative safe harbor if it is exercisable only in favor of a current income beneficiary and the distribution of corpus is "chargeable against the proportionate share of corpus held in trust for the payment of income to the beneficiary as if the corpus constituted a separate trust." I.R.C. § 674(b)(5)(B). For example, suppose that Janet creates a trust to pay all of its current income to her son Ken for life, with remainder at his death to his issue then living. Janet can retain an unrestricted power to invade corpus for Ken during his lifetime without being treated as the owner of the trust under § 674.

Alternatively, suppose that the trust is to pay all of its current income in equal shares to Janet's two children, Ken and Lily, with remainder at the death

of each beneficiary to his or her issue then living.
Janet can retain an unrestricted power to invade up
to half of the corpus for each of the two children, as
long as any invasion will cause a proportionate
reduction of the recipient's share of future income
distributions. Reg. § 1.674(b)–1(b)(5)(iii) (Example
3). For example, if Janet exercised her power to
distribute half of the corpus to Ken, all of the income
from the remaining half of the corpus must be
distributed to Lily. If Janet can exercise her power to
distribute corpus in favor of either income beneficiary
without a proportionate reduction in future
distributions, she will be treated as the owner of the
trust unless the power is subject to a reasonably
definite standard.

The provision for powers to invade corpus is
complemented by a separate safe harbor for a power
to withhold income temporarily from a current
income beneficiary. The grantor or any other person
may hold a power "to distribute or apply income to or
for any current income beneficiary or to accumulate
the income," as long as the accumulated income is
ultimately payable to the beneficiary from whom it
was withheld, to the beneficiary's estate, to the
beneficiary's appointees, or to alternate takers in
default of appointment. I.R.C. § 674(b)(6)(A). If the
accumulated income is not payable directly to the
beneficiary (e.g., because the distribution occurs after
the beneficiary's death), the statute requires that the
accumulated income be subject to disposition by the
beneficiary, either through the beneficiary's estate or
by exercise of a power of appointment which does not
exclude as possible appointees any person other than

the beneficiary's estate (or creditors of the beneficiary or of the estate).

For example, suppose that Cecily creates a trust to pay income to her son Dan until he reaches age 30 or until his earlier death; the corpus will be distributed to Dan at age 30, or upon his earlier death to his estate. Cecily can retain a power to accumulate the income and add it to the corpus which will be distributed to Dan or his estate without causing her to be treated as owning any part of the trust. The result is the same if, upon Dan's death before reaching age 30, the remainder is payable not to Dan's estate but instead as he may appoint by will, as long as the permissible appointees do not exclude any person other than his estate, or creditors of himself or of his estate. (This limitation on Dan's power of appointment does not represent a significant constraint on his power of disposition, but it will prevent the remainder from being includible in his gross estate for estate tax purposes.)

The accumulated income need not be distributed to the beneficiary from whom it was withheld if it is distributable instead, on termination of the trust or in conjunction with a distribution of corpus, to "the current income beneficiaries in shares which have been irrevocably specified in the trust instrument." I.R.C. § 674(b)(6)(B). In the preceding example, suppose that Cecily's trust provides for all of its income to be paid currently in equal shares to her two sons, Dan and Evan, until the younger son reaches age 30 and then for the corpus and any accumulated income to be distributed in equal shares to the sons or their estates. Cecily can retain a power to withhold income from either or both of her sons, as long as the accumulated income will ultimately be distributed along with corpus to both sons in prescribed shares. Reg. § 1.674(b)–1(b)(6)(ii) (Example 1). Note that this safe harbor allows the grantor to shift part of the accumulated income from one income beneficiary to the other.

Furthermore, the trust instrument may provide that, in the event the beneficiary does not survive a distribution date which could reasonably be expected to occur within the beneficiary's lifetime, the beneficiary's share of accumulated income shall be paid to the beneficiary's appointees under "any power of appointment, general or special," or if the beneficiary has no power of appointment to "one or more designated alternate takers (other than the grantor or the grantor's estate) whose shares have been irrevocably specified in the trust instrument." Reg. § 1.674(b)–1(b)(6).

For example, suppose that Simon creates a trust to pay income to his daughter Tricia until Simon's death, subject to a retained power to accumulate income; at Simon's death, the corpus and any accumulated income will be distributed to Tricia, or if she is not living to the appointees named in her will, or in default of appointment to her surviving issue. Simon's retained accumulation power falls within the safe harbor because Tricia can reasonably be expected to survive her father. Reg. § 1.674(b)–1(b)(6)(ii) (Example 3). The safe harbor does not apply, however, if any person has a power to add beneficiaries to those designated in the trust instrument (except to provide for after-born or after-adopted children).

A grantor or any other person may exercise a discretionary power to withhold the trust's ordinary income from an income beneficiary, accumulate it, and add it to corpus while the beneficiary is under a legal disability or before the beneficiary reaches age 21. I.R.C. § 674(b)(7). Unlike § 674(b)(6), this provision does not require that the accumulated income ultimately be distributed to the income beneficiary from whom it was withheld or be subject to the beneficiary's control. For example, Penny, the grantor of a trust to pay income to her son Robert for life with remainder at Robert's death to his issue then living, may retain a power to accumulate all or part of the trust's ordinary income while Robert is under age 21 and add it to corpus, without being treated as the owner of the trust under § 674. Reg. § 1.674(b)–1(b)(7). The safe harbor does not apply if any person has a power to add beneficiaries to those designated in the trust instrument (except to provide for after-born or after-adopted children).

The last enumerated power that may be retained by the grantor or any other person is a power "to allocate receipts and disbursements between corpus and income, even though expressed in broad language." I.R.C. § 674(b)(8). Such a power will not cause the grantor to be treated as owning any portion of the trust, even though an exercise of the power clearly may have a substantial impact on the rights of different beneficiaries. For example, a grantor may be authorized under the trust instrument and local law to allocate all or part of a trust's realized capital gains to ordinary income in order to make up for a lack of current income in previous years due to underproductive investments. Similarly, the grantor may have discretion to allocate trustee's fees and other administrative expenses between corpus and income. The legislative history suggests that this provision was intended to accommodate powers held by a trustee for the purpose of conforming to appropriate fiduciary accounting principles, but the statute is not so limited and the regulations indicate that it is "immaterial" whether the power of allocation is held in a fiduciary capacity. Reg. § 1.674(b)–1(a).

The statute provides a somewhat more flexible safe harbor for a power "to distribute, apportion, or accumulate income to or for a beneficiary or beneficiaries, or to, for, or within a class of beneficiaries," if the power is "limited by a reasonably definite external standard which is set forth in the trust instrument." This safe harbor applies, however, only if the power is "solely exercisable (without the approval or consent of any other person) by a trustee or trustees, none of whom is the grantor or spouse living with the grantor." I.R.C. § 674(d).

The § 674(d) power to distribute or accumulate income is similar to the power over income permitted under § 674(b)(6), with two key differences. First, the scope of the power is considerably broader. Under § 674(d), the income may be distributed to or accumulated for any one or more beneficiaries. If the income is distributed currently, it may be sprinkled among current and future beneficiaries; if the income is accumulated, there is no requirement that it be held for the beneficiary from whom it was withheld or be subject to disposition by that beneficiary. Thus, the power may be exercised not merely to postpone a particular beneficiary's enjoyment or disposition of income but to shift the income among different beneficiaries, subject only to the requirement of a "reasonably definite external standard." As in the case of a "reasonably definite standard" under § 674(b)(5), the statutory requirement is satisfied by a standard expressed in terms of a beneficiary's education, support, health, accustomed standard of living, or emergency needs; the variation in the statutory language is not significant.

The second major point of contrast with § 674(b)(6) concerns the holder of the power over trust income. The § 674(d) safe harbor applies only if the power is exercisable solely by one or more trustees, and neither the grantor nor the grantor's spouse may be among the trustees. Thus, in exercising the power, the trustees are constrained not only by a reasonably definite external standard but also by basic fiduciary duties of fairness and good faith. Furthermore, since the power must be exercisable solely by the trustees, without the consent of any other person, neither the grantor nor any other person may have a veto power. As a practical matter, the statute allows the grantor considerable freedom to choose trustees who are likely to be responsive to the grantor's wishes. The § 674(d) safe harbor does not apply if any person has a power to add beneficiaries to those designated in the trust instrument (except to provide for after-born or after-adopted children).

The most flexible safe harbor applies to two powers which are exercisable solely by one or more "independent" trustees, without the approval or consent of any other person. For this purpose, trustees are independent only if none of them is the grantor (or the grantor's spouse) and no more than half of them are "related or subordinate parties who are subservient to the wishes of the grantor." If these requirements are met, the independent trustees may hold the following powers: (1) "to distribute, apportion, or accumulate income to or for a beneficiary or beneficiaries, or to, for, or within a class of beneficiaries"; and (2) "to pay out corpus to or for a beneficiary or beneficiaries or to or for a class of beneficiaries (whether or not income beneficiaries)." I.R.C. § 674(c). The first power resembles the power to distribute or accumulate income permitted under § 674(d), except that the trustees' discretion need not be constrained by any standard. The second power to invade corpus is similarly unconstrained. In effect, § 674(c) allows independent trustees to exercise virtually unlimited discretionary powers over trust income and corpus, except that the safe harbor does not apply if any person has a power to add beneficiaries to those designated in the trust instrument (except to provide for after-born or after-adopted children).

The only significant restrictions under § 674(c) arise from the requirements that neither the grantor nor the grantor's spouse may be a trustee, that no more than half of the trustees may be "related or subordinate parties" who are subservient to the grantor, and that the powers must be exercisable solely by the trustees without the consent of the grantor or any other person. Thus, in addition to the grantor (and the grantor's spouse), who are categorically excluded from the group of permissible trustees, the grantor's parents, issue, and siblings, as well as various employees and corporations affiliated with the grantor, as enumerated in § 672(c) (see § 8.6, *supra*), are prohibited (unless they are adverse parties or not subservient to the grantor) from constituting a majority of the trustees. This constraint is not especially onerous. For example, a child of the grantor and an independent corporate fiduciary may exercise broad discretionary powers as co-trustees without causing the grantor to be treated as a deemed owner under § 674(c). Nevertheless, to ensure compliance with § 674(c), the trust instrument should expressly prohibit the grantor and the grantor's spouse from being appointed as trustees, and should also require that no more than half of the trustees may be related or subordinate parties.

In theory, the question of whether related or subordinate parties are "subservient" to the grantor's wishes depends on the facts and circumstances of each case, but in practice it may be difficult to rebut the statutory presumption of subservience. In any event, the range of permissible trustees is normally wide enough to allow the grantor to select persons who can be counted on to comply with the grantor's wishes.

In one case, a grantor appointed two lawyers as trustees of an irrevocable discretionary trust that he had created for his three sons. Although the grantor retained no powers or interests, the nominally "independent" trustees in fact entrusted the administration of the trust to the sole discretion of the grantor, who "kept all the records, made all of the investments and decided the amount to be distributed to the beneficiaries. The trustees merely acquiesced in these actions." Nevertheless, the Tax Court refused to treat the grantor as the owner of the trust's income under § 674, observing that the trustees were technically independent and their powers complied with the § 674(c) safe harbor. Estate of Goodwyn v. Commissioner, 35 T.C.M. (CCH) 1026 (1976). Taking the trust instrument at face value, the court assumed that the trustees could have exercised control over the trust had they chosen to do so. In effect, the court presumed that the grantor acted as the agent of the trustees rather than the other way around. Another court might take a different view when confronted with similar facts, however, and a prudent trustee should be careful to avoid any appearance of acting as a de facto agent of the grantor.

As already noted, the safe harbors for trustee powers under § 674(c) and (d) exclude the grantor (or the grantor's spouse) as a permissible trustee. This restriction would be of little consequence, however, if the grantor (or the grantor's spouse) held an unrestricted power to remove and replace the trustees. Even without exercising the power, a grantor could exert substantial influence over the acting trustees, who could hardly ignore the implied threat of removal and replacement if they failed to carry out the grantor's wishes. Accordingly, the regulations provide that a power in the grantor (or the grantor's spouse) to "remove, substitute, or add trustees (other than a power exercisable only upon limited conditions which do not exist during the taxable year, such as the death or resignation of, or breach of fiduciary duty by, an existing trustee)" may disqualify powers that would otherwise be permissible under § 674(c) and (d). Reg. § 1.674(d)–2(a). Specifically, if the grantor has an unrestricted power to remove an independent trustee and substitute any person (including the grantor or the grantor's spouse) as trustee, the safe harbors of § 674(c) and (d) are inapplicable. However, if the power to remove, substitute, or add trustees is limited so that it cannot be exercised to designate an impermissible trustee, the power is unobjectionable. Thus, for example, a grantor may retain a power to remove an independent trustee as long as the vacancy must be filled with another independent trustee.

As noted above, the safe harbors of § 674(b)(5), (b)(6), (b)(7), (c), and (d) do not apply if any person holds a power to add beneficiaries to those designated in the trust instrument (other than to provide for after-born or after-adopted children). This restriction prevents such a power from being exercised to expand a permitted power beyond its scope under the original terms of the trust. Nevertheless, the prohibition does not prevent a trust beneficiary from designating a successor owner of his or her interest by will or assigning the interest during life (if the assignment is not prohibited by a spendthrift clause). Reg. § 1.674(d)–2(b).

§ 8.11   ADMINISTRATIVE POWERS

Section 675 describes several administrative powers which may cause the grantor to be treated as owning all or part of a trust even though they do not directly affect the timing or amount of distributions or the interests of the beneficiaries. Instead, the enumerated administrative powers generally reflect the possibility that under the terms of the trust or the circumstances of its operation, administrative control may be exercisable "primarily for the benefit of the grantor rather than the beneficiaries of the trust." Reg. § 1.675–1(a). Of particular concern are powers that might allow borrowing or other transactions on terms that are imprudent, unfair, or not subject to customary fiduciary protections. Standard fiduciary powers and duties generally should not give rise to grantor trust status under § 675, but if the trust instrument includes unusual provisions expanding a trustee's powers, limiting its duties, exonerating the trustee from liability, or granting powers to other persons, those provisions should be tailored to avoid unwanted tax consequences.

The grantor is treated as the owner of a portion of a trust if the grantor (or the grantor's spouse) or any nonadverse party holds a power which can be exercised, without the consent of an adverse party, to enable the grantor or any other person to "purchase, exchange, or otherwise deal with or dispose of the corpus or the income therefrom for less than an adequate consideration in money or money's worth." I.R.C. § 675(1). This is essentially a mild constraint on transactions involving conflicting interests. For example, if the terms of a trust expressly authorize the trustee, with the approval of a nonadverse party, to sell trust property to the grantor at a price below fair market value, or to purchase property for the trust from the grantor for more than fair market value, the grantor will be treated as the owner of the trust.

Section 675 includes two separate provisions concerning loans of trust funds to the grantor. The first provision treats the grantor as owning a portion of the trust if the grantor (or the grantor's spouse) or any nonadverse party holds a power which can be exercised to enable the grantor "to borrow the corpus or income, directly or indirectly, without adequate interest or without adequate security except where a trustee (other than the grantor) is authorized under a general lending power to make loans to any person without regard to interest or security." I.R.C. § 675(2). This rule initially appears to require adequate interest and security for any loan to the borrower, but the general rule is swallowed up by the safe harbor for general lending powers. For example, suppose that the trust instrument expressly authorizes the trustee (a nonadverse party) to make an unsecured, interest-free loan from trust corpus or income to the grantor. Under § 675(2), the grantor will be treated as owning the entire trust. However, this result can be avoided if the trustee's power is framed as a "general lending power" to make an unsecured, interest-free loan to any person, including the grantor. The only restriction is that the general lending power must be held by a trustee other than the grantor or the grantor's spouse. Moreover, the regulations state that a general lending power held by the grantor as sole trustee, under which the grantor has discretion to determine interest rates and the adequacy of security "is not in itself an indication that the grantor has power to borrow the corpus or income without adequate interest or security." Reg. § 1.675–1(b)(2). To avoid any uncertainty, however, the trust instrument should expressly require adequate interest and security for any loans made by the grantor (or the grantor's spouse) to the grantor pursuant to such a general lending power.

The second provision concerning loans of trust funds applies if "[t]he grantor has directly or indirectly borrowed the corpus or income and has not completely repaid the loan, including any interest, before the beginning of the taxable year." This rule does not apply, however, to "a loan which provides for adequate interest and adequate security" if the loan is made by "a trustee other than the grantor and other than a related or subordinate trustee subservient to the grantor." I.R.C. § 675(3). Unlike the other provisions concerning administrative powers, § 675(3) is triggered by the actual loan of funds to the grantor or the grantor's spouse.

The Service takes the position that the grantor may be treated as owning the trust under § 675(3) even if the funds are borrowed and repaid within the same taxable year. For example, suppose that Jerome creates an irrevocable trust for his children and names himself as sole trustee. The trust instrument authorizes the trustee to make loans of trust funds at a market rate of interest and with adequate security. In compliance with these requirements, Jerome borrows the entire corpus of the trust on March 1 and repays the loan in full, with interest, on August 31. Under the Service's reading of § 675(3), Jerome is taxable on all of the trust's income for the taxable year. Rev. Rul. 86–82, 1986–1 C.B. 253. In contrast, if Jerome appointed his lawyer (a nonadverse party who is not a "related or subordinate party" within the meaning of § 672(c)) as trustee and the lawyer lent the trust funds on the same terms to Jerome, § 675(3) would not apply.

Neither the statute nor the regulations prescribe a method for determining the portion of the trust's income which is attributable to a grantor under § 675(3) by reason of a loan from the trust. The case law is suggestive but inconclusive. Several possible formulas might be appropriate in a particular case, depending on the amount borrowed, the duration of the loan, and whether the loan is deemed to have been made from ordinary income, from corpus, or from a combination thereof.

Trust income may also be attributed to the grantor if certain administrative powers are held "in a nonfiduciary capacity by any person without the approval or consent of any person in a fiduciary capacity." The proscribed powers consist of (1) "a power to vote or direct the voting of stock or other securities of a corporation in which the holdings of the grantor and the trust are significant from the viewpoint of voting control"; (2) "a power to control the investment of the trust funds either by directing investments or reinvestments, or by vetoing proposed investments or reinvestments, to the extent that the trust funds consist of stocks or securities of corporations in which the holdings of the grantor and the trust are significant from the viewpoint of voting control"; and (3) "a power to reacquire the trust corpus by substituting other property of an equivalent value." I.R.C. § 675(4). Whether the holdings of the grantor and the trust in a corporation are "significant from the viewpoint of voting control" raises the same factual question that arises in identifying related or subordinate parties under § 672(c) (see § 8.6, *supra*).

Any one or more of the powers enumerated in § 675(4), if exercisable by any person in a nonfiduciary capacity without the consent of a person in a fiduciary capacity, may cause the grantor to be a deemed owner. In determining whether a power is exercisable in a fiduciary or nonfiduciary capacity, the regulations presume that a power is exercisable in a fiduciary capacity if it is held by a trustee, but in any other case the determination depends on "all the terms of the trust and the circumstances surrounding its creation and administration." Reg. § 1.675–1(b)(4). Thus, a grantor normally can avoid deemed ownership under § 675(4) if the trust instrument provides that the enumerated powers may be exercised only by the trustee in a fiduciary capacity (i.e., acting in good faith for the benefit of the beneficiaries). Even in such a case, however, the presumption may be rebutted by evidence of a contrary intent. For example, the trustee's fiduciary duties may be illusory if the trust instrument contains an extraordinarily broad exculpatory provision or if the trustee in fact acts as the grantor's agent.

A grantor's retained power to substitute property of equal value, exercisable in a nonfiduciary capacity, is especially useful as a technique for triggering grantor trust status if the grantor wishes to be treated as the owner of the entire trust for income tax purposes but not for estate tax purposes. The Service has ruled that such a power will not cause the trust property to be included in the grantor's gross estate for estate tax purposes, as long as the trustee has a fiduciary duty to ensure that the substituted property is in fact of equal value and as long as the power cannot be used to shift benefits among the trust beneficiaries. Rev. Rul. 2008–22, 2008–1 C.B. 796 (no inclusion under §§ 2036 and 2038); Rev. Rul. 2011–28, 2011–49 I.R.B. 830 (no inclusion under § 2042).

§ 8.12 OWNER OTHER THAN GRANTOR

Section 678 is unique among the grantor trust rules in treating a person other than the grantor as the owner of all or part of a trust. Under the general rule of § 678(a)(1), a "person other than the grantor" is deemed to own any portion of a trust with respect to which "such person has a power exercisable solely by himself to vest the corpus or the income therefrom in himself." Thus, for example, a trust beneficiary who holds an unrestricted power to withdraw income or corpus may be a deemed owner for income tax purposes, even though the beneficiary neither created the trust nor transferred property to it.

Section 678 reflects the holding of Mallinckrodt v. Nunan, 146 F.2d 1 (8th Cir.), cert. denied, 324 U.S. 871 (1945), which involved an irrevocable trust from which the grantor's son was entitled to receive current income on request. The Eighth Circuit held that the son was taxable on the undistributed income based on his unrestricted power of withdrawal, observing that "it is the possession of power over the disposition of trust income which is of significance in determining whether, under [the predecessor of § 61], the income is taxable to the possessor of such power," and "logically it makes no difference whether the possessor is a grantor who retained the power or a beneficiary who acquired it from another." The *Mallinckrodt* holding was initially reflected in the *Clifford* regulations and was subsequently codified in 1954 by the enactment of § 678.

The general rule of § 678(a)(1) applies only to a power exercisable "solely" by the holder to withdraw income or corpus from the trust. It does not apply if the power is exercisable only with the consent of another person. In this respect, the reach of § 678 is quite limited compared to the other grantor trust provisions, presumably because the holder of a § 678 power (who by definition is someone other than the grantor) does not necessarily have the ability to select a compliant third party from whom consent can readily be obtained.

For example, suppose that Rowan, the income beneficiary of a testamentary trust of which his sister Sally is trustee, has a power, exercisable with Sally's consent, to withdraw $10,000 from the trust corpus. Since Rowan cannot exercise the power alone without Sally's consent, he is not a deemed owner under § 678. The result is the same if Rowan and Sally are co-trustees and the power is exercisable by both trustees acting jointly. Rev. Rul. 67–268, 1967–2 C.B. 226. Moreover, if Rowan has an unrestricted power to invade the trust corpus for his wife Tina, neither Rowan nor Tina is treated as an owner under § 678. Rowan is the sole holder of the power, but he cannot exercise it in favor of himself; Tina is not the holder of the power, although it is exercisable for her sole benefit. The result is not affected by the spousal attribution rule of § 672(e), which has no application to the spouse of any person other than the grantor.

If the holder of a § 678 power is incapable of exercising it, by reason of minority or other legal disability, the holder is still generally treated as a deemed owner. The requirement that the power be exercisable solely by the holder for his or her own benefit is satisfied as long as there is no impediment under the trust instrument or local law to the appointment of a legal guardian who can exercise the power on behalf of the holder, regardless of whether a guardian has actually been appointed.

For example, a minor beneficiary is frequently given a power to withdraw corpus from a trust in connection with a contribution of property by the grantor, in order to qualify the grantor's contribution for the gift tax annual exclusion. Assuming that there is no barrier to the appointment of a guardian, the minor beneficiary is treated under § 678(a)(1) as the owner of the portion of the trust that is subject to the power of withdrawal. Rev. Rul. 81–6, 1981–1 C.B. 385. The same rationale supports the conclusion that the minor beneficiary receives a "present interest" in the property contributed by the grantor for purposes of the gift tax annual exclusion, even though no guardian is appointed and the power remains unexercised. Rev. Rul. 73–405, 1973–2 C.B. 321. To ensure the desired gift tax treatment, however, it is advisable to provide notice to the holder of a power of withdrawal as well as a reasonable opportunity to exercise it. Rev. Rul. 81–7, 1981–1 C.B. 474.

The holder of a § 678 power may be treated as owning all or a portion of the trust, depending on whether the power relates to trust corpus or income. For example, suppose that Norma has an unrestricted power to require that all of the current income of a testamentary trust created by her deceased husband be distributed to her currently during her lifetime, and any income not distributed to her will be accumulated and added to corpus to be paid at her death to the remainder beneficiaries. (This power may be useful in qualifying the trust for the estate tax marital deduction. See Reg. § 20.2056(b)–5(f)(8).) Norma will be treated under § 678(a)(1) as owning the ordinary income portion of the trust, regardless of whether the income is actually distributed to her or accumulated. Reg. § 1.671–3(b)(1) and (c).

In the preceding example, if Norma also has an unrestricted, presently exercisable power to withdraw the entire corpus of the trust, she will be treated as owning the entire trust, including items attributable to corpus as well as ordinary income. Reg. § 1.671–3(a)(1) and (b)(3). Alternatively, if Norma has a noncumulative annual power to withdraw the greater of $5,000 or 5% of the value of the trust corpus, she will generally be treated as owning a fractional portion of the entire trust based on the ratio of the amount subject to her power of withdrawal and the value of the trust property at the beginning of the taxable year. Reg. § 1.671–3(a)(3). Such a "5-or-5 power" is often used to allow a surviving spouse limited access to trust corpus. If the power is exercisable annually on a noncumulative basis, it will lapse each year to the extent that it is not exercised. Lapses occurring during the holder's lifetime are disregarded for gift and estate tax purposes, but the power itself causes the holder to be a deemed owner under § 678(a)(1) for income tax purposes. Rev. Rul. 67–241, 1967–2 C.B. 225; see also I.R.C. §§ 2514(e) (gift tax) and 2041(b)(2) (estate tax). Failure to exercise the power in successive years may lead to complications in measuring the portion of the trust owned by the power holder under § 678(a)(2), discussed below.

It seems clear that § 678 applies only to powers which are presently exercisable. If a power is subject to a condition that has not yet occurred, the holder is not treated as a deemed owner under § 678. For example, suppose that Julia, the income beneficiary of a testamentary trust, is entitled to withdraw the trust property at age 30. Upon reaching age 30, Julia will be treated as owning the entire trust under § 678, but until the age contingency is met she is treated as an income beneficiary under the normal conduit rules.

Section 678 clearly applies to a beneficiary's unfettered power to withdraw income or corpus from a trust. Its application is less clear if the power is constrained by an ascertainable standard or by fiduciary duties to other beneficiaries. The legislative history indicates that § 678 is aimed at an "unrestricted power" to withdraw income or corpus, and there is some support in the case law for confining § 678 to powers that are substantially unfettered. Thus, one court held that a life tenant's power to consume property for her own "needs, maintenance and comfort" fell outside the reach of § 678, and another court reached a similar result under pre-1954 law in a case involving a trustee's discretionary power to invade corpus for her own "needs." United States v. DeBonchamps, 278 F.2d 127 (9th Cir. 1960); Funk v. Commissioner, 185 F.2d 127 (3d Cir. 1950); but cf. Koffman v. United States, 300 F.2d 176 (6th Cir. 1962) (life tenant's unfettered power of invasion). Even if § 678 does not apply, a power holder who actually withdraws income or corpus will be taxed on a corresponding portion of the trust's income under the normal conduit rules. Accordingly, the practical significance of § 678 is greatest when the power remains unexercised.

In the event of a conflict between § 678 and the other grantor trust rules, the trust is treated as owned by the grantor, not by the holder of a § 678 power. This ordering rule appears in § 678(b), which makes § 678(a) inapplicable if the grantor is treated as the owner of the trust under §§ 671–677. (The same ordering rule also applies to a U.S. transferor's deemed ownership of a foreign trust under § 679.) Taken literally, the ordering rule of § 678(b) refers only to a power over "income," but the legislative history indicates that it is intended to apply equally to a power over corpus. This broad reading is consistent with the scope of § 678(a) and seems sensible as a matter of statutory interpretation. For example, suppose that Rachel creates a revocable trust to pay income to her son Stanley for life with remainder at his death to his issue then living; the trust instrument gives Stanley an unrestricted power to withdraw the trust corpus upon reaching age 30. As long as Rachel is alive and retains her power of revocation, she will be treated as owning the entire trust under § 676, and Stanley will not be a deemed owner. However, if Rachel's power of revocation lapses at her death and Stanley has reached age 30, he will thereafter be treated as the owner of the entire trust under § 678.

Although § 678(a) refers to a power to vest trust corpus or income in the holder, the statute is interpreted to reach any power exercisable solely by the holder "to apply the income or corpus for the satisfaction of his legal obligations." Reg. § 1.678(a)–1(b). This interpretation is consistent with the treatment under § 677(a) of a discretionary power to apply corpus or income to discharge a grantor's legal obligations. The rationale is that a discretionary power to pay the holder's obligations represents an indirect benefit to the holder and should be taxed accordingly. Note that § 678(a) applies only to a discretionary power exercisable by the holder for his or her own benefit. If trust income or corpus is required to be used to discharge the beneficiary's obligations, or may be so used in the discretion of another person (other than the grantor), the beneficiary is taxable on amounts so used under the normal conduit rules. Reg. §§ 1.678(a)–1(b) and 1.678(c)–1(c).

An important qualification to the general rule of deemed ownership appears in § 678(c), which makes § 678(a) inapplicable to a power which enables the holder "in the capacity of trustee or co-trustee, merely to apply the income of the trust to the support or maintenance of a person whom the holder of the power is obligated to support or maintain except to the extent that such income is so applied." This safe harbor resembles the parallel provision in § 677(b), and it involves the same considerations relating to the determination of support obligations under applicable local law (see § 8.9, *supra*). Thus, if the holder of a § 678 power is authorized to use trust income to discharge his or her obligation to support another person, the mere existence of the unexercised power will not cause the holder to be treated as owning any portion of the trust, but the holder will be taxable on any amount actually used to discharge the support obligation. Amounts so used are deemed to be paid first from any available ordinary income and then from corpus. Amounts deemed paid from ordinary income are taxed directly to the power holder under § 678(a), while amounts deemed paid from corpus or accumulated income are treated as distributions to the power holder and are taxed under the normal conduit rules. Reg. §§ 1.678(c)–1(a) and 1.677(b)–1.

Note that the § 678(c) safe harbor applies only to a power exercisable by the holder as a trustee. Reg. § 1.678(c)–1(b). This requirement provides some protection against arbitrary or excessive exercise of the power by invoking basic fiduciary standards of loyalty, prudence, fairness, and good faith. For example, suppose that Zack, the sole trustee of a testamentary trust, holds a discretionary power to use the trust's ordinary income or corpus for the support of his minor children. If Zack exercises his fiduciary power, he will be treated as owning the trust only to the extent of the amount actually used to discharge his support obligation. However, if Zack is not a trustee, so that he holds the power in a nonfiduciary capacity, he will be a deemed owner under § 678(a) of any portion of the trust that could have been used to discharge his support obligation, regardless of whether he actually exercises the power. Similarly, if Zack holds a power to benefit himself by paying his legal obligations other than the support of his dependents, he will be a deemed owner under § 678(a) regardless of whether he holds the power in a fiduciary or nonfiduciary capacity. However, if Zack can exercise the power only with the consent of another person, the power falls outside

§ 678(a), and Zack will be taxed, if at all, only as a beneficiary under the normal conduit rules.

The holder of a § 678 power is normally treated as the owner of a portion of the trust from the time the power becomes exercisable until it is exercised or released. If the holder exercises the power for his or her own benefit, of course, the holder becomes the actual owner (rather than the deemed owner) of the property withdrawn from the trust. Conversely, if the power is exercised in favor of another person or completely released, § 678 will cease to apply and the holder will no longer be treated as owning any portion of the trust (unless the holder retains a residual power or interest that gives rise to continuing deemed ownership under § 678(a)(2), discussed below). If the holder does not intend to exercise the power and wishes to disclaim it, either to avoid deemed ownership or for other reasons, the holder may be able to escape being treated as a power holder under § 678 from the time the power came into existence. Section 678(a) is expressly inapplicable to any power which is "renounced or disclaimed within a reasonable time after the holder of the power first became aware of its existence." I.R.C. § 678(d). This provision is reminiscent of the gift tax regulations concerning disclaimers of interests created before 1977. See Reg. § 25.2511–1(c)(2). Although § 2518 now provides detailed rules concerning disclaimers, those rules apply only for gift, estate, and generation-skipping transfer tax purposes and not for income tax purposes. As a practical matter, however, a disclaimer that satisfies the requirements of § 2518 is likely to be effective under § 678(d) as well. A valid disclaimer of a § 678 power should be effective to prevent the disclaimant from being treated as a deemed owner of any portion of the trust from its inception under § 678(a).

The holder of a § 678 power may continue to be treated as a deemed owner, even after releasing the power, if the holder retains an interest or power of a type that would give rise to grantor trust treatment in the hands of a grantor. In the words of the statute, the power holder is treated as an owner to the extent that "such person has previously partially released or otherwise modified such a power and after the release or modification retains such control as would, within the principles of sections 671 to 677, inclusive, subject a grantor of a trust to treatment as the owner thereof." I.R.C. § 678(a)(2). In effect, once a § 678 power becomes exercisable, the holder is treated not only as an owner but also as a grantor for purposes of determining the income tax consequences of a subsequent modification or release of the power. This provision is intended to prevent the power holder from escaping the consequences of deemed ownership under § 678 by relinquishing or cutting back a taxable power while retaining interests or powers described in §§ 673–677. In short, if the power holder wishes to terminate deemed ownership under § 678, he or she must give up residual control to the same extent as a grantor who wishes to avoid deemed ownership under the other grantor trust rules.

For example, suppose that Hubert is the life income beneficiary of a testamentary trust. He also holds a nongeneral testamentary power to appoint the remainder among his issue who are living at his death, as well as an unrestricted power to withdraw the entire corpus at any time during his life. Hubert will initially be treated as the owner of the entire trust under § 678(a)(1). If he subsequently releases his power of withdrawal but retains his life income interest and his testamentary power of appointment, he will continue to be treated under § 678(a)(2) as the owner of the entire trust, just as a grantor who retained a life income interest and a testamentary power over corpus would be. (A grantor would be treated as owning the ordinary income portion of the trust under § 677(a) because of the retained life income interest, as well as the corpus portion under § 674(a) because of the testamentary power of appointment; the safe harbor of § 674(b)(3) for testamentary powers would not apply to the extent that the corpus portion included items accumulated during the grantor's lifetime. See § 8.10, *supra*.) Alternatively, if Hubert released both his lifetime power of withdrawal and his testamentary power of appointment, retaining only the life income interest, he would be taxable only on the ordinary income portion of the trust. Only if he relinquished the life income interest as well as both powers would he completely terminate his status as a deemed owner under § 678. Note that if Hubert never had a lifetime power to withdraw trust corpus but held only a life income interest and a testamentary power of appointment, he would not be treated as owning any portion of the trust under § 678, although he would be taxed on the current income as a beneficiary under the normal conduit rules. The result would be the same if he made a timely disclaimer of his lifetime power of withdrawal, since the effect of the disclaimer would be to treat the power as if it never came into existence.

Suppose that Esther, the income beneficiary of a testamentary trust worth $1 million, holds a noncumulative annual power to withdraw the greater of $5,000 or 5% of the value of the trust corpus. If she allows the power to remain unexercised, it lapses at the end of the taxable year and she becomes entitled to withdraw another $5,000 or 5% of the trust corpus in the following taxable year. In the first year, Esther is treated as owning 5% of the entire trust under § 678(a)(1). (She is also taxable on the ordinary income distributed to her under the normal conduit rules.) Thereafter, the computation of her deemed ownership under § 678 becomes more complicated. Neither the statute, the regulations, nor the Service's published revenue rulings provide much guidance for measuring the portion of the trust owned by Esther. In private letter rulings, however, the Service has consistently taken the position that the annual lapse of a 5-or-5 power constitutes a partial release, and that the percentage of the trust owned by the power holder increases each year by 5% of the portion of the trust not already owned. In the preceding example, if Esther's power remains unexercised, her ownership percentage under the Service's method would increase from 5% in the first year to 9.75% in the second year [5% + (5% × 95%)], to 14.26% in the third year [9.75% + (5% × 90.25%)], and so on. Although Esther's ownership percentage increases each year, it does so at a diminishing rate and would never reach 100%. An argument can be made that the annual lapse of the power is technically distinguishable from a "partial release" and that § 678(a)(2) therefore should not apply, but there is no support for such an approach in the regulations, rulings, or case law.

CHAPTER 9
CHARITABLE TRUSTS

§ 9.1 OVERVIEW

Charitable trusts come in many different forms. Some trusts serve purely charitable purposes and have no private beneficiaries; others provide mixed benefits for both charitable and private beneficiaries. Broadly speaking, a charitable trust may be classified for tax purposes as exempt or as nonexempt. An exempt trust, as its name implies, is generally exempt from income tax and is not subject to the rules of Subchapter J. In contrast, a nonexempt trust is generally subject to tax under Subchapter J, and the trust's income, net of the § 642(c) deduction for charitable payments, is taxable either to the beneficiaries (to the extent of taxable distributions under the conduit rules) or to the trust itself (to the extent of residual accumulations). See Chapters 5–7, *supra*. In determining the structure of a charitable trust and the time and manner of its funding, a grantor should consider not only whether the trust itself will be tax-exempt but also whether a deduction will be allowed for amounts contributed to the trust. In general, the grantor is entitled to an income tax deduction, subject to numerous limitations and restrictions, for charitable contributions of cash or other property. Charitable gifts and bequests, if made in qualifying form, are also deductible for gift and estate tax purposes.

Exempt charitable trusts. A trust may be eligible for tax-exempt status under § 501(c)(3) if it is organized and operated exclusively for charitable purposes; the trust must not engage in substantial lobbying or participate in political campaigns, and no part of its net earnings may inure to any private beneficiary. I.R.C. § 501(a) and (c)(3). In addition, the trust must notify the Service of its application for recognition of its § 501(c)(3) tax-exempt status. I.R.C. § 508(a). Although an exempt trust generally pays no income tax, it must file an annual information return (Form 990), and it is subject to tax on any "unrelated business taxable income." I.R.C. §§ 501(b) and 511(b).

An exempt § 501(c)(3) organization will be classified either as a "public" charity or as a "private foundation." To qualify as a public charity, the organization must provide benefits directly to the public through its charitable operations, receive substantial public support, or function as a "supporting organization" for a public charity. Otherwise, the organization will be classified by default as a private foundation. I.R.C. § 509. A charitable trust created and funded by an individual grantor will almost certainly be classified as a private foundation unless it is operated, supervised, or controlled by or in connection with one or more public charities. For example, if a grantor creates an irrevocable trust for purely charitable purposes, giving an independent trustee discretion to determine the time and amount of distributions and to select charitable objects, the trust will be treated as a private foundation.

The distinction between public charities and private foundations has considerable practical

significance because the former enjoy markedly
preferential tax treatment compared to the latter.
Specifically, private foundations are subject to a
special 1.39% excise tax on net investment income
(I.R.C. § 4940), as well as penalty taxes that are
intended to deter abuses involving self-dealing
transactions, income accumulations, excessive
business holdings, imprudent investments and
prohibited expenditures (I.R.C. §§ 4941–4945).
Indeed, a private foundation will qualify for tax-
exempt status only if its governing instrument
includes provisions that effectively prohibit activities
that would trigger the penalty taxes. I.R.C. § 508(e).
A private foundation that willfully engages in
repeated or flagrant violations of the statutory
requirements may lose its tax-exempt status and
incur a substantial termination tax. I.R.C. § 507.
While charitable contributions to tax-exempt
organizations are generally deductible for income tax
purposes, the percentage limitations are
substantially less generous for private foundations
than for public charities. I.R.C. § 170(b)(1)(A)–
(b)(1)(D). Finally, private foundations are subject to
special reporting and disclosure requirements. For
example, a private foundation must disclose the
sources of its contributions, while a public charity
need not do so. The rationale for the differential tax
treatment of public charities and private foundations
is that the former are presumed to be more
responsive to public scrutiny while the latter require
more intrusive regulation to compensate for their
lack of public accountability.

Nonexempt charitable trusts. A trust may be created for purely charitable purposes yet fail to qualify for tax-exempt status. For example, a charitable trust may fail to apply for recognition as an exempt § 501(c)(3) organization, or its governing instrument may omit required safeguards against violation of the statutory requirements. Alternatively, a trust may initially qualify as an exempt private foundation but subsequently lose its tax-exempt status.

In general, a nonexempt charitable trust is taxable under the rules of Subchapter J. Nevertheless, under pre-1969 law, such a trust could be functionally tax-exempt because § 642(c) allowed an unlimited deduction not only for amounts actually paid from gross income for charitable purposes but also for amounts permanently set aside for charitable purposes. When Congress enacted the private foundation provisions in 1969, it repealed the charitable set-aside deduction for trusts (though not for estates) and left intact the unlimited deduction for amounts paid from gross income for charitable purposes pursuant to the terms of the governing instrument. (See I.R.C. § 642(c)(2), discussed in § 5.8, *supra*.) Consequently, under current law a nonexempt charitable trust is taxable on amounts of income that are accumulated rather than paid out currently, even if the accumulated income is irrevocably set aside for future payment to charity. Of course, if the trust could reduce its taxable income to zero by paying all of its gross income to charity, it might achieve de facto tax-exempt status while circumventing the statutory restrictions imposed on tax-exempt private foundations. To forestall such an end-run, the Code makes the private foundation provisions—including the governing instrument requirements, termination rules, and excise and penalty taxes, but not the determination of § 501(c)(3) status—applicable to any purely charitable nonexempt trust that received tax-deductible contributions. I.R.C. § 4947(a)(1).

To illustrate, suppose that Frances creates an irrevocable trust which pays out all of its income each year to provide scholarships for needy students selected by an independent trustee. The trust's purposes are purely charitable and its governing instrument contains all of the terms that would be required for a tax-exempt private foundation, but the trust fails to apply for tax-exempt status under § 501(c)(3). Nevertheless, Frances is allowed an income tax deduction for her contribution to the trust. Although the trust is a taxable entity under Subchapter J, it will also be subject to excise and penalty taxes as if it were a private foundation. The trust can offset its regular income tax liability against the 1.39% excise tax on net investment income and the tax on unrelated business income, but it may incur substantial additional liabilities if it engages in self-dealing or other prohibited activities. I.R.C. § 4940(b). In addition, the trust's § 642(c) deduction for amounts paid for charitable purposes will be disallowed to the extent that it is allocable to unrelated business income. I.R.C. § 681(a). Furthermore, if the trust's governing instrument failed to include the terms required for a private foundation, the trust's charitable deduction would be subject to the limitations of § 170 (instead of § 642(c)). I.R.C. § 642(c)(6); Reg. § 1.642(c)–4. In sum, § 4947(a)(1) ensures that a purely charitable nonexempt trust cannot be used to enjoy the tax benefits of a private foundation without bearing its correlative burdens.

Split-interest trusts. A trust that provides mixed benefits for both charitable and private beneficiaries is automatically ineligible for tax-exempt status under § 501(c)(3) because it violates the prohibition on private inurement. Nevertheless, the charitable portion of such a split-interest trust may be effectively exempt from tax in some circumstances.

Under pre-1969 law, the trust was allowed to deduct amounts of gross income that were either actually paid or permanently set aside for charitable purposes under § 642(c); in addition, the trust was entitled to a deduction for amounts distributed to private beneficiaries under the normal conduit rules. Furthermore, if the charitable interest was actuarially ascertainable and not subject to material contingencies, the grantor was entitled to deduct a corresponding portion of amounts contributed to the trust for income, gift, and estate tax purposes. For example, suppose that Gordon creates an irrevocable trust to pay income to his wife Helen for her life, with remainder at her death to a tax-exempt university foundation. Under pre-1969 law, the trust's ordinary income was taxable to Helen under the conduit rules and any capital gains (or other items of gross income allocable to corpus) qualified for the charitable set-aside deduction under § 642(c), leaving the trust itself with no taxable income. In addition, Gordon could deduct the present value of the charitable remainder for income and gift tax purposes. To the extent that the value of the property received by the charity fell short of its estimated value under the Treasury tables, Gordon's charitable deductions would be overstated. Moreover, the problem of misvaluation would be exacerbated if the trustee exercised its administrative powers to favor the income beneficiary at the expense of the charitable remainder beneficiary in selecting investments and allocating receipts and expenses to income or principal.

When Congress repealed the charitable set-aside deduction for trusts in 1969, it also curtailed the deductibility of contributions to split-interest trusts. The charitable interest in a split-interest trust is no longer deductible for income, gift, or estate tax purposes unless the trust qualifies as a charitable remainder trust, a charitable lead trust, or a pooled income fund. I.R.C. § 170(f)(2); see also I.R.C. §§ 2055(e)(2) (estate tax) and 2522(c)(2) (gift tax). The requirements for each type of trust are intended to ensure that there is a reasonable correlation between the amount deducted by the grantor and the benefits ultimately received by the charity, and to prevent deductible contributions from being diverted to private beneficiaries. The problem of mismatching does not arise in the case of a purely charitable trust that has no private beneficiaries, and the restrictions do not apply to such a trust. I.R.C. § 170(f)(2)(D). To illustrate the split-interest trust provisions, consider the example given in the preceding paragraph involving the trust created by Gordon to pay income to Helen for life with remainder to charity. The trust does not come within any of the statutory safe harbors. Accordingly, if the trust is created after 1969, Gordon will not be allowed any charitable deduction for his contributions. Furthermore, the trust's ordinary income will be taxed to Gordon (under the grantor trust rules, while Gordon is alive) or to Helen (under the conduit rules, after Gordon's death), and the trust will be taxable on any capital gains (or other items of gross income allocable to corpus).

A *charitable remainder trust* is a trust that pays a specified amount annually to one or more private beneficiaries for a specified period and then distributes the remaining property to charity. The annual payments may be stated either as a fixed dollar amount (i.e., an annuity) or as a fixed percentage of the annually-determined value of the trust property (i.e., a unitrust amount). I.R.C. § 664(d). By limiting the permissible private interests to an annuity or a unitrust amount, the statute ensures that the trustee has no discretion to favor the private beneficiaries at the expense of the charitable remainder beneficiary. A charitable remainder trust is exempt from income tax (except for unrelated business income, which is subject to a 100% excise tax), and the private beneficiaries are taxed on their annual payments under special rules. I.R.C. § 664(b) and (c). The net effect is to treat the trust as tax-exempt with respect to amounts held or accumulated for charity while imposing tax on amounts distributed to the private beneficiaries. A grantor who contributes cash or property to the trust is entitled to deduct the present value of the charitable remainder interest. I.R.C. § 170(f)(2)(A); Reg. §§ 1.170A–6(b), 1.664–2(c), and 1.664–4. The deduction may be eligible for a favorable 50% limitation* if, upon termination of the annual payments to the private beneficiaries, the trust property is to be paid "to" a public charity (rather than held in trust "for the use of" the charity). I.R.C. § 170(b)(1)(A); Reg. § 1.170A–8(a)(2) and (b). Charitable remainder trusts are discussed in § 9.2, *infra*.

A *pooled income fund* is a trust maintained by a public charity and funded solely with property contributed by multiple donors. The trust distributes its net income annually to the donors or their designated beneficiaries for their lifetimes, and at the death of each beneficiary the charity receives a proportionate share of the trust property. The trust itself is not tax-exempt, but it generally has little or no taxable income because its fiduciary accounting income is taxed to the private beneficiaries under the normal conduit rules and the trust receives a special deduction for long-term capital gains that are accumulated for the charitable remainder beneficiary. I.R.C. § 642(c)(3). This special deduction for pooled income funds replaces the charitable set-aside deduction formerly allowed under pre-1969 law. Donors who contribute cash or property to a

---

* The 50% limitation is increased to 60% for cash contributions to public charities for taxable years beginning after 2017 and before 2026. I.R.C. § 170(b)(1)(G).

pooled income fund are entitled to deduct the present value of the charitable remainder interest, and the deduction may be eligible for a favorable 50% limitation* if the underlying property is payable to the charity (rather than held in trust for its use) at the death of the life income beneficiary. I.R.C. § 170(b)(1)(A) and (f)(2)(A); Reg. §§ 1.170A–6(b), 1.170A–8(a)(2) and (b), and 1.642(c)–6. Pooled income funds are discussed in § 9.3, *infra*.

A *charitable lead trust* is the mirror image of a charitable remainder trust. It provides specified annual payments to charity for a fixed term or the lives of one or more living individuals, with remainder to private beneficiaries. The annual payments to charity must be stated either as an annuity or a unitrust amount. I.R.C. § 170(f)(2)(B). The mandatory annuity or unitrust format is intended to protect the charity's interest from discretionary investment or administrative decisions that might favor the private remainder beneficiary; the rationale is essentially the same as in the context of a charitable remainder trust. Contributions to a charitable lead trust are deductible only if the grantor is treated as the owner of the charitable lead interest under the grantor trust rules. In that case, the grantor is entitled to deduct the present value of the charitable lead interest; to prevent a double tax benefit, however, neither the grantor nor the trust is allowed to deduct the annual charitable payments

---

* The 50% limitation is increased to 60% for cash contributions to public charities for taxable years beginning after 2017 and before 2026. I.R.C. § 170(b)(1)(G).

when they are actually made. I.R.C. § 170(f)(2)(B) and (f)(2)(C); Reg. § 1.170A–6(c)(3). Because the contributed property is held in trust "for the use of" the charitable lead beneficiary (rather than paid "to" the charity), the deduction is subject to a 30% limitation. I.R.C. § 170(b)(1)(B); Reg. § 1.170A–8(a)(2) and (b). If the grantor trust rules do not apply, the grantor is not entitled to a charitable deduction, but the trust will be allowed to deduct the annual charitable payments under § 642(c). Charitable lead trusts are discussed in § 9.4, *infra*.

Because charitable remainder trusts, pooled income funds and charitable lead trusts have mixed charitable and private beneficiaries, they cannot qualify for tax-exempt status under § 501(c)(3). Nevertheless, split-interest trusts enjoy substantial direct and indirect tax benefits comparable to those of private foundations. Accordingly, a split-interest trust that was funded with deductible contributions is treated as if it were a private foundation for purposes of the termination rules and the governing instrument requirements as well as the penalty taxes on self-dealing transactions and prohibited expenditures; the penalty taxes on excess business holdings and imprudent investments may also apply in some cases. I.R.C. § 4947(a)(2) and (b)(3).

§ 9.2   CHARITABLE REMAINDER TRUSTS

A charitable remainder trust is a trust that provides specified annual payments to one or more private beneficiaries for life or a term of years, with remainder upon termination to be distributed to or held for the use of one or more charitable organizations. The trust may take one of two forms, namely a charitable remainder annuity trust (CRAT) or a charitable remainder unitrust (CRUT). The primary difference between the two types of charitable remainder trust involves the computation of the annual payment to the private beneficiary: in a CRAT the payment consists of a "sum certain" (i.e., an annuity) that is not less than 5% nor greater than 50% of the initial value of the trust property, while in a CRUT the payment consists of a "fixed percentage"—again, not less than 5% nor greater than 50%—of the annually-determined value of the trust property (i.e., a unitrust amount). I.R.C. § 664(d)(1)(A) and (d)(2)(A). The 5% floor, which corresponds to the 5% payout requirement for a private foundation, limits the trust's ability to accumulate income on a tax-exempt basis. The 50% ceiling, enacted in 1997, limits the private beneficiary's opportunity to receive tax-free corpus distributions.

In the case of a CRUT, the annual payment may be limited to the lesser of the unitrust amount or the trust's net income, if the trust instrument so provides. I.R.C. § 664(d)(3); Reg. § 1.664–3(a)(1)(i)(b). Thus, in any year when the trust's net income is less than the specified unitrust amount, the private beneficiary will be entitled only to the net income. The trust instrument may also provide for "make-up" payments in subsequent years from net income in excess of the unitrust amount, up to the aggregate amount by which the amounts payable were less than the unitrust amount in previous years. For example, suppose that a CRUT requires annual payments to Agnes equal to 5% of the trust's value (determined annually) for life, subject to a "net income with make-up" provision. Assume that the trust has a net value of $1 million at all relevant times, resulting in a unitrust amount of $50,000. If the trust has only $40,000 of net income in the first year, Agnes's first-year payment will be limited to $40,000 (rather than the $50,000 unitrust amount). If the trust has $70,000 of net income in the second year, Agnes's second-year payment will be $60,000 ($50,000 unitrust amount plus $10,000 to make up for the shortfall in the previous year). The net income limitation, with or without a make-up feature, may be useful to avoid the need to increase cash flow by selling trust property in years when the trust has insufficient net income to pay the full unitrust amount. The net income limitation has no effect on the deductible value of the charitable remainder interest, which is determined based on a unitrust amount equal to the greater of 5% or the percentage specified in the trust instrument. I.R.C. § 643(e); Reg. § 1.664–4(a)(3); Estate of Schaefer v. Commissioner, 145 T.C. 134 (2015). The regulations also permit a CRUT that initially includes a net income limitation (with or without a make-up feature) to "flip" back to a simple unitrust amount. Reg. § 1.664–3(a)(1)(i)(c). For example, a CRUT funded with closely held stock may provide for annual payments limited to net income (if less than the unitrust amount) until the stock is sold and thereafter require annual payments of the full unitrust amount. Reg. § 1.664–3(a)(1)(i)(e) (Example 2).

The required payments must be made at least annually, and no other distributions may be made to any private beneficiary. I.R.C. § 664(d)(1)(B) and (d)(2)(B). Thus, for example, a trust cannot qualify as a charitable remainder trust if the trustee has a power to invade corpus for the support of the private beneficiary, even if the possibility of invasion is remote. Reg. §§ 1.664–2(a)(4) and 1.664–3(a)(4). Similarly, a trust cannot qualify as a charitable remainder trust if the grantor's debts or estate tax liability might be payable from the trust property at the grantor's death. Reg. § 1.664–1(a)(6) (Example 3); see also Rev. Rul. 82–128, 1982–2 C.B. 71 (estate tax); Rev. Proc. 2005–24, 2005–1 C.B. 909 (spouse's elective share). Furthermore, the charitable remainder must be worth at least 10% of the initial value of the trust property at the creation of the trust (and at the time of any subsequent contribution, in the case of a CRUT). I.R.C. § 664(d)(1)(D) and (d)(2)(D). This requirement, enacted in 1997, is intended to ensure that the charitable remainder beneficiary receives a significant benefit from the trust.

A charitable remainder trust may be disqualified if there is more than a 5% probability that the trust property will be exhausted before the scheduled termination date, leaving nothing to be paid over to charity. Rev. Rul. 70–452, 1970–2 C.B. 199; Rev. Rul. 77–374, 1977–2 C.B. 329. When the duration of a CRAT is measured by the lifetime of a private beneficiary, there may be a substantial risk that the annuity payments will exhaust the trust property during the beneficiary's life, especially if the beneficiary is young and interest rates are low. In such a case, however, the CRAT can avoid disqualification if the trust instrument provides for early termination (and acceleration of the charitable remainder) in the event that an annuity payment would cause the value of the trust property (multiplied by a specified discount factor) to fall below 10% of its initial value. Rev. Proc. 2016–42, 2016–34 I.R.B. 269. The effect of such a saving clause is to allow the CRAT to "wait and see" whether the trust property will be depleted, while ensuring that the charity will receive at least 10% of the trust's initial value.

The statutory provisions limiting private benefits to annuity or unitrust payments serve a dual purpose. Most obviously, they ensure that the trust's property and income cannot be diverted from the charitable remainder beneficiary to private beneficiaries. If the private beneficiary is entitled to receive only a fixed dollar amount (i.e., an annuity), the trustee cannot favor the income beneficiary at the charity's expense by investing in wasting assets or by making unusual allocations of receipts and expenses to income or principal accounts. Similarly, in the case of a CRUT, the unitrust format results in a proportionate allocation of the trust's total investment return between the private and charitable interests, regardless of how receipts and expenses are treated for fiduciary accounting purposes. A second, related function of the statutory restrictions is to ensure that the trust provides benefits to charity that are reasonably correlated with the tax deduction allowed to the grantor.

Although the deductible value of a charitable remainder interest is only a rough estimate of what the charity will receive in the future, the strict limitation of the private beneficiary's interest to an annuity or unitrust amount (rather than a simple income interest) greatly reduces the opportunities for manipulation and misvaluation.

The duration of a charitable remainder trust is limited to a fixed term of up to 20 years or the lifetimes of one or more individuals alive at the creation of the trust. I.R.C. § 664(d)(1)(A) and (d)(2)(A). The annual payments may be made to named individuals for their respective lives, for a fixed term of up to 20 years, or for the shorter (but not the longer) of those periods. For example, a trust may provide annual payments to Natalie and then to Oscar for their respective lives, with remainder to charity. Alternatively, the payments may be made to Natalie and Oscar for their respective lives or a fixed 20-year term, whichever is shorter. However, a trust that provides annual payments to Natalie for life and then to Oscar for 10 years is not permitted because the trust might last longer than the lifetimes of Natalie and Oscar and longer than 20 years. Reg. §§ 1.664–2(a)(5)(i) and 1.664–3(a)(5)(i). An individual beneficiary may receive annual payments for his or her own lifetime or for a term of years, but not for a period measured by another individual's lifetime. If an annuity or unitrust amount is payable to a class of beneficiaries (rather than named individuals), all of the class members must be alive and ascertainable at the creation of the trust unless the payment period is limited solely to a fixed term of years. For example, a testamentary trust may provide for annual payments to the testator's children who survive the testator for their respective lives, with remainder to charity. Reg. §§ 1.664–2(a)(3)(i) and 1.664–3(a)(3)(i).

The trust instrument may provide that the annual payments will terminate upon the occurrence of a specified contingency before the trust's scheduled termination date; such a contingency will not disqualify the trust as a charitable remainder trust, but it will be disregarded in valuing the charitable remainder interest. I.R.C. § 664(f). For example, a testamentary trust might provide for annual payments to the testator's spouse until the spouse's death or remarriage, with remainder to charity, and in that case the charitable remainder would be valued as if it took effect only at the spouse's death (without regard to the possibility of early termination upon remarriage). The trust may also provide that the annual payments will end with the last regular payment before the terminating event, thereby avoiding the need to compute a prorated amount for a final short period. Reg. §§ 1.664–2(a)(5) and 1.664–3(a)(5).

The regulations require that a charitable remainder trust must qualify "in every respect" as either a CRAT or a CRUT; a hybrid trust combining elements of both types is not recognized. For example, a trust that provides for an annual payment equal to the greater (or lesser) of an annuity or a unitrust amount is neither a CRAT nor a CRUT and therefore does not qualify as a charitable remainder trust. Reg. § 1.664–1(a)(2). Moreover, the trust must "function exclusively" as a charitable remainder trust from the time of its creation. For this purpose, an inter vivos trust is created when it is first funded with property and is not treated as entirely owned by the grantor (or any other person) under the grantor trust rules. Reg. § 1.664–1(a)(4). A testamentary trust is created at the testator's death, even though the funding of the trust may be deferred for a reasonable period of administration and the required annual payments (computed from the date of death, with interest) need not actually be made until the end of the year in which the trust is fully funded. Reg. § 1.664–1(a)(5). Following the termination of the required annual payments, the trust will continue to be recognized as a charitable remainder trust for a reasonable period while the trustee completes the administration of the trust and distributes the remaining trust property to the charitable remainder beneficiary. Reg. §§ 1.664–2(a)(6) and 1.664–3(a)(6).

A charitable remainder trust must be irrevocable from its inception, but the grantor (or another person) may have a limited power to select or designate the charitable remainder beneficiary. Rev. Rul. 76–7, 1976–1 C.B. 179 (special power held by beneficiary of testamentary trust); Rev. Rul. 76–8, 1976–1 C.B. 179 (power retained by grantor of inter vivos trust). The grantor may also retain a testamentary power to revoke or terminate the annual payments to a private beneficiary, but neither the grantor nor any other person may hold a power to alter the amount of those payments if the power would cause the grantor (or any other person) to be treated as the owner of any portion of the trust under the grantor trust rules. Reg. §§ 1.664–2(a)(3) and (a)(4), and 1.664–3(a)(3) and (a)(4).

The Service has published sample forms to provide guidance in drafting charitable remainder trusts. Rev. Proc. 2003–53 et seq., 2003–2 C.B. 230 (CRAT forms); Rev. Proc. 2005–52 et seq., 2005–2 C.B. 326 (CRUT forms). If a trust fails to satisfy the technical definition of a charitable remainder trust due to a drafting error, a remedy may be available through a "qualified reformation." I.R.C. § 2055(e)(3); see also I.R.C. §§ 170(f)(7) and 2522(c)(4).

In deciding whether to structure a charitable remainder trust as a CRAT or a CRUT, a grantor should consider the advantages and drawbacks of both types of trust. A major advantage of a CRAT is its administrative convenience. The annual payment is a fixed dollar amount which is determined at the creation of the trust and does not vary from year to year. Moreover, once the initial value of the trust assets has been determined, the trust is not permitted to receive any additional contributions and there is no need for subsequent revaluations. Reg. § 1.664–2(b). In contrast, a CRUT requires that the trust assets be revalued each year to determine the amount of the unitrust payment. If the trust assets are hard to value (e.g., real estate or closely held business interests), the administrative burden of a CRUT may be substantial. The major advantage of a CRUT is its flexibility. A CRUT (unlike a CRAT) may receive additional contributions. Reg. § 1.664–3(b). Moreover, the annual unitrust payments in a CRUT automatically adjust to changes in the value of the trust property, allowing the private beneficiary to participate in the trust's total investment return. By the same token, the private and charitable beneficiaries of a CRUT share ratably in the trust's total investment return. In a CRAT, however, the private beneficiary receives a fixed priority return and the charity receives any residual net gain or loss. Thus, if the total investment return on a CRAT is insufficient to make the required annuity payments, there may be little or no trust property left for the charitable remainder beneficiary upon termination.

A charitable remainder trust is generally exempt from income taxation, though it is subject to a 100% excise tax on any unrelated business income. I.R.C. § 664(c). A charitable remainder trust may also incur penalty taxes if it engages in acts of self-dealing or makes prohibited expenditures (or, in some cases, if it has excess business holdings or makes imprudent investments). I.R.C. § 4947(a)(2) and (b)(3).

Although a charitable remainder trust is tax-exempt, the private beneficiaries are taxable on the annuity or unitrust amounts required to be distributed to them. Distributions to private beneficiaries are deemed to carry out the trust's current and accumulated income and corpus in the following order of priority: (1) gross income other than capital gain; (2) net capital gain; (3) tax-exempt income; and (4) corpus. I.R.C. § 664(b). This distinctly unfavorable ordering rule is amplified in the regulations, which rank the items within each category by applicable income tax rates in descending order. Reg. § 1.664–1(d)(1)(ii).

To illustrate, suppose that a CRAT makes a $50,000 annuity payment to Robin in a year when the trust has $5,000 of taxable interest, $10,000 of qualified dividends, $15,000 of net short-term capital gain, $30,000 of net long-term capital gain, and $10,000 of tax-exempt interest. Robin will include all of the taxable interest, qualified dividends, and net short-term capital gain, as well as $20,000 of long-term capital gain, in her gross income for the year in which the distribution was required to be made. Moreover, in a subsequent year she will have to absorb the remaining $10,000 of long-term capital gain (in addition to any other items of current and accumulated income) before she can treat any portion of her annuity payments as tax-exempt interest or tax-free corpus.

The items of income in each category are reduced (but not below zero) by deductions directly attributable to that category as well as a ratable portion of other deductions. Reg. § 1.664–1(d)(2). If there are two or more recipients, each recipient is taxed on a ratable portion of the aggregate distributions. Reg. § 1.664–1(d)(3). Because all charitable remainder trusts are required to report on a calendar-year basis and most individual taxpayers elect to do so, the taxable years of the trust and its private beneficiaries are generally identical. I.R.C. § 644. Distributions are includible in a beneficiary's gross income for the taxable year in which the amounts are required to be paid, even if they are actually paid after the close of the taxable year. If a cash-basis beneficiary dies during the taxable year, only amounts actually received before death are included on the beneficiary's final return, and any amount payable to the beneficiary's estate constitutes an item of income in respect of a decedent. Reg. § 1.664–1(d)(4). Under general tax principles, a distribution of property other than cash in satisfaction of a required payment may cause the trust to recognize gain or loss (see § 7.7, *supra*).

The ordering rule of § 664(b) severely restricts a trustee's ability to exercise investment discretion in a manner that favors the private beneficiaries of a charitable remainder trust. Nevertheless, the Service remains vigilant in addressing new forms of abusive transactions, as illustrated by two recent examples. The first example involves the use of a CRUT to avoid recognizing gain on a sale of appreciated assets. Suppose that Walter creates a CRUT to pay 50% of its net asset value to himself for two years, with remainder to charity. He funds the trust with a zero-basis asset worth $1,000 that produces no current income. At the end of the first year, when the asset is still worth $1,000, the trust borrows $500 and uses the borrowed cash to pay the $500 unitrust amount to Walter. During the second year, the trust sells the asset for $1,000 and repays the $500 loan; at year-end, the trust pays a unitrust amount of $250 (50% of $500) to Walter and makes a terminating distribution of the remaining $250 to charity. Because the trust had no income during the first year, Walter reports the first unitrust payment of $500 as a tax-free corpus distribution, and he reports the second payment of $250 as capital gain, thereby hoping to avoid tax on all of the remaining capital gain realized by the trust. This gambit has been foreclosed by the regulations, which treat the trust as selling half of the asset when the trust makes the first unitrust payment. Reg. § 1.643(a)–8(b)(1) and (c) (Example 1). The regulations also warn that transactions having the purpose or effect of circumventing the deemed-sale rule will be disregarded. Reg. § 1.643(a)–8(b)(2); cf. Notice 94–78, 1994–2 C.B. 555 (in similar transaction, trust makes first-year unitrust payment after selling asset at beginning of second year).

The second example involves another use of a charitable remainder trust to avoid gain recognition, this time through an early termination. Suppose that Violet contributes an asset with a basis of $500 to a CRAT in which she retains the annuity interest. The trust then sells the original asset for $1,500, distributes a $100 annuity payment to Violet, and reinvests the remaining $1,400 in new assets. Shortly afterward, when the new assets are still worth $1,400, Violet and the charity sell their interests to a third party for a total price of $1,400, causing the trust to terminate. Violet receives $800 of the sale proceeds and the charity receives $600, in proportion to the actuarial values of their respective trust interests. Violet includes the entire $100 annuity payment as capital gain. However, she seeks to avoid reporting any taxable gain from the sale of her annuity interest, claiming that her share of the sale proceeds ($800 amount realized) is fully offset by her share of the trust's uniform basis in the new assets ($1,400 × 800/1,400). Reg. §§ 1.1014–5(a) and 1.1015–1(b). (Note that Violet's basis in her annuity interest is not disregarded, because all of the trust interests are sold in a single transaction. I.R.C. § 1001(e); Reg. § 1.1001–1(f).) To block this avenue of tax avoidance, the regulations now require that Violet's basis in her annuity interest be reduced by her ratable share of the trust's undistributed net ordinary income and net capital gain. The required basis reduction is $514 ($900 × 800/1,400), leaving Violet with a basis in her annuity interest of only $286 ($800 − $514), and she must recognize additional gain of $514. As a result, Violet will be taxed on her share of the trust's undistributed net ordinary income and net capital gain. Reg. § 1.1014–5(c) and (d) (Example 8); cf. Notice 2008–99, 2008–47 I.R.B. 1194 (describing similar "transaction of interest").

§ 9.3   POOLED INCOME FUNDS

A pooled income fund is maintained by a public charity and funded solely with contributions from multiple donors. The fund's net income is payable annually to the donors or their designated beneficiaries for their respective lifetimes, and at each beneficiary's death a proportionate share of the underlying property is paid to or held for the use of the public charity. I.R.C. § 642(c)(5). In effect, the arrangement provides the private beneficiaries with lifetime enjoyment of the income from the commingled contributions (as well as tax-free diversification and professional fund management), while allowing the donors to deduct the value of the remainder interest transferred to charity. Because the public charity that maintains and controls the fund is also its sole remainder beneficiary, the concerns that prompted Congress to impose strict annuity or unitrust requirements on charitable remainder trusts do not apply to pooled income funds.

The remainder interest in a pooled income fund must be irrevocably vested in a specific public charity at the time of each donor's contribution. Reg. § 1.642(c)–5(b)(1). Thus, a private foundation may not be named as the remainder beneficiary, and neither the donor nor any other person may hold a power to appoint the remainder to a different public charity. Each donor must designate one or more living individuals to receive income from the contributed property for their lifetimes. The life income interest may be retained by the donor or created in other beneficiaries, and if there are two or more designated beneficiaries their interests may be concurrent or consecutive. Reg. § 1.642(c)–5(b)(2). For example, Dana might direct that income be paid half to Austin and half to Brenda during their respective lives, or to Austin for his life and then to Brenda (if she survives Austin) for her life, or equally to Austin and Brenda for their joint lifetime and then to the survivor for life. The measuring lives must be those of the designated beneficiaries; an income interest measured by another person's life is not permitted. Rev. Rul. 79–61, 1979–1 C.B. 220. In the case of a class gift (e.g., income to the donor's children), the members of the class must be living and ascertainable at the time of the contribution. The donor may retain a testamentary power to revoke or terminate the interest of an income beneficiary, but otherwise the beneficiaries and their income shares must be specified at the time of the contribution.

Although a pooled income fund must be "maintained by" the same charity that is named as the remainder beneficiary, the fund need not be administered directly by the charity as long as the charity "exercises control directly or indirectly over the fund." I.R.C. § 642(c)(5)(E); Reg. § 1.642(c)–5(b)(5). This requirement is generally met, for example, if the charity has the power to remove and replace the fund's trustees. Rev. Rul. 74–132, 1974–1 C.B. 152 (public charity had power to remove and replace directors of supporting organization named as fund's trustee); Rev. Rul. 92–107, 1992–2 C.B. 120 (fund maintained by national organization on behalf of itself and its local affiliates); Rev. Rul. 96–38, 1996–2 C.B. 44 (fund maintained by community trust on behalf of one or more component funds under common control). The purpose of the statutory requirement is to ensure that the public charity can protect its remainder interest and to prevent the income beneficiaries from interfering in the administration of the fund. Accordingly, neither the donor nor any individual income beneficiary may serve as a trustee of the fund, although the donor may be an officer or director of the charitable remainder beneficiary. Reg. § 1.642(c)–5(b)(6).

A pooled investment fund must be funded exclusively with cash or other property contributed by the donors, and the contributions must be commingled for investment purposes. Moreover, the fund is prohibited from investing in municipal bonds or other tax-exempt securities. I.R.C. § 642(c)(5)(B)–(c)(5)(D); Reg. § 1.642(c)–5(b)(3) and (b)(4). These requirements ensure that all of the income beneficiaries share proportionately in the fund's net income, and also prevent donors from converting appreciated assets into a stream of tax-exempt income through deductible contributions to the fund.

A pooled income fund is required to distribute all of its net income annually, within 65 days after the close of each taxable year, to the income beneficiaries in proportion to their interests in the fund. Each income beneficiary is entitled to receive a ratable share of the fund's net income annually for life; when the beneficiary dies, his or her income interest may terminate with the last regular payment before death or be prorated for the final short period ending at death, as provided in the governing instrument. Reg. § 1.642(c)–5(b)(7). Upon the death of a beneficiary, an amount corresponding to the deceased beneficiary's interest in the fund must be severed and paid over to (or held for the use of) the charitable remainder beneficiary. Reg. § 1.642(c)–5(b)(8).

In allocating the fund's net income among living beneficiaries or determining the amount payable to charity at a beneficiary's death, each beneficiary's interest in the fund may be expressed in terms of "units of participation." Reg. § 1.642(c)–5(c)(2). Each unit represents a fractional interest in the fund, and the aggregate value of all units outstanding at any particular time is equal to the fund's net asset value. Thus, the value of a unit will vary over time, reflecting fluctuations in the fund's net asset value, even if the number of outstanding units remains constant. Moreover, the total number of units will increase when the fund issues additional units (in exchange for new contributions) or decrease when the fund retires outstanding units (upon the death of a beneficiary).

The number of units assigned to a newly-issued interest may be expressed as $a \times b \div c$, where a is the value of the contributed property, b is the number of units outstanding, and c is the fund's net asset value. To illustrate, suppose that Clara contributes $20,000 and Dennis contributes $10,000 to a newly-created pooled income fund, each retaining a life income interest. Assuming an initial value of $100 per unit ($30,000 net asset value ÷ 300 outstanding units), 200 units will be allocated to Clara and 100 units to Dennis. Later, when the fund's net asset value is $36,000, Emily contributes $12,000, retaining a life income interest. Immediately before her contribution, the fund's net asset value was $36,000 and the number of outstanding units was 300, so each outstanding unit was worth $120 ($36,000 ÷ 300). Accordingly, the fund will allocate 100 new units to Emily. After Emily's contribution, the fund's net asset value is $48,000 and the number of outstanding units is 400; each outstanding unit is still worth $120 ($48,000 ÷ 400). Reg. § 1.642(c)–5(c)(4) (Example 1).

The Service has published sample forms to provide guidance in drafting governing instruments for pooled income funds. Rev. Rul. 82–38, 1982–1 C.B. 96 (sample provisions); Rev. Rul. 85–57, 1985–1 C.B.

182 (same); Rev. Proc. 88–53, 1988–2 C.B. 712 (form of trust declaration).

A pooled income fund is classified as a trust for tax purposes (though not necessarily under local law), and it is generally treated as a complex trust under Subchapter J, without regard to the grantor trust rules. Reg. § 1.642(c)–5(a)(2). Because the fund is required to distribute all of its net income annually, the income distributions are deductible by the trust and includible by the income beneficiaries as first-tier distributions under the normal conduit rules. The fund and its beneficiaries generally have the same taxable year, since most individuals report on a calendar-year basis and pooled income funds are required to do so. I.R.C. § 644. Income distributions are includible in a beneficiary's gross income for the taxable year in which they are required to be paid, even though payment may actually be made up to 65 days after the close of the taxable year. Reg. § 1.642(c)–5(b)(7). If a cash-basis beneficiary dies during the taxable year, only amounts actually received before death are included on the beneficiary's final return, and any amount payable to the beneficiary's estate constitutes an item of income in respect of a decedent. Because a pooled income fund is expressly prohibited from holding tax-exempt securities, the net income distributions generally consist of fully taxable items.

Although a pooled income fund is treated as a nonexempt trust, it is entitled to a special deduction for long-term capital gain that is permanently set aside for charitable purposes pursuant to the terms of the governing instrument. I.R.C. § 642(c)(3). This provision applies even though the realized gain is not currently payable but is accumulated for future distribution to the charitable remainder beneficiary; it was added in 1969, when Congress repealed the general charitable set-aside deduction for trusts, to provide targeted relief for pooled income funds. The deduction for long-term capital gain, in conjunction with the deduction for required current income distributions, generally ensures that a pooled income fund reports little or no taxable income. The fund may have taxable income, however, if it realizes an item of gain that does not qualify as long-term capital gain (i.e., ordinary gain or short-term capital gain).

Under traditional fiduciary accounting principles, proceeds of asset sales are generally allocated to corpus. Consequently, long-term capital gains realized by a pooled income fund are normally deductible under § 642(c)(3) because such gains are permanently set aside for the charitable remainder beneficiary and cannot be distributed to or appropriated by the income beneficiaries. In some cases, however, the fund's net income may be defined in terms of a unitrust amount, or the trustee may have a power to adjust between income and corpus. I.R.C. § 643(b); Reg. § 1.643(b)–1. The possibility that capital gains may be allocated to income, and thus be diverted from the charitable remainder beneficiary to the income beneficiaries, raises two concerns in the context of pooled income funds. One concern involves the extent of the trustee's discretion in making such an allocation. If the trustee has broad discretion to allocate sale proceeds to income instead of corpus, the income beneficiaries may receive an unwarranted benefit at the expense of the charitable remainder beneficiary. To protect the value of the charitable remainder, the regulations require that the trustee, in exercising a power to adjust, must allocate sale proceeds to corpus to the extent of the value of the assets at the time they were contributed to or acquired by the fund. Reg. § 1.642(c)–5(a)(5)(i). This provision allows the trustee to reallocate post-acquisition capital gains to income, while ensuring that the initial value of the assets acquired by the fund is preserved intact for the charitable remainder beneficiary.

A second, related concern involves the scope of the charitable set-aside deduction for long-term capital gains realized by the fund. To the extent that such gains may become distributable to the income beneficiaries, they are not permanently set aside for the charitable remainder beneficiary and therefore should not be deductible in computing the fund's taxable income. For example, if the annual payment to the income beneficiaries is defined in terms of a unitrust amount, the current year's payment may include capital gains realized in the current year or a prior year or even unrealized capital appreciation that will not be realized until a subsequent year. Accordingly, to prevent an unwarranted tax benefit, the regulations provide that the charitable set-aside deduction is not allowed if the income beneficiaries' right to the fund's net income can be satisfied either by payment of a unitrust amount or by an amount that takes into account unrealized appreciation in the fund's assets. By the same token, the charitable set-aside deduction does not apply to the extent that sale proceeds are allocated to income and distributed to the income beneficiaries. Reg. § 1.642(c)–2(c).

§ 9.4 CHARITABLE LEAD TRUSTS

A charitable lead trust provides annual payments to charity for a specified period followed by a remainder interest in private beneficiaries. Under pre-1969 law, a grantor who contributed cash or property to a charitable lead trust could claim a charitable deduction for the present value of the lead interest under § 170; in addition, the trust could deduct the annual payments made to charity from gross income under § 642(c), so that in many cases the trust was effectively tax-exempt. This tax-favored arrangement came to an end in 1969, when Congress enacted far-reaching restrictions on the charitable deduction for amounts contributed to split-interest charitable trusts.

Under current law, the grantor is not allowed to deduct any amount contributed to a charitable lead trust unless the charitable lead interest takes the form of a "guaranteed annuity" or a unitrust interest payable annually to charity and the grantor is treated as the owner of the lead interest under the grantor trust rules. I.R.C. § 170(f)(2)(B); Reg. § 1.170A–6(c)(1). Furthermore, if the grantor deducts amounts contributed to the trust, no deduction is allowed to the grantor (or any other person) for the annual charitable payments. I.R.C. § 170(f)(2)(C); Reg. § 1.170A–6(d)(1). Thus, the grantor can receive an immediate deduction for the value of the charitable lead interest, but only at the cost of remaining taxable on the trust's gross income, which will be attributed to the grantor (under the grantor trust rules) even though no distributions can be made to the grantor (or any other private beneficiary) during the charitable lead term. On one hand, the grantor may be taxable on gain realized by the trust if the trust sells appreciated property. On the other hand, the grantor's continuing tax liability may be reduced or eliminated if the trust invests in tax-exempt securities, but such an investment strategy is also likely to erode the value of the property payable to the private beneficiaries at the termination of the trust.

A grantor who is willing to forego an immediate charitable deduction may choose instead to create a charitable lead trust as a nongrantor trust. In that case, the grantor will not be allowed a deduction for any amounts contributed to the trust, but the trust itself will be treated as a complex trust and will be entitled to an unlimited charitable deduction for amounts paid to charity from gross income (other than unrelated business income) pursuant to the terms of the trust instrument. I.R.C. § 642(c)(1) and (c)(4); see, e.g., Rev. Rul. 83–75, 1983–1 C.B. 114 (allowing charitable deduction for gain realized on distribution of appreciated property in satisfaction of guaranteed annuity). Although a nongrantor trust may be entitled to a § 642(c) deduction for amounts payable to charity in almost any form, such payments will almost always be structured as a guaranteed annuity or a unitrust interest, so that the grantor can deduct the charitable lead interest for gift or estate tax purposes. I.R.C. §§ 2055(e)(2)(B) and 2522(c)(2)(B). As a practical matter, in deciding whether to create a charitable lead trust as a grantor trust or a nongrantor trust, a charitably minded grantor who wishes to obtain an immediate income tax deduction will choose the former (especially if the trust property will revert to the grantor or the grantor's spouse at the end of the trust term); in contrast, a grantor who wishes to transfer a future interest to children or grandchildren at a discounted value for gift and estate tax purposes is likely to opt for a nongrantor trust.

A grantor is entitled to deduct contributions to a charitable lead trust under § 170 only if the trust provides annual payments to charity for a fixed term of years or for the lifetimes of one or more specified individuals alive and ascertainable at the time of the contribution. The regulations restrict the permissible measuring lives to a limited group comprising the donor, the donor's spouse, and anyone who is an ancestor (or the spouse of an ancestor) of all the remainder beneficiaries (disregarding beneficiaries who are not descendants if their chances of receiving any trust corpus are less than 15%). Reg. § 1.170A–6(c)(2)(i)(A) and (c)(2)(ii)(A). This restriction was imposed to curb the use of "vulture trusts" in which an unrelated person, seriously but not terminally ill, was selected as the measuring life for a charitable lead trust, in the hope of obtaining an inflated charitable deduction based on the person's actuarial life expectancy.

The annual charitable payments must be irrevocable and must be in the form of either a guaranteed annuity or a unitrust interest. In the case of a guaranteed annuity, the payments must be "determinable," that is, they must be ascertainable at the time of the contribution. The annuity payments may increase or decrease by a stated amount over the term of the trust, but they may not be redetermined by reference to a "fluctuating index" such as a cost-of-living index. In the case of a unitrust interest, the payments must be determined as a "fixed percentage" of the annually-determined value of the trust property. Reg. § 1.170A–6(c)(2)(i)(A) and (c)(2)(ii)(A). The charity's lead interest must qualify as a guaranteed annuity or a unitrust interest "in every respect"; a hybrid interest equal to the greater (or lesser) of an annuity or a unitrust amount does not qualify. Reg. § 1.170A–6(c)(2)(i)(B) and (c)(2)(ii)(B). The trust must not permit any payments for private purposes before the expiration of the charitable lead interest, except in strictly limited circumstances. Reg. § 1.170A–6(c)(2)(i)(E) and (c)(2)(ii)(D). Furthermore, although the trust may be permitted to pay amounts to charity in excess of the required annuity or unitrust amount, such payments will be disregarded in valuing the charitable lead interest. In sum, while the charitable lead interest bears a marked resemblance to the annuity or unitrust interest of the private beneficiary in a charitable remainder trust, it is less rigidly defined. A charitable lead trust, unlike a charitable remainder trust, is not subject to a 20-year maximum term of years; the annual payments are not subject to a 5% floor or a 50% ceiling; and the value of the lead interest is not subject to a 10% floor. However, a charitable lead trust is subject to special investment restrictions if the required annuity payments to charity are worth more than 60% of the value of the trust property at the time of the transfer. Reg. § 1.170A–6(c)(2)(i)(D).

A grantor's contributions to a charitable lead trust are deductible under § 170 only if the grantor is treated as the owner of the lead interest under the grantor trust rules. If the trust property will revert to the grantor (or the grantor's spouse) at the termination of the charitable lead interest, the trust will almost certainly qualify as a grantor trust, and the grantor will be treated as owning the entire trust. I.R.C. § 673 (see § 8.7, *supra*). Alternatively, if the remaining trust property will pass to other beneficiaries, grantor trust status may be achieved if any person holds a nonfiduciary power to purchase property from the trust. I.R.C. § 675(4) (see § 8.11, *supra*). Such a power should be held by a person other than the grantor, the trustee, or a disqualified person, to avoid violating the provisions of § 4941 concerning acts of self-dealing.

If the grantor loses his or her status as deemed owner under the grantor trust rules before the charitable lead interest expires, any deduction previously allowed for the grantor's contributions to the charitable lead trust will be recaptured. Upon early termination of grantor trust status, the grantor will be treated as receiving income equal to the amount previously allowed as a deduction, reduced by the discounted value of the required annual charitable payments that were actually made before the termination of grantor trust status. I.R.C. § 170(f)(2)(B); Reg. § 1.170A–6(c)(4). For example, suppose that Tess contributes $50,000 to a charitable lead trust that will pay $5,000 to charity each year for 10 years and then distribute the remaining trust property to Tess. The trust qualifies as a grantor trust under § 673, and Tess receives a $40,000 charitable deduction (equal to the present value of the charitable lead interest). If Tess dies after the trust has made one annual payment to charity, the trust will no longer be a grantor trust. Tess must report gross income on her final return equal to the excess of $40,000 (previously allowed as a charitable deduction) over the present value of $5,000 (discounted back to the date of her original contribution). Reg. § 1.170A–6(c)(5) (Example 3). After Tess's death, the trust will be treated as a complex (nongrantor) trust and will be entitled to deduct the annual amounts of gross income paid to charity during the rest of the trust term. Reg. § 1.170A–6(d)(2).

The Service has published sample forms to provide guidance in drafting governing instruments for charitable lead trusts of both the grantor and the nongrantor types. Rev. Proc. 2007–45 and 2007–46, 2007–2 C.B. 89, 102 (charitable lead annuity trust); Rev. Proc. 2008–45 and 2008–46, 2008–30 I.R.B. 224, 238 (charitable lead unitrust).

CHAPTER 10
FOREIGN TRUSTS

§ 10.1   OVERVIEW

For federal tax purposes, trusts are classified as domestic or foreign. A trust qualifies as a domestic trust only if (1) it is subject to the supervisory jurisdiction of a domestic court and (2) its administration is controlled by U.S. persons. Any trust that fails to satisfy one or both tests is a foreign trust. Although most trusts that are administered exclusively by domestic trustees within the United States routinely qualify as domestic trusts, foreign trust status is readily available. For example, a trust with a foreign trustee may be classified as a foreign trust even though the grantor and all of the beneficiaries are U.S. persons and the trust is administered in the United States. The criteria for classifying domestic and foreign trusts are discussed in § 10.2, *infra*.

For federal income tax purposes, a foreign trust is generally treated as a nonresident alien and is therefore taxed only on income derived from U.S. sources or effectively connected with the conduct of business in the United States. I.R.C. §§ 641(b) and 872(a). In effect, a foreign trust is exempt from tax on income from foreign sources. In contrast, a domestic trust is taxed on its worldwide income. Thus, foreign trusts enjoy a significant tax advantage over domestic trusts, and the advantage may be enhanced if a trust is treated as owned by a foreign grantor under the grantor trust rules. For example, suppose that a nonresident alien grantor creates a revocable foreign trust and is treated as owning the entire trust under § 676. The trust's foreign source income will escape U.S. tax in the grantor's hands, and distributions from the trust to U.S. beneficiaries will be excluded from the beneficiaries' gross income as gifts or bequests. Rev. Rul. 69–70, 1969–1 C.B. 182. Even if the trust is a nongrantor trust, it will be able to accumulate foreign source income free of U.S. tax, and the U.S. beneficiaries will not be taxed on such income unless or until it is distributed to them. In contrast, if the trust were classified as a domestic trust (or treated as owned by a U.S. grantor), the trust's worldwide income would be subject to U.S. tax in the hands of the trust or its beneficiaries (or the U.S. grantor).

Congress has enacted several provisions that sharply limit opportunities for deferral or complete avoidance of U.S. income taxation through foreign trusts. Section 679, enacted in 1976, treats a U.S. grantor who transfers property to a foreign trust as owning the trust for income tax purposes if the trust has one or more U.S. beneficiaries. This provision, when applicable, denies nongrantor status to the foreign trust and subjects the trust's worldwide income to U.S. tax in the hands of the U.S. grantor. Section 679 applies even though the grantor retains no beneficial interests or powers that would trigger grantor trust status under §§ 671–677. The operation of § 679 is discussed in § 10.3, *infra*.

Section 672(f), enacted in 1990 and amended in 1996, generally restricts the application of the grantor trust rules to situations where the deemed owner of a trust's income is a U.S. citizen or resident (or a domestic corporation). The provision applies equally to domestic and foreign trusts. Consequently, a nonresident alien generally will not be treated as the owner of a trust for income tax purposes, even if he or she holds beneficial interests or powers that otherwise would trigger grantor trust status under §§ 671–678. The operation of § 672(f) is discussed in § 10.4, *infra*.

To the extent that the grantor trust rules do not apply, foreign trusts are generally taxed in the same manner as nongrantor domestic trusts, with a few important modifications. Specifically, under § 643(a)(6), the distributable net income of a foreign trust includes foreign source income as well as net capital gains. As a result, these items are included in taxable distributions to U.S. beneficiaries under the normal conduit rules, even if the items were excluded from the foreign trust's gross income or allocated to corpus for trust accounting purposes. If a foreign trust distributes amounts in excess of distributable net income, such amounts may be taxed to U.S. beneficiaries as accumulation distributions under the throwback rules. Under § 643(h) and (i), certain loans and indirect payments made by foreign trusts to U.S. persons may be recharacterized as distributions in accordance with substance-over-form principles. The treatment of foreign nongrantor trusts is discussed in § 10.5, and the throwback rules are discussed in Chapter 11, *infra*.

Under § 684, a U.S. person who transfers appreciated property to a foreign trust must recognize gain equal to the excess of the property's fair market value over its adjusted basis; a similar rule applies when a domestic trust becomes a foreign trust. The operation of § 684 is discussed in § 10.6, *infra*.

The Code imposes special information reporting requirements in connection with foreign trusts. The reporting requirements apply to a U.S. grantor who creates or transfers property to a foreign trust; to a U.S. grantor who is treated as owning a foreign trust under the grantor trust rules; and to a U.S. beneficiary who receives a distribution from a foreign trust. A grantor or a beneficiary who fails to comply with the reporting requirements may incur a substantial penalty. The reporting requirements are discussed in § 10.7, *infra*.

§ 10.2   FOREIGN TRUST

For federal tax purposes, a trust is classified as a foreign trust unless it meets the statutory definition of a domestic trust. I.R.C. § 7701(a)(31)(B). To qualify as domestic rather than foreign, a trust must be subject to the supervisory jurisdiction of a domestic court (the "court test"), and its administration must be controlled by U.S. persons (the "control test"). I.R.C. § 7701(a)(30)(E); Reg. § 301.7701–7(a)(1). Both requirements must be satisfied concurrently; a trust that fails to satisfy either the court test or the control test will be classified as a foreign trust. Furthermore, a trust's status may change from domestic to foreign or vice versa, potentially triggering substantive tax liability and information reporting requirements.

The objective two-pronged definition of a domestic trust was enacted in 1996 to replace the vague, open-ended test of prior law, which depended on whether a trust more closely resembled a resident or nonresident alien individual. See, e.g., Jones Trust v. Commissioner, 132 F.2d 914 (4th Cir. 1943). The current statutory provisions provide greater certainty and make it relatively easy for trusts to qualify as foreign rather than domestic. In contrast, decedents' estates continue to be classified under the open-ended test of prior law. I.R.C. § 7701(a)(30)(D) and (a)(31)(A). Thus, in some circumstances the estate of a deceased nonresident alien may be classified as a domestic estate, and the estate of a deceased U.S. citizen may be classified as a foreign estate. Rev. Rul. 62–154, 1962–2 C.B. 148; Rev. Rul. 81–112, 1981–1 C.B. 598.

A trust satisfies the court test only if a domestic court "is able to exercise primary supervision over the administration of the trust." I.R.C. § 7701(a)(30)(E). According to the regulations, this means that a domestic court must have "the authority to determine substantially all issues regarding the administration of the entire trust," including recordkeeping, tax return filing, investment management, and distributions. Reg. § 301.7701–7(c)(3). The court test is not violated merely because a foreign court has jurisdiction over a trustee, a beneficiary or trust property, as long as a domestic court also has jurisdiction to determine matters of trust administration. In many cases, trust administration proceeds smoothly without any need for court proceedings. Moreover, it may be unclear whether a particular court would have jurisdiction to resolve a matter of trust administration if the need arose. To avoid the difficulty of hypothetical jurisdictional determinations, the regulations provide a safe harbor. A trust is deemed to satisfy the court test if (1) the trust instrument does not direct that the trust be administered outside the United States, (2) the trust is in fact administered exclusively in the United States, and (3) the trust is not subject to an "automatic migration provision." Reg. § 301.7701–7(c)(1). A prohibited automatic migration provision (sometimes referred to as a "flee clause") refers to a provision that would cause the trust to migrate from the United States if a domestic court attempts to assert jurisdiction or supervise the administration of the trust. Such a provision will generally cause the trust to be treated as a foreign trust. Reg. § 301.7701–7(c)(4)(ii); see also Reg. § 301.7701–7(d)(3).

The control test requires that one or more U.S. persons "have the authority to control all substantial decisions of the trust." I.R.C. § 7701(a)(30)(E). For this purpose, a decision is "substantial" unless it is "ministerial." The regulations provide a nonexclusive list of substantial decisions, including determinations involving distributions, principal and income allocations, trust investments, and trustee removal or replacement. Reg. § 301.7701–7(d)(1)(ii). In applying the control test, it is necessary to consider all persons who have the power, by vote or otherwise, to make substantial decisions of the trust. Such persons are not limited to trustees but may also include grantors, beneficiaries, and other power holders. The control test is satisfied only if all substantial decisions of the trust are subject to the control of one or more U.S. persons without the veto or required consent of any other person. Reg. § 301.7701–7(d)(1)(iii). Thus, a trust is classified as a foreign trust if any foreign person has control over any substantial decision, including the ability to block a decision made by domestic trustees. For example, a trust with two domestic trustees and one foreign trustee satisfies the court test if all substantial decisions can be made by majority vote, but not if any substantial decision requires the agreement of all three trustees. Reg. § 301.7701–7(d)(1)(v) (Examples 1 and 2). Similarly, the test is not met if a trust is treated as owned by a foreign grantor under the grantor trust rules. Reg. § 301.7701–7(d)(4) (Example 2). If trustees delegate investment authority to an agent, the trustees are deemed to retain control over the agent's decisions if they can terminate the agency at will.

Even if U.S. persons initially have authority to make all substantial decisions of a trust, control may shift to a foreign person as a result of a controlling person's death, incapacity, resignation, or change of residence. To prevent a shift in control from triggering an "inadvertent" change of status from a domestic trust to a foreign trust (or vice versa), the regulations allow a 12-month grace period for the trust to preserve its status by making any necessary changes in the identity or the residence of the persons who control substantial trust decisions. Unless the necessary changes are made within the 12-month grace period, the trust's status changes on the date of the shift in control. Reg. § 301.7701–7(d)(2).

§ 10.3   U.S. GRANTOR AS DEEMED OWNER: § 679

Under § 679, a U.S. person who transfers property to a foreign trust that has one or more U.S. beneficiaries is treated as owning the portion of the trust attributable to the transferred property. This provision extends grantor trust treatment to foreign trusts solely by reference to the U.S. citizenship or residence of the transferor and the beneficiaries. Unlike the other grantor trust rules of §§ 673–677, § 679 does not require that the deemed owner retain any beneficial interest or power. It was enacted in 1976 to prevent U.S. grantors from using foreign trusts to avoid current taxation of income accumulated for U.S. beneficiaries. Although grantor trust status may be advantageous in a few situations (e.g., in qualifying a foreign trust as a permissible shareholder of an S corporation), the primary consequence of § 679 is to subject the worldwide income of a foreign trust to current U.S. taxation in the hands of a U.S. grantor.

Section 679 applies only if a U.S. person transfers property to a foreign trust that has at least one U.S. beneficiary. I.R.C. § 679(a)(1); Reg. § 1.679–1(a). In determining whether a transferor or a beneficiary is a "U.S. person," the regulations refer to § 7701(a)(30), which defines the term to include a U.S. citizen or resident as well as a domestic partnership, corporation, estate or trust. Reg. § 1.679–1(c)(2). In addition, a foreign trust is treated as having a U.S. beneficiary if its beneficiaries include a controlled foreign corporation, a foreign partnership with a U.S. partner, or a foreign estate or trust with a U.S. beneficiary. I.R.C. § 679(c)(2); Reg. § 1.679–2(b)(1). Thus, grantor trust status cannot be avoided simply by naming a foreign entity owned or controlled by U.S. persons as the beneficiary of a foreign trust; under the "look-through" rule, the U.S. persons will be treated as indirect beneficiaries of the foreign trust. Certain types of foreign trusts (e.g., employee benefit trusts and charitable trusts) are expressly exempt from grantor trust treatment under § 679. I.R.C. § 679(a)(1); Reg. § 1.679–4(a)(2) and (a)(3).

A foreign trust is treated as having U.S. beneficiaries unless (1) no income or corpus can be paid or accumulated to or for the benefit of any U.S. person during the taxable year and (2) no income or corpus could be paid to or for the benefit of any U.S. person if the trust were to terminate during the taxable year. I.R.C. § 679(c)(1); Reg. § 1.679–2(a)(1). This determination is made without regard to whether income or corpus is actually distributed to a U.S. person and without regard to whether a beneficiary's interest is contingent on a future event, but the regulations acknowledge the possibility that remote contingent interests may be disregarded. Reg. § 1.679–2(a)(2). Moreover, if any person has a discretionary power—whether as trustee, as the holder of a power of appointment, or otherwise—to make trust distributions, the trust is treated as having U.S. beneficiaries unless the permissible beneficiaries are limited to a specifically identified class that does not include any U.S. persons during the taxable year. I.R.C. § 679(c)(4). In determining whether a trust has U.S. beneficiaries, the terms of the written trust instrument are not conclusive; informal agreements and understandings may be taken into account, as well as the possibility of a trust amendment or judicial reformation. I.R.C. § 679(c)(5); Reg. § 1.679–2(a)(4). Beneficiaries of a trust are not limited to actual or potential recipients of trust distributions, but also include persons who receive indirect benefits in the form of a below-market loan or rent-free use of trust property. I.R.C. § 679(c)(6). More generally, any foreign trust funded by a U.S. transferor is presumed to have U.S. beneficiaries unless the transferor demonstrates the contrary. I.R.C. § 679(d).

To illustrate the expansive concept of U.S. beneficiaries, suppose that Amy, a U.S. resident, transfers property to a foreign trust to pay income to her son Ben, a nonresident alien, for life; at Ben's death, the trust will terminate and the remaining property will be distributed to his surviving issue, or in the absence of issue to his heirs (other than Amy). All of Ben's closest living relatives—three children, two brothers and their respective children—are nonresident aliens. However, Ben also has a first cousin, a U.S. resident, who might share in the remainder if none of the other relatives survive him. If Amy can show that the first cousin's interest is so remote as to be negligible, the trust will not be treated as having a U.S. beneficiary. In contrast, if one of Ben's brothers' children is a U.S. resident, the trust probably will be treated as having a U.S. beneficiary. Furthermore, if the trustee has a discretionary power to distribute income or corpus to the first cousin, or if Ben has a power to appoint the remainder to a class of beneficiaries that includes the first cousin, the trust will be treated as having a U.S. beneficiary. Reg. § 1.679–2(a)(2)(iii) (Examples 7–11).

The determination of whether a foreign trust has U.S. beneficiaries is made on an annual basis. Reg. § 1.679–2(a)(1). Changes in the trust's status may be triggered by various events, including birth or death of beneficiaries, termination of a beneficiary's interest, exercise or lapse of discretionary powers, and changes in a beneficiary's citizenship or residence. Thus, a foreign trust that formerly had no U.S. beneficiaries may be treated as a grantor trust under § 679 beginning in the taxable year when it acquires a U.S. beneficiary. In that case, the U.S. grantor will be treated as receiving a distribution of any undistributed net income (determined immediately before the beginning of the grantor's taxable year in which § 679 becomes applicable) attributable to the grantor's earlier contributions and transferring the same amount back to the trust. I.R.C. § 679(b); Reg. § 1.679–2(c)(1). The net effect is to negate the tax advantage for the U.S. grantor of accumulating income in a foreign trust.

For example, suppose that Carlos, a U.S. resident, created and funded a foreign trust in 2017. The trust initially had no U.S. beneficiaries, but in 2020 one of the beneficiaries becomes a U.S. resident, causing Carlos to be treated as the owner of the trust beginning in 2020. If the trust has $30,000 of undistributed net income from taxable years before 2020, Carlos will be treated as receiving an accumulation distribution of $30,000 and transferring the same amount back to the trust. The distribution will be taxed as an accumulation distribution under the "throwback rules" of §§ 665–668, including an interest charge, as discussed in Chapter 11, *infra*. Reg. § 1.679–2(c)(3) (Example 1).

In determining whether a foreign trust has U.S. beneficiaries, the possibility that a nonresident alien beneficiary might eventually acquire U.S. citizenship or residence is disregarded until the beneficiary actually becomes a U.S. person. Moreover, in applying § 679 to a transfer by a U.S. grantor to a foreign trust, a beneficiary who first becomes a U.S. person more than five years after the transfer will not be treated as a U.S. person. I.R.C. § 679(c)(3); Reg. § 1.679–2(a)(3)(i). In the previous example, suppose that the beneficiary does not become a U.S. resident until 2023, six years after Carlos funded the trust in 2017. In that case, the trust will not be treated as having a U.S. beneficiary for purposes of applying § 679 to Carlos's transfer. Accordingly, Carlos will not be treated as owning the trust and will not be taxed on the trust's undistributed net income. Reg. § 1.679–2(a)(3)(ii) (Example 2).

A foreign trust may lose its grantor trust status under § 679 if it ceases to have any U.S. beneficiaries.

If the trust is not treated as a grantor trust under §§ 673–678, the U.S. grantor will be treated as transferring the trust property to a nongrantor foreign trust on the first day of the next taxable year. Consequently, the termination of grantor trust status may trigger a deemed sale of any appreciated property held by the trust, causing the U.S. grantor to recognize gain under § 684, as discussed in § 10.6, *infra*. For example, suppose that Debbie, a U.S. resident, was treated under § 679 as owning a foreign trust that she created in 2017. In 2020 the trust ceases to have any U.S. beneficiaries as a result of a beneficiary's change of residence. Beginning in 2021, neither Debbie nor any other person is treated as owning the trust under §§ 673–679. When the trust loses its grantor trust status, Debbie will be treated as transferring the trust property to a nongrantor foreign trust, and she will recognize gain under § 684 on any appreciated property held in the trust. Reg. § 1.679–2(c)(3) (Example 2).

If a U.S. grantor transfers property to a foreign trust that has one or more U.S. beneficiaries, § 679 treats the trust as wholly or partially owned by the grantor. For this purpose, a "transfer" means a gratuitous lifetime transfer of any type of property, including cash. The statute expressly excludes a transfer occurring by reason of the transferor's death. I.R.C. § 679(a)(2)(A); Reg. § 1.679–4(a)(1). In the case of an individual transferor, the limitation to lifetime transfers reflects the notion that only a living grantor can be treated as owning a trust for income tax purposes. The statute also excludes a transfer made in exchange for consideration of at least equivalent fair market value, in accordance with the general scope of the grantor trust rules. I.R.C. § 679(a)(2)(B); Reg. § 1.679–4(a)(4). For this purpose, consideration includes property received from the trust, services rendered by the trust, and the right to use trust property, but does not include a beneficial interest in the trust itself. Reg. § 1.679–4(b). Moreover, in determining the fair market value of consideration received, an obligation of the trust, a grantor or beneficiary, or any related person is not taken into account unless it is a "qualified obligation" described in the regulations. I.R.C. § 679(a)(3); Reg. § 1.679–4(c). For example, if a U.S. grantor transfers property to a foreign trust with U.S. beneficiaries and receives the trust's note in exchange, the note will be counted as consideration only if it has a term of no more than five years, has a yield to maturity within specified limits, and meets the other requirements of a qualified obligation set forth in the regulations. Reg. § 1.679–4(d).

The concept of a transfer is broadly defined to include not only direct transfers but also indirect and constructive transfers. Reg. § 1.679–3(a). Thus, § 679 cannot be circumvented by interposing an intermediary between a U.S. transferor and a foreign trust that has U.S. beneficiaries. Reg. § 1.679–3(c)(1)–(c)(4). Suppose that, as part of a tax avoidance plan, Elise, a U.S. resident, gives stock to her uncle, a nonresident alien, and the uncle sells the stock and contributes the proceeds to a foreign trust for the benefit of Elise's relatives, some of whom are U.S. residents. The uncle will be treated as Elise's agent, and she will be treated as transferring property to the trust for purposes of § 679. Reg. § 1.679–3(c)(5) (Example 2). Similarly, if a domestic revocable trust transfers property to a foreign trust that has U.S. beneficiaries, the deemed owner of the revocable trust will be treated as the transferor for purposes of § 679. Reg. § 1.679–3(b).

If a nonresident alien individual becomes a U.S. resident within five years after transferring property to a foreign trust, the individual is treated as making a transfer to the trust on the "residency starting date." The amount of the deemed transfer is equal to the portion of the trust property attributable to the earlier transfer, including any undistributed net income. I.R.C. § 679(a)(4); Reg. § 1.679–5(a) and (b)(2). This five-year look-back rule is aimed at foreign grantors who transfer property to foreign trusts shortly before moving to the United States.

For example, suppose that Franz, a nonresident alien, creates and funds an irrevocable foreign trust in 2016 for the benefit of his relatives, some of whom are U.S. residents. In 2020 Franz becomes a U.S. resident. Franz will be treated as making a transfer to the trust of all of the property (including any undistributed net income) held in the trust and will be treated as the deemed owner of the trust from the date he becomes a U.S. resident. Reg. § 1.679–5(c) (Example 1). Alternatively, suppose that Franz initially retained a power to revoke the trust and was treated as owning the entire trust from its inception. In 2020, while still a nonresident, Franz releases his power of revocation and the trust loses its grantor trust status. In 2022 Franz becomes a U.S. resident.

For purposes of § 679, Franz's original transfer to the trust is deemed to occur when he ceases to be treated as owning the trust. Accordingly, the five-year look-back period runs from 2020 (not 2016), and § 679 will apply from the time Franz becomes a U.S. resident in 2022. Reg. § 1.679–5(b)(1) and (c) (Example 2).

Section 679 has no application to domestic trusts. However, if a domestic trust becomes a foreign trust (e.g., upon the appointment of a foreign trustee), the change in status may trigger a deemed transfer under § 679. Specifically, if a U.S. grantor transfers property to a domestic trust that subsequently becomes a foreign trust, the U.S. grantor is treated as making a transfer to the trust on the date that the trust becomes a foreign trust. The amount of the deemed transfer is equal to the portion of the trust property attributable to the original transfer, including any undistributed net income. I.R.C. § 679(a)(5); Reg. § 1.679–6(a) and (b). The special rule for "outbound trust migration" applies only if the change in the trust's residence occurs while the U.S. grantor is still alive. For example, suppose that Gertrude, a U.S. resident, creates and funds a domestic trust for the benefit of her children (who are also U.S. residents). Gertrude retains no beneficial interests or powers that would cause her to be treated as owning any portion of the trust under §§ 673–677. Ten years later, the original U.S. trustee resigns and is replaced by a foreign trustee, causing the trust to become a foreign trust. Gertrude will be treated as transferring all of the trust's property (including any accumulated income) on the date of the foreign

trustee's appointment and will become the deemed
owner of the trust under § 679. Reg. § 1.679–6(c).

§ 10.4   FOREIGN GRANTOR AS DEEMED OWNER: § 672(f)

Section 672(f), originally enacted in 1990 and
amended in 1996, sharply restricts the application of
the grantor trust rules to foreign persons as deemed
owners. The provision is intended to prevent the
grantor trust rules from operating to attribute trust
income to a foreign deemed owner and thereby avoid
U.S. tax on foreign source income that is distributed
to or accumulated for U.S. beneficiaries. Subject to
two important exceptions described below, § 672(f)
generally provides that the grantor trust rules apply
only to the extent that they cause a trust to be treated
as owned in whole or in part by a U.S. citizen or
resident or by a domestic corporation. I.R.C.
§ 672(f)(1); Reg. § 1.672(f)–1(a). Section 672(f) applies
equally to domestic and foreign trusts, other than
certain trusts created to compensate employees for
services. I.R.C. § 672(f)(2)(B); Reg. § 1.672(f)–3(c)(1).
In applying § 672(f), it is necessary first to identify
the persons who would be treated as owning the trust
under the grantor trust rules (other than § 672(f))
and then to disregard any deemed owner who is not
a U.S. citizen or resident or a domestic corporation.
For this purpose, a controlled foreign corporation, a
passive foreign investment company, and a foreign
personal holding company are treated as domestic
corporations. I.R.C. § 672(f)(3); Reg. § 1.672(f)–2(a)
and (c). Thus, § 672(f) generally prevents nonresident
aliens and foreign entities from being treated as

owning any portion of a trust under the grantor trust rules, unless the trust comes within a specific statutory safe harbor. Any portion of a trust that is not treated as a grantor trust as a result of § 672(f) will be subject to the normal conduit rules. For example, suppose that Aldo, a nonresident alien, creates a trust for his children and grandchildren. The trust is irrevocable, but Aldo retains an unrestricted power to sprinkle income or corpus among the beneficiaries. But for § 672(f), Aldo would be treated as owning the trust under § 674. Because he is a nonresident alien, however, § 672(f) precludes grantor trust status, and the trust is subject to the normal conduit rules.

Notwithstanding the general rule limiting deemed owner status to U.S. citizens or residents and domestic corporations, § 672(f) allows the grantor trust rules to operate without regard to the identity of the deemed owner in two specific situations. The first statutory safe harbor applies where a grantor retains a power to revoke the trust (i.e., a power to "revest" title "absolutely" in the grantor). The power must be exercisable by the grantor alone (i.e., "without the consent or approval of any other person") or by the grantor "with the consent of a related or subordinate party who is subservient to the grantor." I.R.C. § 672(f)(2)(A)(i); Reg. § 1.672(f)– 3(a)(1). A power of revocation is attributed to the grantor if it is exercisable without restriction on the grantor's behalf by a guardian, conservator, or agent. A power held by the grantor's spouse is also attributed to the grantor under § 672(e) (see § 8.6, *supra*). However, a power that requires the consent of another person (other than the grantor's spouse) does not come within the statutory safe harbor unless the other person is "related or subordinate" and also "subservient" within the meaning of § 672(c) (see § 8.6, *supra*).

For example, suppose that Bianca, a nonresident alien, creates a trust for the benefit of her children with her brother as trustee, and reserves a power to revoke the trust with the trustee's consent. Since Bianca can revoke the trust only with the consent of her brother (a related party), she will be treated as the owner of the trust unless the facts indicate that her brother is not subservient to her. However, if the trustee is not a related or subordinate party (e.g., an uncle or a brother-in-law), Bianca will not be treated as the owner of the trust, even if she has an unrestricted power to remove and replace the trustee. Reg. § 1.672(f)–3(a)(4) (Examples 1 and 3).

To come within the statutory safe harbor, a power of revocation must be exercisable by the grantor for at least 183 days during the taxable year (or each day of the taxable year, in the case of a first or final taxable year of less than 183 days). Reg. § 1.672(f)–3(a)(2). If a power of revocation falls outside the statutory safe harbor for any taxable year, § 672(f) denies grantor trust status for that taxable year and all subsequent taxable years. Reg. § 1.672(f)–3(a)(1). Note that the statutory safe harbor applies only to a grantor's power of revocation, not to another person's power of withdrawal. Thus, a nonresident alien beneficiary of a trust created by another person will not qualify as a deemed owner, even if the beneficiary holds an unrestricted power to withdraw property from the trust.

The second statutory safe harbor applies where distributions of trust income or corpus during the grantor's lifetime can be made only to the grantor or the grantor's spouse. I.R.C. § 672(f)(2)(A)(ii); Reg. § 1.672(f)–3(b)(1). For example, suppose that Claude, a nonresident alien, creates an irrevocable trust to pay income (and corpus in the trustee's discretion) to himself and his wife Diana (also a nonresident alien) while either of them is living and thereafter to their 25-year-old child. Because the trust permits distributions only to Claude and his spouse during Claude's lifetime, Claude will be treated as the owner of the trust until his death. After Claude's death the trust will no longer be a grantor trust; even if Diana survives him and has an unrestricted power to withdraw property from the trust, she is not a grantor and therefore cannot be treated as a deemed owner. If the couple's child is entitled or permitted to receive any distributions while Claude is alive, the trust will be a nongrantor trust from its inception. Reg. § 1.672(f)–3(b)(4) (Examples 1–3). For this purpose, payments from a trust that discharge a legal obligation of the grantor (or the grantor's spouse) are generally treated as distributions to the grantor (or the spouse). An obligation owed to a related party, however, is taken into account only if it is bona fide and contracted for full money's-worth consideration or if it is an obligation of support owed to a dependent who is permanently and totally disabled or under 19 years of age. Reg. § 1.672(f)–3(b)(2).

Even if § 672(f) would otherwise allow a foreign grantor to be treated as the owner of a trust, a U.S. beneficiary of the trust (rather than the foreign grantor) may be treated as the owner to the extent that the U.S. beneficiary transferred property directly or indirectly to the foreign grantor for less than full money's-worth consideration. I.R.C. § 672(f)(5). In effect, this rule disregards the nominal foreign grantor and treats the U.S. beneficiary who indirectly furnished consideration for the trust as the real grantor. Consequently, the trust's worldwide income will be subject to U.S. taxation in the hands of the U.S. beneficiary. The rule does not apply to a transfer that was eligible for the gift tax annual exclusion, nor to a transfer that was "wholly unrelated to any transaction involving the trust." Reg. § 1.672(f)–5(a). To illustrate the operation of § 672(f)(5), suppose that Edgar, a U.S. resident, gives $1 million in cash to his sister Frieda, a nonresident alien. Frieda creates a trust of $1 million for the benefit of Edgar and his children, retaining an unrestricted power of revocation exercisable by her alone. Edgar, not Frieda, will be treated as the owner of the trust. The result would be the same if Edgar was a nonresident alien when he made the gift to Frieda and subsequently became a U.S. resident. Reg. § 1.672(f)–5(a)(2) (Examples 1 and 2). Note that the rule of § 672(f)(5) attributing ownership to a U.S. transferor may overlap with § 679 in the case of a foreign trust (see § 10.3 *supra*).

§ 10.5   NONGRANTOR FOREIGN TRUSTS

Many foreign trusts are classified as nongrantor trusts, either because they never qualified for grantor trust status or because the grantor who was formerly treated as owning the trust is no longer alive. For example, a trust created by a foreign grantor will generally be classified as a nongrantor trust unless it comes within an exception to § 672(f), and a trust that was treated as owned by a U.S. grantor under § 679 will generally become a nongrantor trust when the grantor dies.

A nongrantor foreign trust is treated as a nonresident alien and its taxable income is computed in the same manner as that of a domestic trust, subject to a few important modifications. I.R.C. § 641(b). Thus, a foreign trust is generally subject to tax at the entity level only on income derived from U.S. sources or effectively connected with the conduct of a business in the United States; it is effectively exempt from tax on foreign source income. I.R.C. § 872(a). Nevertheless, in computing distributable net income (DNI), a foreign trust must take its worldwide income into account. The expanded definition of DNI ensures that the foreign trust cannot be used as a vehicle to shelter income from tax in the hands of U.S. beneficiaries. The normal conduit rules ensure that U.S. beneficiaries who receive taxable distributions from the foreign trust are taxed on their ratable share of items included in the trust's DNI for the current taxable year (see Chapter 7, *supra*), and the "throwback rules" serve the same function for "accumulation distributions" of

DNI accumulated in previous years (see Chapter 11, *infra*). Consequently, items of a foreign trust's worldwide income that escape tax at the entity level will ultimately be taxed to the extent that they are distributed to U.S. beneficiaries.

A foreign trust generally computes DNI in the same manner as a domestic trust under § 643(a), starting with taxable income (determined before allowing any deductions for distributions or for a personal exemption) and including net tax-exempt interest (see Chapter 6, *supra*). In addition, a foreign trust must include in DNI three additional items that are excluded from its taxable income. First, DNI of a foreign trust includes gross income derived from foreign sources, reduced by otherwise deductible expenses allocable to such income. I.R.C. § 643(a)(6)(A). Second, DNI includes U.S. source income, determined without regard for treaty provisions exempting particular types of income. I.R.C. § 643(a)(6)(B). Third, DNI includes net capital gains, regardless of whether such gains are allocated to income or to corpus and regardless of whether they are distributed currently or accumulated for future distribution. I.R.C. § 643(a)(6)(C). As a result, if a foreign trust makes taxable distributions in a year when it has a net capital gain, the amount reported by a beneficiary will include a ratable share of capital gain along with other items entering into DNI. For example, suppose that a foreign trust distributes $25,000 to a U.S. beneficiary in a year when the trust has $10,000 of foreign-source rent, $10,000 of U.S. portfolio interest, and a $30,000 net capital gain from U.S. stock sales. The trust is not subject to U.S. tax on any of its income; the rent is derived from foreign sources, and the portfolio interest and capital gain are excluded by statute. Nevertheless, the beneficiary will report $5,000 of rent, $5,000 of interest, and $15,000 of capital gain.

If the beneficiary receives a distribution of income on which U.S. tax was withheld at the source, the amount of the distribution is grossed up by the amount of tax withheld and the beneficiary is entitled to credit the tax withheld against his or her personal income tax. For example, suppose that a foreign trust has $10,000 of U.S. dividends from which the issuing corporation withholds $3,000 of tax. If the trust distributes the net amount of $7,000 to a U.S. beneficiary, the beneficiary will report $10,000 of dividend income and will be entitled to a $3,000 credit for the tax previously withheld. Reg. §§ 1.1441–3(f) and 1.1462–1(b).

When a foreign trust makes a distribution that carries out DNI accumulated in previous years, the beneficiary is taxed on the accumulation distribution under the throwback rules of §§ 665–668, which include an interest charge to compensate for the deferral of tax (discussed in Chapter 11, *infra*). The throwback rules apply primarily to foreign trusts (or domestic trusts that were formerly foreign trusts); they no longer apply to most domestic trusts. I.R.C. § 665(c).

To the extent that an accumulation distribution consists of tax-exempt interest, it retains its tax-exempt character in the beneficiary's hands. The taxable portion of the accumulation distribution received by a U.S. beneficiary, however, is taxed as ordinary income in the beneficiary's hands; the character of items other than tax-exempt interest is not preserved in the hands of the U.S. beneficiary. I.R.C. § 667(a). (In contrast, an accumulation distribution does preserve the character of its component items in the hands of a foreign beneficiary. I.R.C. § 667(e). This rule ensures that the foreign beneficiary will be taxed only on the portion of the distribution attributable to income from U.S. sources or effectively connected with a U.S. business.) Consequently, the throwback rules have an especially harsh impact on a foreign trust that makes an accumulation distribution to a U.S. beneficiary of capital gains accumulated in previous years. As a practical matter, the trust can mitigate the beneficiary's tax burden by making distributions at least equal to DNI in years when the trust realizes capital gains, since the net gain will be included in DNI and its character will be preserved in the beneficiary's hands.

Congress enacted two anti-abuse rules in 1996 to discourage tax avoidance by foreign trusts that make disguised or indirect distributions to U.S. beneficiaries. The first rule treats a loan of cash or marketable securities made by a foreign trust to a U.S. person as a taxable distribution if the borrower is a grantor or beneficiary of the trust or a related person. I.R.C. § 643(i). This provision also applies to uncompensated use of other trust property. If a loan is recharacterized as a taxable distribution, any subsequent repayment, modification, or cancellation of the loan is disregarded for tax purposes.

The second anti-abuse rule treats a U.S. person who receives an amount "indirectly" from a foreign trust through an intermediary as receiving payment directly from the trust. I.R.C. § 643(h). According to the regulations, this provision applies only if the U.S. person receives property from an intermediary who received it from a foreign trust "pursuant to a plan one of the principal purposes of which was avoidance of United States tax." Reg. § 1.643(h)–1(a)(1). A tax avoidance purpose is presumed to exist if (1) the U.S. person is related to the trust's grantor, (2) within two years before or two years after receiving property from the trust, the intermediary transfers the same property (or its proceeds or substitute property) to the U.S. person, and (3) the U.S. person cannot demonstrate that the transfer was a bona fide gift from the intermediary. Reg. § 1.643(h)–1(a)(2). The intermediary is generally treated as an agent of the foreign trust, and the deemed distribution from the foreign trust occurs at the time of the transfer from the intermediary to the U.S. person. Reg. § 1.643(h)–1(c). The purpose of the rule is to recharacterize the form of the transaction to reflect its substance, and to ensure that a taxable distribution from a foreign trust to a U.S. person is not disguised as a tax-free gift from an intermediary.

For example, suppose that a foreign trust created by Fabio (a nonresident alien) for his issue distributes $50,000 to Fabio's daughter Greta (also a nonresident alien), and less than two years later Greta transfers an equivalent amount to her son Harry (a U.S. resident). Unless Harry can show that the transfer was a bona fide gift from Greta, it may be recharacterized as a taxable distribution from the trust. The result would be the same if Greta received stock from the trust and then sold the stock and transferred the proceeds to Harry within two years. Reg. § 1.643(h)–1(g) (Examples 1 and 2).

According to the regulations, the rule of § 643(h) does not apply to the extent that (1) the transfer from the foreign trust or from the intermediary is made for fair market value, or (2) the intermediary is the grantor of the portion of the foreign trust from which the transferred property is derived. Reg. § 1.643(h)–1(b). The rule is also inapplicable if the aggregate value of all property transferred to the U.S. person from all foreign trusts during the taxable year does not exceed $10,000. Reg. § 1.643(h)–1(d).

§ 10.6   DEEMED SALE ON TRANSFER TO FOREIGN TRUST

Although the funding of a trust is generally a tax-free gift for income tax purposes, a transfer to a foreign trust may be treated as a taxable sale or exchange. Under § 684, a transfer of property by a U.S. person to a nongrantor foreign trust (or a foreign estate) is treated as a sale, and the transferor must recognize gain equal to the excess of the property's fair market value over its adjusted basis in the transferor's hands. I.R.C. § 684(a). This provision was enacted in 1997 to replace a longstanding excise tax on the transfer of appreciated property to a foreign trust, estate, or partnership. It requires immediate recognition of built-in gain on an asset-by-asset basis, but does not allow any built-in loss to be recognized or offset against gain from other assets. Reg. § 1.684–1(a). Thus, a grantor who transfers two assets, one with a built-in gain of $300 and the other with a built-in loss of $200, must recognize $300 of gain. Reg. § 1.684–1(d) (Example 2). The rule of gain recognition applies without regard to whether the transfer is wholly gratuitous or made for full or partial consideration, and it overrides any deferral that might otherwise result from a bargain sale, private annuity, or installment sale. Reg. § 1.684–1(d) (Examples 3–5). According to the regulations, however, § 684 does not apply to a transfer to a charitable foreign trust or a transfer to an unrelated foreign trust for fair market value. Reg. § 1.684–3(b) and (d).

A transfer may be direct, indirect, or constructive. Reg. § 1.684–2(a). For example, if a U.S. person transfers property to a foreign intermediary who then contributes the property to a foreign trust, the U.S. transferor must recognize any built-in gain at the time of the transfer to the foreign trust. Reg. § 1.684–2(b).

No gain is recognized under § 684 if the foreign trust is treated as owned by any person under the grantor trust rules. I.R.C. § 684(b); Reg. § 1.684–3(a). For example, suppose that Irene, a U.S. resident, transfers appreciated property to a foreign trust for the benefit of her children, one of whom is also a U.S. resident. Irene is treated as the owner of the trust under § 679, and accordingly she recognizes no gain under § 684. Reg. § 1.684–3(g) (Example 1). However, if the foreign trust ceases to be a grantor trust during

Irene's lifetime (e.g., because it no longer has any U.S. beneficiaries), the termination of grantor trust status will be treated as a transfer under § 684 and Irene will recognize any built-in gain in the trust property. Reg. § 1.684–2(e)(1) and (e)(2) (Example 1). Alternatively, suppose that Irene retained an unrestricted power to revoke the foreign trust. As long as the trust remains revocable, even if it ceases to have any U.S. beneficiaries, Irene will continue to be treated as owning the trust under § 676 and no deemed transfer will occur under § 684. Irene will be taxed on the built-in gain in the trust property, however, if she releases her power of revocation during her lifetime and causes the trust to lose its grantor trust status. Reg. § 1.684–2(e)(2) (Example 3). The result would be the same if Irene caused the revocable trust to transfer appreciated property to a separate nongrantor foreign trust. Reg. § 1.684–2(d)(1).

A constructive transfer may occur when a domestic trust becomes a foreign trust. I.R.C. § 684(c); Reg. § 1.684–4(a). For example, suppose that Jasper, a U.S. resident, creates an irrevocable, nongrantor domestic trust for the benefit of his children. One year later, while Jasper is still alive, the original trustee is replaced by a foreign trustee, causing the trust to become a foreign trust. If the trust has U.S. beneficiaries, Jasper will be treated as owning the trust under § 679 and the change in the trust's status will not give rise to a constructive transfer under § 684. (If the trust subsequently ceases to have any U.S. beneficiaries, however, Jasper may be required to recognize gain when the trust loses its grantor trust status.) Alternatively, if the trust has no U.S. beneficiaries at the time it becomes a foreign trust (and is not treated as owned by Jasper or any other person under the grantor trust rules), the trust will be required to recognize any built-in gain on a constructive transfer of its property under § 684. Reg. § 1.684–4(d) (Examples 1 and 2). The transfer is deemed to occur immediately before, but on the same date as, the trust becomes a foreign trust. Reg. § 1.684–4(b).

According to the regulations, the gain recognition rule of § 684 does not apply to a deathtime transfer if the foreign trust receives the transferred property with a fresh-start basis (generally equal to fair market value) under § 1014(a). Reg. § 1.684–3(c)(1). This exception preserves a tax-free basis step-up under § 1014(a) for appreciated property which is included in the gross estate of a deceased transferor. For example, suppose that Kate, a U.S. resident, transfers appreciated property to a foreign trust, retaining an unrestricted power to revoke. Kate is treated as owning the trust under § 676 and therefore recognizes no gain on the transfer under § 684. Kate retains her power of revocation until her death several years later. The trust property is included in Kate's gross estate and acquires a fresh-start basis equal to fair market value in the trust's hands under § 1014(a); neither Kate nor her estate recognizes any built-in gain as a result of a deathtime transfer under § 684. Reg. § 1.684–3(g) (Examples 1 and 2). The result is the same if Kate owns property at her death and leaves it by will to the foreign trust. Alternatively, suppose that the foreign trust is irrevocable and has at least one U.S. beneficiary, so that Kate is treated as the trust's owner under § 679 until her death. Moreover, Kate does not retain any interest or power that would cause the trust property to be included in her gross estate. If the property does not receive a fresh-start basis in the trust's hands under § 1014(a), Kate will be treated as transferring the property to the foreign trust immediately before her death and will recognize any built-in gain on her final income tax return. Reg. § 1.684–3(g) (Example 3).

§ 10.7 REPORTING

The substantive provisions concerning the taxation of foreign trusts are buttressed by various reporting requirements and related penalties. Information reports generally must be filed by three categories of U.S. persons: (1) a U.S. person who creates or transfers property to a foreign trust; (2) a U.S. person who is treated as the owner of a foreign trust under the grantor trust rules; and (3) a U.S. beneficiary who receives a distribution from a foreign trust. I.R.C. § 6048(a)–(c). The required information is generally reported annually on Form 3520.

The creation of a foreign trust by a U.S. grantor is a reportable event regardless of whether the grantor actually transfers property to the trust or whether the trust has U.S. beneficiaries. Thus, the reporting requirement may apply even if the trust is not treated as a grantor trust under § 679 and no gain is recognized under § 684. The death of a U.S. grantor or transferor is also a reportable event if the decedent was treated as owning any portion of a foreign trust for income or estate tax purposes; in that case, the reporting obligation falls on the decedent's executor.

Reporting requirements also apply to any U.S. person who is treated as owning any portion of a foreign trust at any time during the taxable year. In addition to disclosing information concerning the trust, the deemed owner is responsible for ensuring that the trust files a U.S. information return (Form 3520-A) and for ensuring that the trust provides statements to its deemed owners and beneficiaries.

A U.S. beneficiary who receives a distribution, directly or indirectly, from a foreign trust is required to report the distribution, as well as any amount received from the trust as a loan. The reporting requirements apply regardless of whether the foreign trust is a grantor trust or a nongrantor trust.

A person who is required to report information concerning a foreign trust and fails to file a timely, complete and accurate report may incur a penalty, unless the failure is due to reasonable cause and not due to willful neglect. In the case of a transferor or a beneficiary, the penalty is equal to the greater of $10,000 or 35% of the reportable amount (i.e., the value of property transferred or the amount distributed); in the case of a deemed owner, the ceiling is reduced to 5% of the reportable amount (i.e., the value of the deemed owner's portion of the trust). I.R.C. § 6677. Furthermore, failure to comply with the reporting requirements extends the limitation period for assessment of tax with respect to "any tax return, event, or period to which such information relates." I.R.C. § 6501(c)(8).

CHAPTER 11
THROWBACK RULES

§ 11.1   OVERVIEW

The "throwback rules" of I.R.C. §§ 665–668 are intended to limit the potential tax savings resulting from accumulating taxable income in trust for future distribution to beneficiaries. When Subchapter J was enacted in 1954 and for the next 30 years, income tax rates were steeply progressive and the rate brackets for trusts were relatively broad. In many cases, if a trust accumulated taxable income instead of distributing it currently, the income was subject to tax at a lower marginal rate in the hands of the trust than it would have been if distributed to the beneficiaries. If the trust accumulated taxable income for several taxable years and then made large distributions of accumulated income or corpus in a subsequent taxable year, the beneficiaries would not be taxed on those distributions under the conduit rules of § 662 to the extent that the distributed amounts (combined with any first-tier distributions) exceeded the trust's DNI for the taxable year of the distributions. Given the large amounts of taxable income that could be accumulated and taxed to the trust at its relatively low marginal rates, coupled with the trustee's ability to manipulate the timing and amount of discretionary distributions, the use of accumulation trusts to avoid taxes posed a real and substantial problem which was addressed by the throwback rules.

The general purpose of the throwback rules is to tax the beneficiary of a trust which accumulates all or part of its income currently, in most cases, as if the income had been currently distributed to the beneficiary instead of accumulated by the trust. To accomplish this, the statute imposes an additional tax on a beneficiary who receives an "accumulation distribution" from a complex trust, to the extent that the distribution is deemed to consist of "undistributed net income" accumulated by the trust in previous years. The additional tax is separate from, and supplementary to, the regular tax on distributions that carry out DNI from the trust for its current taxable year.

Broadly speaking, the beneficiary is treated as if he or she had received distributions of trust income in equal annual installments in previous years, along with the taxes actually paid by the trust on such income in the years when it was accumulated. I.R.C. § 666. The additional tax imposed on the beneficiary is computed by determining the amount of the average annual increase in the beneficiary's income tax liability resulting from the deemed distributions, multiplying that amount by the number of years in which the accumulations occurred, and reducing the product of the two amounts (but not below zero) by the taxes previously paid by the trust. I.R.C. § 667. Thus, the statutory formula provides an averaging mechanism to prevent a "bunching" of deemed distributions from being taxed at an unduly high marginal rate in the beneficiary's hands. Moreover, by allowing the taxes previously paid by the trust as an offset or credit, the statute generally prevents

double taxation of the deemed distributions. The
beneficiary owes additional tax only to the extent
that the beneficiary's tax on the accumulation
distribution exceeds the taxes actually paid by the
trust when the income was first accumulated.
Neither the beneficiary nor the trust is entitled to a
refund if the taxes paid by the trust turn out to be
greater than the tax on the accumulation
distribution. In the case of an accumulation
distribution from a foreign trust, an interest charge
is imposed to compensate for the advantage of tax
deferral during the accumulation period. I.R.C.
§ 668.

The general concept behind the throwback rules is
quite straightforward, but the same cannot be said of
the operative statutory provisions. The statute
bristles with specially defined terms, cross-
references, and convoluted formulas based on
deemed distributions. Moreover, the problem at
which the throwback rules are aimed—the use of
accumulation trusts to shelter income from the
beneficiaries' high tax rates—has largely
disappeared, at least in the case of domestic trusts.
The introduction in 1986 of the severely compressed
income tax rate schedule of § 1(e), following the
enactment in 1984 of the multiple trust rule of
§ 643(f), greatly reduced the traditional incentives for
accumulating income in trusts. Under current law,
trustees seeking to manipulate the timing and
amount of distributions are more likely to channel
taxable income into the hands of low-bracket
beneficiaries than to accumulate it in trust.

Recognizing that the utility of the throwback rules was often outweighed by their complexity, Congress repealed those rules in 1997 for most domestic trusts. Under current law, the throwback rules continue to apply to trusts created before March 1, 1984, unless the taxpayer shows that the multiple-trust rule of § 643(f), if applicable, would not require the trust to be aggregated with other trusts. I.R.C. § 665(c). The throwback rules have never applied to estates, presumably because their specialized function and limited duration are not considered to pose a substantial risk of abuse.

The situation is somewhat different for foreign trusts, which are often established in jurisdictions that impose little or no tax on accumulated income at the trust level. Consequently, foreign trusts continue to offer opportunities for deferral or exemption. Accordingly, the throwback rules remain in full force for foreign trusts, as well as for domestic trusts which were formerly classified at any time as foreign trusts. I.R.C. § 665(c).

§ 11.2   DEFINED TERMS

The throwback rules come into play only if a trust has "undistributed net income" in one or more taxable years and then makes an "accumulation distribution" in a subsequent taxable year. Each of these terms is specially defined, and both concepts play a key role in the computations required by the statute.

The statute defines the "undistributed net income" (UNI) of a trust for any taxable year as the excess of

DNI over the sum of the trust's distribution deduction and "the amount of taxes imposed on the trust attributable to such [DNI]." I.R.C. § 665(a). As its name implies, the concept of UNI is closely related to DNI. It refers to the residual amount of DNI that remains in the trust's hands after deducting the amounts of DNI carried out to the beneficiaries by first-tier and second-tier distributions and then subtracting the income tax imposed on the trust with respect to the undistributed DNI. In other words, UNI represents the amount of DNI, net of tax thereon, that is accumulated by the trust for the taxable year. This amount, together with the taxes imposed on the trust, will enter into the computation of deemed distributions when the trust makes accumulation distributions in subsequent years, as discussed in § 11.3, *infra*.

An important difference between domestic trusts and foreign trusts involves the treatment of capital gains. In the case of a domestic trust, accumulated capital gains rarely enter into UNI. This is because capital gains usually do not enter into DNI, and when they do they are often distributed currently rather than accumulated in the trust. (See § 6.3, *supra*.) In the usual case, capital gains are excluded from DNI and therefore cannot enter into UNI. They are taxed to the trust in the year of realization and are generally not subject to the throwback rules in a subsequent year. By contrast, in the case of a foreign trust, capital gains (along with the rest of its worldwide income) are included in DNI. I.R.C. § 643(a)(6). Thus, to the extent that a foreign trust does not distribute all of its income currently, the accumulated amounts, including capital gains, will be exposed to the throwback rules when they are ultimately distributed in a subsequent year.

The definition of UNI implies that the throwback rules apply only to complex trusts and not to simple trusts. This proposition, made explicit elsewhere in the statute (e.g., § 666(a), discussed in § 11.3, *infra*), is consistent with the notion that a simple trust cannot accumulate income. Nevertheless, solely for purposes of the throwback rules, a trust which qualifies as a simple trust for a taxable year may be treated as a complex trust to the extent that it receives "outside income" or the trustee does not distribute all of the income that is required to be distributed currently. I.R.C. § 665(e)(2); Reg. § 1.665(e)–1A(b). The regulations define outside income as amounts that are included in DNI but not in fiduciary accounting income (FAI), and offer the following examples: items of income in respect of a decedent (IRD); unrealized accounts receivable that are assigned to the trust; and "trapping" distributions that carry out DNI or UNI from another trust (but not an estate). Reg. § 1.665(e)–1A(b). For example, suppose that a simple trust receives a $100 taxable distribution from an individual retirement account (an item of IRD) and a $200 taxable distribution from another trust. Both items are includible in the trust's gross income and enter into the trust's DNI. To the extent that they are allocated to corpus (rather than income) on the trust's books, however, they cannot be distributed currently because under § 651 a simple trust is prohibited from making any distributions of amounts other than the income required to be distributed currently. Accordingly, to the extent that these items are allocated to corpus, they constitute outside income which will be treated as UNI for purposes of the throwback rules. Similarly, suppose that the trust receives a taxable stock dividend which the trustee in good faith allocates to corpus and therefore does not distribute to the current income beneficiaries. If it is subsequently determined that the dividend should have been allocated to income, the trust is not disqualified as a simple trust, but it will have UNI equal to the amount that was erroneously taxed to the trust instead of passed through to the income beneficiaries. Reg. § 1.665(e)–1A(b) (Example 2).

The definition of UNI requires that DNI be reduced not only by the trust's distribution deduction but also by the taxes imposed on the trust with respect to the undistributed DNI. For this purpose, the "taxes imposed on the trust" are defined as the federal income taxes payable by the trust (without regard to credits) which are properly allocable to the undistributed portions of DNI and, in the case of a domestic trust, to net capital gains not included in DNI. I.R.C. § 665(d)(1). In the case of a foreign trust, the adjustment for taxes on net capital gains is unnecessary because such gains must be included in DNI in any event under § 643(a)(6). However, in the case of a foreign trust, the adjustment for the trust's taxes also includes an allocable portion of any foreign income taxes imposed on the trust (or on the settlor or other person who would have been treated as the owner of any part of the trust under the grantor trust rules, but for § 672(f)). I.R.C. § 665(d)(2). When a trust eventually makes an accumulation distribution, the trust's taxes will be treated as an additional deemed distribution and allowed as a credit against any additional tax imposed on the beneficiaries, as discussed in §§ 11.3 and 11.4, *infra*.

An "accumulation distribution" is generally defined as the amount by which the trust's second-tier distributions exceed its DNI reduced (but not below zero) by its first-tier distributions for the taxable year. I.R.C. § 665(b). In other words, a second-tier distribution (i.e., an amount properly paid, credited, or required to be distributed, other than a required current income distribution) constitutes an accumulation distribution to the extent that it exceeds the amount of DNI remaining after any first-tier distributions (i.e., required current income distributions) have been taken into account.

The definition of an accumulation distribution prompts two observations. First, it confirms that the throwback rules generally apply only to complex trusts, since these are the only trusts that can make second-tier distributions; simple trusts, by contrast, are required to distribute all of their income currently but are prohibited from making any other distributions. The second observation concerns the relationship between the throwback rules and the conduit rules. An accumulation distribution, by definition, consists of the residual amount of second-tier distributions after all of the trust's DNI for the current taxable year has been carried out by first-tier or second-tier distributions. Therefore, an accumulation distribution can never carry out DNI for the trust's current taxable year; it is neither deductible by the trust nor includible by the beneficiaries under the conduit rules of §§ 661 and 662, and is taxable, if at all, only under the throwback rules.

The statute specifically provides that "[i]f the amounts properly paid, credited, or required to be distributed by the trust for the taxable year do not exceed the income of the trust for such year, there shall be no accumulation distribution for such year." I.R.C. § 665(b). This provision allows a trust to distribute all of its FAI, even if that amount exceeds DNI, without triggering an additional tax under the throwback rules. However, it does not provide an ironclad exemption from the throwback rules for distributions up to the amount of FAI. To illustrate, suppose that a trust has FAI of $100 and DNI of $80 (reflecting a $20 deduction for administration expenses charged to corpus). If the only amount distributed for the year is a $100 discretionary distribution, that distribution will carry out all of the DNI for the current year but will not give rise to an accumulation distribution. However, if the discretionary distribution is $110 (instead of $100), there will be an accumulation distribution of $30 ($110 total distribution less $80 DNI). In other words, if the total first-tier and second-tier distributions exceed FAI, the § 665(b) safe harbor for current income distributions does not apply.

The statute also provides a safe harbor for distributions from a domestic trust of income that was accumulated before the beneficiary was born or before the beneficiary reached age 21. I.R.C. § 665(b). Such amounts may qualify as accumulation distributions which carry out income accumulated in earlier years, but they are not subject to the additional tax imposed on the beneficiary under the throwback rules (unless the trust runs afoul of the multiple-trust rule of § 667(c), discussed in § 11.3, *infra*). Thus, in applying the throwback rules to accumulation distributions made by a domestic trust to a beneficiary over the age of 21, it is necessary to determine the extent to which those distributions are allocable to income accumulations for the periods before and after the beneficiary reached age 21, since the accumulations after age 21 will be subject to additional tax but the accumulations before age 21 will not. This safe harbor is of limited practical significance because it applies only to the few domestic trusts that are subject to the throwback rules. The safe harbor does not apply to foreign trusts.

One final observation concerns distributions of specific sums of money or specific property that are excluded from the conduit rules by § 663(a)(1). (See § 7.6, *supra*.) Such nontaxable distributions are disregarded in applying the throwback rules. They are neither first-tier distributions nor second-tier distributions, and therefore they have no effect on the respective amounts of DNI carried out to beneficiaries or remaining to be taxed in the trust's hands. By the same token, they are never part of an accumulation distribution. The throwback rules may be viewed as a mechanism for reallocating the tax burden from the trust, which initially pays tax when income is accumulated, to the beneficiaries who eventually receive an accumulation distribution.

§ 11.3   DEEMED DISTRIBUTIONS

The throwback rules require two sets of computations. First, the accumulation distributions made by a trust in the current taxable year must be "thrown back" to preceding taxable years in which the trust accumulated income ("throwback years") and allocated to the trust's UNI for those years. An allocable portion of the accumulation distribution is deemed to have been distributed as a second-tier distribution on the last day of each of the throwback years, together with the taxes imposed on the trust, pursuant to a formula set forth in § 666. The additional tax on the total amount of those deemed distributions in the beneficiary's hands is determined in a separate computation under an averaging formula set forth in § 667, as discussed in § 11.4, *infra.*

In allocating the amount of an accumulation distribution to UNI for preceding taxable years, it is necessary to ascertain the amount of UNI, if any, for each of those throwback years. In other words, for each throwback year it must be determined whether there was any residual amount of DNI left in the trust, after subtracting the distribution deductions allowed for first-tier and second-tier distributions and also subtracting the trust's income taxes attributable to the undistributed DNI. The only years taken into account are those in which there was residual DNI left in the trust; if DNI was exhausted by the trust's distributions and tax payments, there is no UNI. The accumulation distribution is thrown back to the trust's preceding taxable years in chronological order, beginning with the earliest year in which the trust had UNI, and is deemed to come from each year's UNI to the extent thereof until the accumulation distribution is fully allocated or the UNI for all preceding years is exhausted. If the trust makes successive accumulation distributions, allocations of the earlier distributions to UNI for each throwback year reduce that year's UNI for purposes of allocating the later distributions. I.R.C. § 666(a). For example, suppose that a trust with UNI of $500 for each year beginning in 2009 makes an accumulation distribution of $2,400 in 2020. The accumulation distribution is deemed to consist of distributions of $500 of UNI for each of the years 2009 through 2012 and a distribution of $400 of UNI for 2013. If the trust makes a second accumulation distribution of $800 in 2021, that accumulation distribution is deemed to consist of $100 of UNI for 2013, $500 of UNI for 2014, and $200 of UNI for 2015.

In addition to the deemed distributions of UNI for each throwback year, the trust is deemed to distribute an amount equal to the taxes imposed on the trust (other than the alternative minimum tax) which are attributable to that year's UNI. For each throwback year in which the allocated amount of the accumulation distribution is equal to or greater than UNI, the deemed distribution includes the entire amount of the trust's taxes attributable to that year's UNI, but for a throwback year in which the accumulation distribution does not fully exhaust UNI, the deemed distribution includes only a ratable portion of the trust's taxes attributable to that year's UNI. I.R.C. § 666(b) and (c).

For example, suppose that a trust makes an accumulation distribution of $160 which is thrown back to two previous taxable years, absorbing the trust's entire $100 of UNI for the first year and $60 of the trust's $100 of UNI for the second year. If the trust paid taxes of $25 attributable exclusively to UNI in each year, the amount of taxes deemed distributed would be $25 for the first year and $15 ($25 × 60/100) for the second year. Thus, the beneficiaries are treated as receiving deemed distributions not only of the trust's UNI for the throwback years but also of their share of the taxes paid by the trust on the UNI. In "grossing up" the deemed distributions of UNI by the trust's taxes, the statutory formula treats the beneficiaries as if they received the trust's undistributed DNI for the throwback year, including the amount of taxes actually paid by the trust. (Recall that the trust's taxes were already subtracted from undistributed DNI in computing UNI.)

In computing the tax imposed on the deemed distributions under § 667, however, the beneficiaries will be allowed an offset or credit for the taxes previously paid by the trust. In effect, therefore, the taxes paid by the trust on its undistributed DNI for the throwback year will be treated as a down payment against the taxes owed by the beneficiaries when they receive the accumulation distribution. No refund or credit is allowed to the trust or to the beneficiaries by reason of the deemed distributions. I.R.C. § 666(e).

To illustrate the computation of deemed distributions under § 666, suppose that a trust had DNI and taxable income of $100 for a previous taxable year. The trust made no distributions in that year and paid $20 of tax on its taxable income. Thus, the trust's UNI for the year was $80 ($100 DNI less $0 distribution deduction less $20 taxes imposed on the trust). In its current taxable year the trust makes an accumulation distribution of $80 which is thrown back to the previous taxable year. The accumulation distribution will carry out the earlier year's UNI, and the beneficiary will receive a deemed distribution of $100, consisting of $80 of UNI and $20 of the trust's taxes. In computing the tax on the distribution under § 667, if the beneficiary is taxed at a 37% rate, the $37 tax will be offset by a $20 credit for the tax previously paid by the trust, and the beneficiary's net tax liability will be $17.

The trustee is responsible for maintaining adequate records to make the required allocations of accumulation distributions under § 666. If adequate records are not available, an accumulation distribution will be thrown back to the trust's earliest taxable year and deemed to consist of UNI for that year. I.R.C. § 666(d); Reg. § 1.666(d)–1A.

A special rule enacted in 1976 seeks to prevent multiple trusts from being used to circumvent the throwback rules. If, as the result of an accumulation distribution from a trust, a beneficiary receives a deemed distribution of UNI for a preceding taxable year, and the same beneficiary has previously received deemed distributions of UNI from two (or more) other trusts for the same preceding taxable year, the deemed distribution under § 666 is computed without regard to the taxes imposed on the third (or subsequent) trust. I.R.C. § 667(c)(1). Thus, the beneficiary is not required to include the trust's taxes in gross income, but the beneficiary is also denied any credit for those taxes in computing the tax on the accumulation distribution under § 667. In effect, the trust's undistributed DNI is taxed to the trust when the income is first accumulated, and again to the beneficiary when it is distributed. Since the trust's taxes are not allowed as an offset against the beneficiary's tax, the accumulated income is subject to double taxation. The multiple trust rule is subject to a de minimis threshold: the rule does not apply if the combined amount of the beneficiary's deemed distributions of UNI from the same trust for the same preceding taxable year is less than $1,000. I.R.C. § 667(c)(2). When it does apply, the rule overrides the exemption for income accumulated by a domestic trust before a beneficiary was born or reached age 21. (See § 665(b), discussed in § 11.2, *supra*.) As a practical matter, the multiple trust rule of § 667(c) has been largely eclipsed by the broader rule of § 643(f), enacted in 1984, which often requires that multiple trusts be treated as a single trust (see § 5.4, *supra*.). Indeed, the tax incentives for creating multiple trusts have been drastically curtailed since the enactment in 1986 of the compressed rate schedule for trusts in § 1(e). Nevertheless, the multiple trust rule of § 667(c) remains on the books.

§ 11.4   COMPUTATION OF ADDITIONAL TAX

The additional tax on the accumulation distribution in the beneficiary's hands is imposed by § 667. Very generally, the objective is to impose a tax which approximates the tax that the beneficiary would have paid if the accumulation distribution, grossed up by the taxes already paid by the trust, had been distributed to the beneficiary in a series of equal annual installments. The tax computation requires four steps: (1) determine the average annual amount of the deemed distributions for the trust's throwback years; (2) add that amount to the beneficiary's taxable income for each of three recent years to determine the average annual increase in the beneficiary's tax liability; (3) multiply the average increase by the number of throwback years; and (4) subtract the amount of taxes previously paid by the trust. I.R.C. § 667(b)(1). In the case of a foreign trust, the additional tax is subject to an interest charge under § 668 (see § 11.5, *infra*). In effect, the beneficiary is taxed on the full amount of the deemed distributions in the year the accumulation distribution is received, but the statutory averaging formula ensures that the marginal tax rate is no greater than if the distributions had been spread equally among the throwback years, and the beneficiary owes additional tax only to the extent that the tax on the distributions exceeds the taxes previously paid by the trust. Each of the steps in the tax computation is examined below.

The first step involves a computation of the average annual amount of the deemed distributions for the trust's throwback years. This is done by taking the total amount of the deemed distributions, consisting of the amounts of the accumulation distribution allocated to UNI for each of the throwback years and the taxes paid thereon by the trust (see § 11.3, *supra*), and dividing that total amount by the number of the throwback years involved. I.R.C. § 667(b)(1)(A) and (b)(1)(C).

If the deemed distribution of UNI for any of the throwback years is less than 25% of the average annual deemed distribution of UNI for all years, that year is disregarded in determining the number of throwback years. I.R.C. § 667(b)(3). For example, suppose that in 2020 a trust makes an accumulation distribution of $2,500, which is allocated to UNI in the amounts of $100 for 2010 and $600 for each of the years 2011 through 2014. At first glance, the average annual amount of deemed distributions of UNI appears to be $500 ($2,500 total UNI divided by 5 throwback years). However, because the $100 deemed distribution of UNI for 2010 is less than 25% of the average annual amount (25% × $500 = $125), the deemed distributions will be treated as if they were made in four (rather than five) throwback years. Thus, in computing the additional tax under § 667, the average annual amount of deemed distributions of UNI will be $625 ($2,500 total UNI divided by 4 throwback years). The taxes paid by the trust will also be spread over four throwback years.

The second step requires a computation of the average annual increase in the beneficiary's tax resulting from the deemed distributions. This is done by adding the average annual amount of the deemed distributions (determined in step one) to the beneficiary's taxable income for three of the five preceding taxable years, ignoring the two years in which the beneficiary's taxable income was highest and lowest respectively. I.R.C. § 667(b)(1)(B) and (b)(1)(C).

For purposes of this computation, the beneficiary's taxable income in each taxable year is deemed to be not less than zero; as a result, net losses cannot be used to offset the deemed distributions. I.R.C. § 667(b)(2). Since the average annual deemed distribution is added directly to the beneficiary's taxable income, no adjustments are made in deductions for medical expenses, charitable contributions, miscellaneous itemized deductions, or carryovers determined by reference to adjusted gross income. However, the beneficiary's taxable income includes any deemed distributions resulting from previous accumulation distributions made during that year. I.R.C. § 667(b)(4). Any tax-exempt interest included in the deemed distributions retains its character, but the character of other specially treated items does not flow through to the beneficiary. Thus, for example, any capital gains included in a deemed distribution will be taxed to the beneficiary at ordinary income rates. The beneficiary's tax for each of the three relevant years is then recomputed and compared with the tax originally due. In the case of a foreign trust, the increase in the beneficiary's tax is reduced by a credit (subject to the limitations in § 904) for foreign taxes paid by the trust and included in the deemed distributions. I.R.C. § 667(d).

The average annual increase in the beneficiary's tax is the total amount of annual tax increases divided by three. I.R.C. § 667(b)(1)(D). For example, suppose that a beneficiary had taxable income of $125,000 in 2015, $180,000 in 2016 through 2018, and $200,000 in 2019. In 2020 the beneficiary receives an accumulation distribution which results in an average annual deemed distribution of $1,000. The $1,000 average deemed distribution is added to the beneficiary's taxable income of $180,000 for 2016 through 2018 (ignoring the years with the highest and lowest taxable income). If the beneficiary is taxed at a 37% rate, the average annual tax increase will be $370.

The third and fourth steps are a simple matter of arithmetic. The average annual increase in the beneficiary's tax must be multiplied by the number of throwback years involved in computing the average annual deemed distribution. I.R.C. § 667(b)(1). By stating the increase in the beneficiary's tax as an average annual amount, based on the average annual amount of deemed distributions and the beneficiary's average taxable income, the statute avoids the need for laborious recomputations of the beneficiary's actual tax liability for each of the throwback years. Moreover, although the beneficiary is taxed on the entire accumulation distribution (which may consist of deemed distributions from several preceding taxable years) in a single taxable year, the statutory averaging formula ensures that the tax is calculated at roughly the same marginal rate as if the deemed distributions for each of the throwback years had been made in equal annual installments. Accordingly, multiplying the average annual increase in the beneficiary's tax by the number of throwback years yields the beneficiary's tax on the entire accumulation distribution.

All that remains in the final step is to compare the beneficiary's tax with the taxes previously paid by the trust (and deemed distributed to the beneficiary as described above). I.R.C. § 667(b)(1). The net tax liability under § 667 is limited to the excess of the beneficiary's tax over the trust's tax; if the trust's tax is greater than the beneficiary's tax, no refund or credit is allowed to the trust or to the beneficiary. I.R.C. §§ 666(e) and 667(b)(1). A beneficiary who receives accumulation distributions from two or more trusts in the same taxable year may report them consecutively in whichever order the beneficiary chooses. I.R.C. § 667(b)(5). Because each successive distribution is "stacked" in the beneficiary's taxable income on top of any previous distributions, careful ordering of distributions may work to a beneficiary's advantage. For example, suppose that a beneficiary receives accumulation distributions from Trust A and Trust B in the same taxable year. The tax previously paid by the trust exceeds the beneficiary's tax (before any offset for the trust's tax) on the Trust A distribution, but the reverse is true for the Trust B distribution. The beneficiary may choose to treat the Trust B distribution as occurring first, if doing so will increase the amount of the beneficiary's tax that is offset by the trust's tax on the Trust A distribution.

§ 11.5   INTEREST CHARGE

If a beneficiary receives an accumulation distribution from a foreign trust, the beneficiary's tax on the distribution is subject to an interest charge. I.R.C. § 668. Since the foreign trust may have paid little or no U.S. income tax on its income during the accumulation period, the interest charge is intended to compensate for the deferral of U.S. tax liability. The amount of the § 668 interest charge reflects a weighted average of the trust's UNI for the period between the year in which the income was initially accumulated and the year of the accumulation distribution.

To compute the interest charge, it is necessary to determine the number of preceding taxable years in which the trust had UNI and the beneficiary was a U.S. citizen or resident ("undistributed income years"). I.R.C. § 668(a)(4). For each undistributed income year, the amount of the trust's UNI is multiplied by the number of taxable years between that year and the year of the distribution (including the undistributed income year but not the distribution year). The products for all of the undistributed income years are then added together, and the sum is divided by the trust's aggregate UNI. I.R.C. § 668(a)(3). The result is equal to the "applicable number of years," and the interest charge is imposed for a period consisting of the applicable number of years ending on the date of the distribution. I.R.C. § 668(a)(2). The rate of interest is generally the same as for underpayments of tax. I.R.C. § 668(a)(1). The total amount of interest, however, cannot exceed the amount of the accumulation distribution that gave rise to the beneficiary's tax. I.R.C. § 668(b). Solely for the purpose of computing the interest charge, each accumulation distribution is treated as reducing UNI proportionately for each of the undistributed income years. I.R.C. § 668(a)(5).

To illustrate the computation of the interest charge, suppose that a foreign trust makes an accumulation distribution in 2020 to a beneficiary who has been a U.S. citizen at all relevant times. The trust had UNI of $100 for 2017, zero for 2018, and $150 for 2019. Only 2017 and 2019 count as undistributed income years, and the products for those respective years are $300 ($100 UNI × 3 intervening years) and $150 ($150 UNI × 1 intervening year). The sum of the products divided by aggregate UNI is 1.8 [($300 + $150)/$250]. Thus, the applicable number of years is 1.8. The beneficiary's tax on the accumulation distribution bears interest at the rate for underpayments of tax for the period of 1.8 years (one year and 292 days) ending on the date of the distribution.

The interest charge imposed under § 668 is not deductible for federal tax purposes. I.R.C. § 668(c).

§ 11.6 INTERACTION WITH GRANTOR TRUST RULES

The throwback rules have no application to a trust which is treated as entirely owned by the grantor (or by another person) under the grantor trust rules of §§ 671–678. (See Chapter 8, *supra*.) This perfectly sensible and unsurprising result follows from the statutory scheme. During the period when a trust is treated as a grantor trust, all of the trust income is taxed directly to the grantor (or other deemed owner), not to the trust as a separate taxable entity. It is also clear as a technical matter that the conduit rules do not apply; the trust has no DNI, makes no distributions, and therefore has no UNI. Consequently, there are no preceding taxable years to which any subsequent distributions can be thrown back. For example, suppose that a trust which was revocable by the grantor during life becomes irrevocable at the grantor's death and distributes all of its property at that time to the beneficiaries who survive the grantor. The distributions made after the grantor's death may constitute taxable distributions which carry out the current year's DNI under the conduit rules of §§ 661 and 662, or they may be excluded from those rules by § 663(a)(1), but they are not taxed as accumulation distributions under the throwback rules. Any income accumulated by the trust during the grantor's lifetime has already been taxed to the grantor and is not subject to an additional tax in the hands of the beneficiaries. Similarly, any amounts distributed by the trust while it was still revocable during the grantor's lifetime would be treated as transfers made directly by the grantor and would not be subject to the conduit rules.

The situation is somewhat more complicated if the grantor (or another person) is treated as the owner of only a portion of a trust under the grantor trust rules. As a general matter, the trust must be bifurcated into a grantor portion and a nongrantor portion. The grantor portion is governed exclusively by the grantor trust rules, while the nongrantor portion is subject to the normal provisions of Subchapter J concerning the trust's taxable income and distributions. In some cases it may be unclear whether a distribution made by a trust should be deemed to come from the grantor portion or the nongrantor portion. The regulations expressly recognize that no accumulation distribution will be deemed to occur by reason of the exercise of a power of appointment that affects only taxable income previously attributed to a deemed owner under the grantor trust rules. However, the regulations take the position that an accumulation distribution may include amounts that are paid, credited, or required to be distributed pursuant to the exercise of a power of appointment or withdrawal over trust corpus or accumulated income, even though not all of those amounts are treated as second-tier distributions under the conduit rules. Reg. § 1.665(b)–1A(a)(2). According to an example in the regulations, if the beneficiary of a testamentary trust exercises a noncumulative power to withdraw $5,000 annually from trust corpus, the full amount withdrawn may be treated as an accumulation distribution without any reduction for the amount of trust income attributed to the power holder under § 678. Reg. § 1.665(b)–1A(d) (Example 4).

If a foreign trust acquires a U.S. beneficiary and becomes subject to § 679, the U.S. grantor may be treated as receiving an accumulation distribution of any undistributed net income attributable to the grantor's previous contributions. See § 10.3, *supra.*

CHAPTER 12

SPECIALLY TREATED TRUSTS

§ 12.1 ELECTING SMALL BUSINESS TRUSTS

An eligible domestic corporation may elect, with the consent of its shareholders, to be taxed as a pass-through entity under Subchapter S and thereby avoid a corporate-level tax. An S corporation must have no more than one class of stock and no more than 100 shareholders. I.R.C. § 1361(b)(1). (The 100-shareholder limit is less onerous than it appears because for this purpose all members of a family, including spouses, are counted as a single shareholder. I.R.C. § 1361(c)(1).) In addition, the permitted shareholders of an S corporation are limited to U.S. individuals, estates, and certain trusts and tax-exempt organizations; other domestic entities and all nonresident aliens are prohibited. I.R.C. § 1361(b)(1) and (c)(2).

In 1996, the list of permitted S corporation shareholders was expanded to include an "electing small business trust" (ESBT). I.R.C. § 1361(c)(2)(A)(v). A trust is eligible to elect ESBT status only if its beneficiaries are limited to individuals, estates, or certain tax-exempt organizations, and none of them acquired an interest in the trust by purchase. A trust cannot qualify as an ESBT if it is a "qualified subchapter S trust" (QSST),*

---

* A QSST is a trust with one individual U.S. beneficiary who is entitled to receive all of the trust's fiduciary accounting income a tax-exempt trust, a charitable remainder trust, or a foreign trust. I.R.C. § 1361(c)(2)(A) and (e)(1). Unlike a QSST, an ESBT may provide for discretionary current distributions of trust income or corpus to multiple beneficiaries as well as accumulations of income. Although there is no upper limit on the total number of an ESBT's beneficiaries, each beneficiary who is entitled or permitted to receive current distributions of trust income or corpus (a "potential current beneficiary") is counted as a shareholder of each S corporation whose stock is held in the trust. Thus, if an ESBT has a potential current beneficiary who is not a permitted shareholder of an S corporation (e.g., a partnership), the corporation may lose its S status. Reg. § 1.1361–1(m)(8)(ii) (Example 2). A special rule added in 2017 allows an ESBT to have nonresident alien individuals as its beneficiaries without jeopardizing the corporation's S status, even though such individuals are prohibited from owning S corporation stock directly. I.R.C. § 1361(b)(1)(C) and (c)(2)(B)(v).

An ESBT election is made by the trustee on behalf of an eligible trust. To make the election, the trustee must file a statement identifying the trust, its potential current beneficiaries, and the S corporations in which the trust holds stock; the

---

currently and is the sole permissible recipient of any corpus distributions made during his or her lifetime. I.R.C. § 1361(d)(3). If the beneficiary elects QSST status with respect to S corporation stock held by the trust, the trust will qualify as a permitted shareholder and the beneficiary will be treated as the owner of the S corporation stock under § 678. I.R.C. § 1361(d)(1). See § 8.3, *supra.*

statement must also include representations that the trust qualifies as an ESBT and that all of its potential current beneficiaries (other than nonresident alien individuals) qualify as permitted S corporation shareholders. Reg. § 1.1361–1(m)(2)(ii).

For administrative purposes, an ESBT is treated as a single trust which has one taxpayer identification number and files one tax return. For substantive tax purposes, however, the portion of an ESBT consisting of S corporation stock (the "S portion") and the remaining portion (the "non-S portion") are treated as separate trusts. Reg. § 1.641(c)–1(a). In computing the taxable income of the S portion, the trust takes into account only the following items of income, loss, deduction, or credit: (1) pass-through items relating to S corporation stock; (2) gain or loss from the disposition of S corporation stock (without any deduction for a net capital loss); (3) state and local income taxes and administrative expenses allocable to the S portion; and (4) interest on debt incurred to acquire S corporation stock. Tax is imposed at the trust level on the taxable income of the S portion, at a flat rate equal to the top marginal income tax rate for trusts (or the lower rate for capital gain). I.R.C. § 641(c)(1) and (c)(2); Reg. § 1.641(c)–1(d) and (e). Thus, items attributable to the S portion are taxed directly to the trust and are not allocated to its beneficiaries or taken into account by the beneficiaries on their own tax returns.

The non-S portion of the trust is taxed under the normal conduit rules. In computing the distributable net income of the non-S portion, only items attributable to the non-S portion are taken into account; items attributable to the S portion are excluded from the non-S portion. Nevertheless, in computing the trust's distribution deduction, distributions from the S portion as well as the non-S portion are taken into account. Thus, distributions of cash or other property made by the trust to its beneficiaries, including distributions of S corporation stock, carry out DNI of the non-S portion under the conduit rules. I.R.C. § 641(c)(3); Reg. § 1.641(c)–1(g) and (i). If the S portion ceases to be treated as a separate trust (e.g., because the trust sells or distributes all of its S corporation stock), the trust succeeds to any excess deductions or loss carryovers upon termination of the ESBT election. I.R.C. § 641(c)(4); Reg. § 1.641(c)–1(j).

To illustrate, suppose that an ESBT's gross income for the taxable year consists of $10,000 of ordinary S corporation pass-through items and $5,000 of investment income from other sources; the trust has no expenses. During the taxable year the trust distributes $4,000 in cash to its beneficiaries. The taxable income of the S portion is $10,000, on which the trust is taxed at the top marginal rate under § 1(e). The trust's DNI is $5,000, comprising the investment income attributable to the non-S portion. The trust is allowed a distribution deduction of $4,000 and a personal exemption of $100, reducing the taxable income of the non-S portion to $900 ($5,000 − $4,000 − $100). The $4,000 distribution is fully taxable to the beneficiaries under the normal conduit rules.

In the preceding example, assume the same facts except that at the end of the taxable year the trust also sells the S corporation stock for $30,000, realizing a capital gain of $5,000, and distributes all of the sale proceeds to the beneficiaries. The $5,000 gain is included in the taxable income of the S portion and is taxed to the trust as capital gain under § 1(h). The additional distribution of the sale proceeds increases the trust's distribution deduction by $1,000 and reduces the taxable income of the non-S portion to zero. (Note that the trust's personal exemption is wasted; it is not allowable as a deduction in computing the taxable income of the S portion.) Of the $30,000 additional distribution, $1,000 is taxed to the beneficiaries under the normal conduit rules and the remaining $29,000 is tax-free. The sale of the S corporation stock terminates the trust's ESBT status, and thereafter the trust is fully subject to the general rules of Subchapter J.

To the extent that an ESBT is treated as wholly or partially owned by the grantor or another person under the grantor trust rules (see Chapter 8, *supra*), the items attributable to the "grantor portion" are taxed directly to the deemed owner under § 671. Reg. § 1.641(c)–1(c). Thus, the grantor portion of the trust is governed by the grantor trust rules and not by the provisions described above concerning the S and non-S portions. Nevertheless, a special rule requires that if the deemed owner of the grantor portion is a nonresident alien, any items attributable to the S corporation stock must be reallocated from the grantor trust portion to the S portion. Reg. § 1.641(c)–1(b)(1)(ii) and (b)(2)(ii). This rule is intended to ensure that all of the trust's S corporation income (including foreign source income) will be taxed at the trust level and will not escape U.S. income tax in the hands of a deemed owner who is a nonresident alien.

§ 12.2   ALIMONY TRUSTS

In connection with a divorce or legal separation, a married couple may divide their marital property by agreement or pursuant to a court decree. A transfer of property between spouses, whether made during the marriage or incident to divorce, is generally tax-free for income tax purposes. The transferor spouse recognizes no gain or loss, and the transferee spouse takes the transferred property with a carryover basis. I.R.C. § 1041. In most cases, the transfer is also exempt from gift tax. I.R.C. §§ 2516 and 2523.

In addition to a transfer of marital property, one spouse may be required to pay alimony to the other spouse to satisfy a continuing support obligation. From 1942 until 2019, alimony payments (but not child support payments) were generally includible in gross income by the payee spouse and deductible (above the line) by the payor spouse in computing adjusted gross income. I.R.C. §§ 71 and 215. The special alimony provisions were repealed in 2017, however, and beginning in 2019, alimony payments, like child support payments, must be paid from after-tax dollars; they are no longer deductible by the payor spouse or includible by the payee spouse. The repeal of §§ 71 and 215 applies only to divorce or separation instruments executed after 2018; prior law remains in force for alimony payments made under pre-2019 instruments, unless a post-2018 modification expressly provides to the contrary.

Instead of making periodic cash payments of alimony, one spouse may create a trust for the benefit of the other spouse to provide for full and timely payment of ongoing support obligations. Until 2019, the income tax treatment of such a trust was governed by § 682, which generally provided that when a couple was divorced or legally separated and one spouse was "entitled to receive" trust income that would otherwise be includible in the other spouse's gross income, the income was taxed to the recipient spouse under the normal conduit rules. As a corollary, such income was not attributed to the other spouse under the grantor trust rules. Section 682 was repealed in 2017, along with §§ 71 and 215, but like those provisions § 682 remains in force for divorce or separation instruments executed before 2019 (and not modified thereafter).

To illustrate the operation of § 682, suppose that, pursuant to a divorce settlement, Brian created a trust in 2018 to pay income to Claire until her death or earlier remarriage and then to pay the remaining trust property to their children. In the absence of § 682, Brian would be treated as owning the trust income that is used to satisfy his continuing support obligation (see § 677(a), discussed in § 8.9, *supra*), even though the income tax liability on direct cash payments of alimony would be shifted to Claire under §§ 71 and 215. Section 682 requires a different result. Under § 682, Brian is not taxed on the trust's ordinary income, even though it will be used to satisfy his support obligation. Instead, Claire is taxed as an income beneficiary under the conduit rules. The result would be similar if the amount distributable to Claire was expressed as an annuity rather than a share of trust income.

Section 682 has no application to fixed amounts or shares of income that are designated in a court decree, separation agreement, or trust instrument as payments for the support of minor children. In the preceding example, suppose that the trust instrument specifies that $20,000 of the annual income payable to Claire is to be used for the support of the couple's minor children. Brian will be taxable on the trust income that is used to satisfy his child support obligation under § 677(a), but Claire will be taxed on the rest of the ordinary trust income under § 682.

Section 682 obviously applies to a trust that was created in connection with a divorce or legal separation to satisfy the grantor's spousal support obligation under a court decree or separation agreement. The provision may also apply to a trust that does not provide spousal support payments and was not created in anticipation of divorce or separation. For example, suppose that many years ago Daisy, while married to Eric, created a trust to pay income to Eric for life; at his death, the remaining trust property will be paid to Daisy if she is still alive, otherwise to her surviving issue. Daisy and Eric subsequently divorced in 2018. After the divorce, the ordinary trust income that was payable to Eric will no longer be taxed to Daisy under the grantor trust rules but instead will be taxed to Eric as a beneficiary under the conduit rules. Daisy, however, will continue to be taxed on items of gross income that are allocable to corpus and are not included in the trust's distributable net income (e.g., capital gain). Section 682 prevents Daisy from being taxed on the trust income that is payable to Eric; it does not shield her from tax on amounts that are accumulated for future distribution to her under § 677(a).

As noted above, § 682 has no application to divorce or separation instruments executed after 2018. Moreover, although the regulations indicate that the provisions of § 677(a) referring to the grantor's spouse apply "solely during the period of the marriage, the spousal attribution rule of § 672(e) (discussed in § 8.6, *supra*) contain no such limitation. Reg. § 1.677(a)–1(b)(2). As a result, the grantor trust rules will often apply to a trust created by a married grantor for the benefit of his or her spouse, even after divorce or legal separation. In the case of a trust created during the marriage, any interest or power held by the grantor's spouse will be attributed to the grantor both during the marriage and after divorce or legal separation. I.R.C. § 672(e). Furthermore, the grantor will be treated as owning any trust income that is or may be applied to discharge the grantor's alimony obligations, regardless of whether the trust was created during the marriage or after its termination. I.R.C. § 677(a); Reg. § 1.677(a)–1(d). Nevertheless, with careful planning the grantor may be able to avoid being taxed on trust income that is payable to a former spouse. To accomplish this result, two conditions must be satisfied: (1) the trust must be created when the grantor and the spouse are "legally separated" under a decree of divorce or separate maintenance; and (2) the grantor has no continuing legal support obligation that could be satisfied from the trust property or its income. The first condition blocks the operation of the spousal attribution rule of § 672(e), and the second condition blocks the constructive ownership rule of § 677(a). In sum, the repeal of § 682 makes it considerably more difficult, though not impossible, to ensure that the income of an alimony trust will be taxed to the recipient spouse rather than to the grantor.

§ 12.3   QUALIFIED FUNERAL TRUSTS

A funeral trust is an arrangement which allows a purchaser to pay in advance ("pre-need") for a funeral, burial or cremation, and related goods and services to be provided by a seller (usually a funeral home or a cemetery) at the death of a designated individual beneficiary (who may be either the purchaser or another person). Under applicable local law, some or all of the amounts deposited by the purchaser are typically required to be held in trust until the beneficiary's death, when the trust funds will be disbursed to the seller to pay the costs of the beneficiary's funeral and related items. The trust may be revocable or irrevocable, may be funded with cash or property (e.g., life insurance), and may be administered either by the seller or by a third-party trustee. For federal income tax purposes, the purchaser is generally treated as the owner of the trust under the grantor trust rules. Rev. Rul. 87–127, 1987–2 C.B. 156.

Section 685, enacted in 1997, provides a simplified method for computing and reporting the income of a "qualified funeral trust" (QFT). A QFT is a domestic trust that meets the following requirements: (1) it arises from a contract with a seller engaged in the business of providing funeral or burial services (or related property); (2) its sole purpose is to manage funds which will be used to pay for such services (or property) on behalf of one or more individual beneficiaries at death; (3) it is funded solely with contributions by or on behalf of such individual beneficiaries; (4) it has no beneficiaries other than such individuals; (5) the trustee elects QFT status; and (6) in the absence of a QFT election, the purchaser would be the deemed owner of the trust under the grantor trust rules. I.R.C. § 685(b). The amount of permissible contributions on behalf of each individual beneficiary was originally limited to $7,000 (indexed for inflation), but this restriction was repealed in 2008.

If the trustee elects QFT status, neither the grantor trust rules nor the normal conduit rules apply. Instead, the trust's income is taxed at the trust level, applying the rate schedule for trusts. In applying the tax rate schedule to a trust with two or more individual beneficiaries, each beneficiary's interest is treated as a separate trust. No personal exemption is allowed. I.R.C. § 685(a) and (c). The election is made separately for each trust, and QFT status continues for a 59-day grace period after a beneficiary's death. A trustee who administers multiple trusts may file a single "composite" tax return (Form 1041-QFT) reporting the income attributable to each beneficiary's separate share. Section 685 is intended to alleviate the recordkeeping and compliance burden on individual purchasers of reporting income under the grantor trust rules. As a practical matter, in view of the small amounts of income involved and the lack of a personal exemption, QFT income is generally taxed at a flat rate of 15%.*

§ 12.4   CEMETERY PERPETUAL CARE FUNDS

Cemetery corporations are organized and regulated under local law. For federal income tax purposes, some are classified as taxable associations, while others are tax-exempt (see I.R.C. § 501(c)(13)). A cemetery corporation, whether taxable or tax-exempt, typically agrees to provide "perpetual care" for gravesites and sets aside a portion of amounts received from the sale of burial lots and mausoleum crypts to create an endowment fund for that purpose. Such an endowment fund qualifies as a "cemetery perpetual care fund" if it is created by a taxable cemetery corporation pursuant to local law for the care and maintenance of cemetery property and is treated as a trust for income tax purposes. I.R.C. § 642(i).

---

* The 15% rate applicable to estates and trusts is reduced to 10% for taxable years beginning after 2017 and before 2026. I.R.C. § 1(j)(2)(E).

In general, a cemetery perpetual care fund is treated as a taxable trust under Subchapter J. However, the trust has no ascertainable beneficiaries; its income is devoted to the care and maintenance of gravesites. Accordingly, amounts distributed to the cemetery corporation to pay for gravesite maintenance are not treated as distributions under the normal conduit rules. In this respect, the trust resembles an "honorary trust" created for noncharitable purposes (see § 4.3, *supra*). Nevertheless, § 642(i) allows the trust to deduct amounts paid for the care and maintenance of gravesites in satisfaction of an obligation of the trust or the cemetery corporation. Solely for purposes of determining the trust's distribution deduction under § 651 or § 661, payments for gravesite maintenance are treated as distributions, and the deductible amount is limited to $5 multiplied by the total number of gravesites sold by the cemetery corporation before the beginning of the trust's current taxable year. I.R.C. § 642(i); Reg. § 1.642(i)–1. For example, suppose that Shady Glen, a taxable cemetery corporation, sold 500 burial lots and agreed to provide perpetual care. A trust, created by Shady Glen and funded with proceeds from the sale of the burial lots, pays $6,000 to Shady Glen to defray the cost of gravesite maintenance. The trust will be treated as making a distribution which is eligible for a deduction under § 651 or § 661 in the amount of $2,500 ($5 × 500) or the trust's distributable net income, whichever is less. Note that the special statutory rule allows the trust to claim a limited deduction, but it has no effect on the tax treatment of amounts received from the trust in the hands of the cemetery corporation. Thus, in the previous example, Shady Glen must report the $6,000 payment from the trust as compensation (not as a trust distribution) and must include the full amount in gross income under § 61. Rev. Rul. 87–97, 1987–2 C.B. 155.

INDEX

References are to Sections